Life Histories
of
African Women

Life Histories
of
African Women

Edited By
PATRICIA W. ROMERO

The Ashfield Press
London • Atlantic Highlands, NJ

First published in 1988 by The Ashfield Press Ltd.
17 Pemberton Gardens, London N19 5RR and
171 First Avenue, Atlantic Highlands, New Jersey 07716

Library of Congress Cataloging-in-Publication Data

Life histories of African women.

Includes index.
1. Women—Africa, Sub-Saharan—Biography. 2. Women—
Africa, Sub-Saharan—Social conditions—Case studies.
I. Romero, Patricia W.
HQ1787.A3L54 1988   305.4′0967   87-1441
ISBN 0—948660—04—X
ISBN 0—948660—05—8 (pbk.)

Manufactured in the United States of America

Table of Contents

Contributors

Harold Scheub is Professor of African Languages and Literature at the University of Wisconsin. His research is in folklore, African oral traditions and literature.

Beverly B. Mack is teaching Hausa at Yale University, worked in Washington, D.C., focusing on development issues in Africa. She has taught African history at Georgetown University and African/Afro-American literature at Bayero University in Kano, Nigeria, where she lived for three years doing fieldwork. Her M.A. and Ph.D. in African Languages and Literature are from the University of Wisconsin-Madison. She has published several articles on Hausa women's oral poetry and edited a volume of Hausa women's poetry published in Hausa by a northern Nigerian press in 1983. She is currently working on a longer version of Hajiya Ma'daki's biography.

Enid Schildkrout is Curator of Anthropology at the American Museum of Natural History. She has done research in Ghana and Nigeria. Her book *People of the Zongo* is a study of ethnicity and cultural change in Kumase, Ghana. Most recently she has published on children's economic activities in Kano, Nigeria. She received her Ph.D. from Cambridge University.

Christine Obbo is a social cultural anthropologist trained at the Universities of Makerere and Wisconsin-Madison. Her research interests are social change and work and development, which she sees as an extension of her training in the liberal arts, and in regional and urban planning. Currently she is employed as a migrant laborer in a small liberal arts college in New England, U.S.A.

Ivor Wilks is Professor of History at Northwestern University. His book on *Asante in the Nineteenth Century* is regarded as the classic work on the Asante, whose history he continues to study. Among the many honors Wilks has received is the Herskovits Prize from the African Studies Association in the United States. He received his Ph.D. from Cambridge University.

Patricia W. Romero is an itinerant peddler of African history and a Visiting Fellow at Johns Hopkins University. Her life history of Mama Khadija is part of a larger study on the history of Lamu, Kenya. She received her Ph.D. from Ohio State University.

Anne Cassiers lives in Chateaurenard, France, and has written *Mémoires Ethiopiennes* based on her years in Ethiopia. Chris Prouty Rosenfeld lives in Washington, D.C. She has written an historical biography of an Ethiopian queen. 'Mercha' was reprinted from *Northeastern African Studies* with the permission of the editor, Harold Marcus.

Introduction

This volume contains seven life histories of African women. Most of the women are from different geographical areas on the continent, although all live south of the Sahara desert. One woman was born in South Africa. Two in Northern Nigeria. Another lived in Ghana which, like Nigeria, is in West Africa. Three women represent East Africa, although their backgrounds and cultures are very different from each other. One common thread runs through the history of their nations—direct or indirect contact with Great Britain at some time in their history. South Africa was colonized by the Dutch, but in the nineteenth century Britain was a presence, especially in the south, where we meet Mrs Nongenile Masithathu Zenani. On the other hand, Britain's major involvement with Ethiopia came during and after World War II and had no impact on the traditional Amheric culture depicted in Mercha's life history. The Amhara, who are mostly concentrated in the Ethiopian highlands in the center of the country, were colonial masters too, having imposed their rule over their neighbors in all directions, during the nineteenth and twentieth centuries.

Britain's attempts to conquer Asante, in Ghana, figures largely in the life history of Akyaawa Yikwan, who was active in diplomatic negotiations at an early stage of conquest. We will see the impact of British colonialism on the lives of both Hajiya Mad'aki in northern Nigeria, and that of Bitu in Uganda. The two remaining women—Mama Khadija from Kenya and Hajiya Husaina Ibrahim, also of Nigeria—reflect in their lives more the influence of Islam than that of Britain, although Kenya, too, was a British colony.

Whatever their relation to the larger world in which they lived, each of these women was an unique individual, acting out her life as best she could—whether a commoner or queen. This same individuality is also present in the contributors to this volume. They, like their subjects, have their own cultural baggage which they carry with them to their fields of specialization. Several different scholarly disciplines are represented here—yet even among specialists sharing the same field, methods and questions differ. Harold Scheub is a folklorist. The questions he asks of his living subject, Mrs Zenani, differ from those historian Ivor Wilks requests from his

1

documents. In addition, Scheub as a linguist, is concerned not only with the content of the life history, but also with *how* the story is told. Mrs Zenani's story is long—but it is an exact transcript of what she regarded important in her life, as told to Scheub in a single sitting. You will learn something about the interests of a folklorist and linguist while you share the intimate details of Mrs Zenani's life.

This form of life history is autobiographical—the single voice captured by the tape recorder. The narrative is not interrupted by external questions. Perhaps we feel we know Mrs Zenani better because she is allowed to speak for herself. But, as Scheub cautions in his introduction, some of what she tells us is myth. In any autobiography we can expect myth to be confused with fact: the human psyche is such that each of us tends to jumble what we think is true with what was actually true—especially as we pass further along the corridors of time.[1]

Beverly Mack studied with Harold Scheub and she, too, has the skills of the folklorist. But in the life history she has included here, Mack combines her training in history to give us the larger picture of Hajiya Mad'aki's Hausa society in Northern Nigeria, along with a partial story of Mad'aki's life. Mad'aki was a royal concubine who became a royal wife, and finally a consultant to her brother, the Emir (religious and political leader) of Kano. In the case of Hajiya Mad'aki, (and others in this collection) two voices are speaking about one life: that of the researcher and that of the subject.

Enid Schildkrout and Christine Obbo are anthropologists, yet as each of their woman differ, so do their approaches toward their subjects. It is true of all of us, no matter our station in life, nor our educational background, that behind the facade each of our lives 'harbors a mystery'[2].

Schildkrout's interest in material culture is evident in her life history of Hajiya Husaina Ibrahim, a traditional Muslim woman who lived in the same area of Northern Nigeria where we meet the royal Hajiya Mad'aki. By reading these life histories together one gains a greater insight into the changing ways of traditional society as they affect women: Husaina stayed in seclusion, devoting her energies to providing for her family. Mad'aki, who had no children of her own, broke with tradition, became an international traveler, and at home used her royal position as an advocate for Western education among girls in seclusion. Hajiya Husaina died after the interviews and before Schildkrout wrote her life history. In this case, life history takes on yet another role. It becomes a permanent memorial to a simple woman who lived uneventfully and mostly unremembered, except for the accident of fate which brought her to Schildkrout's attention during her fieldwork in Northern Nigeria.

Bitu, the subject of Christine Obbo's life history, is also dead. Through her story, she, too, will be remembered beyond the mostly female clientele to whom she devoted herself during her life in Uganda. Obbo best illustrates the notion that a theme in life history can tell about the author as well as the subject. Obbo was born in Uganda, attended school during the colonial era (which may have influenced the ambiguity toward Western education found in this piece), and became one of the first African woman to earn a Ph.D in anthropology. Bitu was an early product of Western education for women. She never married—although as Schildkrout explains, marriage and children are of paramount importance to women in African societies. By remaining single, Bitu deprived herself of support in old age from the children she might have borne. Instead, she devoted her maternal instincts and energies to helping young unmarried mothers receive the western education that had been hers; and in so doing, enabled some of them to move from traditional rural labor to professional status. Both Obbo and Bitu exemplify aspects of the European colonial impact on Africa; each has had to make the big leap from one type of ordered society to the less structured, less secure, world of the West.[3] In this life history we have one pioneer describing the life of another. Bitu's story is also an example of biography as life history. Although we get an occasional word from Bitu, the major voice we hear is that of Obbo.[4]

With Ivor Wilks' contribution we meet two new facets of methodology: that of the historical document and oral tradition. Wilks, an historian, is the pre-eminent authority on Asante, a large ethnic group in Ghana, West Africa. During his research on Asante, Wilks came across Akyaawa Yikwan, a queen who lived in the nineteenth century. In those days the Asante, like most African societies, kept no written records of their history. They did, however, keep oral histories of their royals, and oral traditions of special events in their history.

Oral history is not limited to Africa. A good example of this kind of history can be found in the Old Testament. The story of Naomi, the Jewish woman, and Ruth, the Moabite, is a familiar one. Ruth's place is especially important to the history of Western religion because she was the great-grandmother of King David. Yet her story was handed down orally by generation after generation of Hebrews before scribes placed it in writing. The Asante, like the Hebrews, kept genealogies of the people who contributed to their history, and it was through these genealogies that Wilks was able to place Akyaawa Yikwan in historical perspective. He did not depend on oral tradition alone. He made use of travelers accounts—Europeans who did write down their memories of Akyaawa Yikwan—and from these sources he was able to authenticate the Asante oral traditions.

In Asante society, lineage is traced through the mother. (I am Kofi, son of Miriam; my father is Kwame, son of Sara, etc.) But women are rarely remembered as more than mothers; or, in the case of Akyaawa Yikwan, royal mother. What is unusual in the cultural context, is the role Akyaawa Yikwan played on the larger stage of Asante history: as diplomat and negotiator, for instance, with the British during an early stage of conquest. Wilks' deep and penetrating study is, methodologically, political history into which he has woven the fabric of Akyaawa Yikwan's activities on behalf of her people.

Another use of genealogies can be found in my life history of Mama Khadija. She was born into a slave family. Her mother and siblings were all the family Khadija knew, so her concept of extended kinship was that of her owners. And her life began in the twentieth century—not the distant past of Akyaawa Yikwan and the Asante royal family. Khadija produced two living children—both girls—who in turn, have borne several children, and are themselves grandmothers. Thus we have five living generations, beginning with Khadija as progenitor of the line. By tracing these living descendants back to Khadija we establish a kin network that we probably could not have done when people of her class were still slaves; and we develop a small sample of family history in the process. Mama Khadija's family tree differs from the society in which she lives as well as from most African societies, where only the names of men are remembered—if anyone is remembered at all. Mama Khadija is a traditional healer and midwife. These occupations are not unusual in African societies: Bitu's mother was noted for her knowledge of medical herbs; and Bitu's sister trained to be a midwife. Hajiya Husaina learned to treat herself with herbs and traditional medicines. Mrs Zenani eventually turned to the practice of medicine because her illness forced her to accept her calling. Mama Khadija delivered her first baby when her pregnant daughter was giving birth and the midwife did not reach the family in time. After she gained local fame for midwifery—without formal instruction—her practice came to include the use of traditional medicines for all sorts of illnesses she treated.

She is a Muslim, like Hajiya Mad'aki and Hajiya Husaina, although her status within her society differed from that of her counterparts in Northern Nigeria. Slave women in Lamu were never kept in seclusion unless they married their masters, then they were elevated to the status of free women. Among her many husbands (and multiple marriages occurred in the lives of Mrs Zenani and Mercha as well) was an upper class man, but by the time she married him, Mama Khadija was too independent to retire into seclusion. Her life perhaps best illustrates that while Muslim women had to operate within constraints, they could exercise a great deal of choice over their lives—especially where divorce was concerned. Mama Khadija's life history was also written by an historian—but the material was compiled from interviews with her, with members of her immediate family, and with female members of the family which originally owned her—and not from documentary sources more common to the work of historians.

The last life history in this collection came to be written as an outgrowth of friendship between the Ethiopian woman, Mercha, and her ceramics teacher, Anne Cassiers. Cassiers, a French woman, was living in Addis Ababa, the capital of Ethiopia, where she established her workshop. Neither Cassiers, nor her translator, an American who also lived in Ethiopia, are academics: yet Cassiers methodology resembles that of Mack in her life history of Hajiya Mad'aki. Here again we have two voices interwoven together. Mercha talks; and Cassiers interprets the larger picture as we make our way through the somewhat tragic aspects of her life. Mercha, like Mrs Zenani, also interweaves some myth with the facts of her life. For instance, she tells us that her father died at the age of 120. Because so many people in Africa died when still quite young, often those who lived into old age are assumed to be much older than they really are. Mercha, therefore, was repeating the myth which her family perceived as truth.

Mercha, like Hajiya Husaina and Mrs Zenani, was the victim of an early marriage which was forced on her. Her life is full of drudgery—in spite of, and because of, the men in her life. Left finally with children to raise in an urban environment, she longs to return to the traditional, rural life of her youth. Mercha also got caught up in the events surrounding the 1974 revolution in Ethiopia, and her economic situation worsened as a result. Her final comments perhaps best illustrate the dilemma of those women who have had to bridge traditional and modern societies with no special preparation for the transition: 'I wish had been born in another epoch, for nothing of the time in which we live pleases me. In my life, as soon as I find the least joy, it is effaced . . . In itself, the coming into the world of these children is a wonderful thing. But their future torments me so much.'

The future of the children of Africa might be seen as of collective interest to each of the contributors—no matter their individual approach to life history. It was the future of their children—literally or figuratively—which troubled and motivated all of those whose life histories appear in this volume

Patricia W. Romero
Baltimore, Maryland

Notes

1. See for instance, Erik Erikson, *Childhood and Society*, (New York, 2nd Ed., 1963), especially Chapter 7.
2. L. L. Langness and Gelya Frank, *Lives: An Anthropological Approach to Biography*, (Norton, California, 1981), p. 88.
3. Sidney Mintz has written that the 'relationship between culture and personality has never been articulated fully to the satisfaction of anyone', meaning that cultural influences are present in each individual, and because of their influences, it is difficult to separate the person from his culture. In this case, however, Obbo and Bitu share not only a common culture, but the experience in breeching it. Obbo's particular personal insights into this life presents an interesting question: are her observations on her subject more meaningful than those biographers who must always to some extent remain outsiders? Or does the uniqueness of each personality—despite cultural sameness—mean that two voices can never speak as one? See Sidney W. Mintz, 'The Anthropological Interview and the Life History', *Oral History Review*, 1979, p. 21.
4. See Daniel Bertaux (Ed), *Biography and Society: The Life History Approach in the Social Sciences*, (Beverly Hills; 1981).

And So I Grew Up

The autobiography of
Nongenile Masithathu Zenani

HAROLD SCHEUB

For Nongenile Masithathu Zenani, the products of the Xhosa oral imaginative tradition reveal, through the graphic imagery of fantasy, vital truths about her society and its history. The oral tale is the conduit to the past; its alchemizing force allows open and full access to that past. 'The art of composing oral narratives,' she told me, 'is something that was undertaken by the first people—long ago, during the time of the ancestors. When those of us in my generation awakened into earliest consciousness', she said, 'we were born into a tradition that was already flourishing.' It is not surprising that no distinct line demarks Mrs Zenani's creative stories and the events of her own life. The plotting of fictional imagery sometimes gives way to the detailed depiction of, for example, a rite of passage distilled from her history.

If the oral tale provides insights into history, such real life descriptions as are found in this autobiography are frequently framed by the imaginative tradition. The scenes in this account of Mrs Zenani's life in which the *unozakuzaku*, the master of ceremonies, organizes the activities of the bridal party are also a part of a number of her fanciful tales.

The rites of passage remain for her significant centers of the storytelling tradition as of her life. The centerpieces of this autobiography are the teenage girl's puberty ritual and the young woman's marriage. Mrs Zenani treats the problems and exhilaration attendant on the child's move to adulthood. Later, there is the journey of the bride from her home of birth to her home of marriage, with the astonishing behavior of the *unozakuzaku*, an erstwhile sober and respected member of the community, now suffering the taunts and ridicule of the men and women of the groom's home. The behavior surrounding the *unozakuzaku* is typical of an atmosphere of

7

MAP 1

uncertainty experienced during major rites of passage, when new identities are being assumed and the resultant crises wrack people's lives. The world is upside down during such periods; normal strictures do not apply. In this case, a woman is being married, and the topsy-turvy world that characterizes this transitional time of her life is suggested in the contradictory, ambiguous, androgynous figure of the *unozakuzaku*. His acts are not normal to him; the treatment that he receives from others is wholly outside propriety. Only when the ceremony is completed do standard civilities return.

The complex marriage arrangement is indicated by the many seemingly trivial but highly symbolic gifts, each of which represents a stage that more tightly links the bride and groom and their families. The ritual is a dramatic theatrical bridge between the two parts of the young Mrs Zenani's life.

Threading through the autobiography is the conflict between Xhosa traditionalists and Western, Christian influences in southern Africa. The *amaqaba* (singular, *iqaba*) are the traditionalists, a reference to the red ochre which they apply to their garments and bodies, representing the ties to the past. The Christian converts are sometimes called 'trousered' people, a reference to their adoption of Western-style clothing.

Mrs Zenani experienced the struggle between the Xhosa past and the European-dominated present that often demanded an abrupt break with that past. She was not always enamored of Western ideals and customs; some of the ardor that she felt towards the West in this autobiography seems to have diminished in later years. She had seen these ideals expressed in the many forms of apartheid evident even in such remote areas as Nkanga, her home in Willowvale District in the Transkei (Map 1). She had been made to endure the routine racism of the white-run bureaucracy: the white magistrate would not accept her word that she was, in 1976, seventy years old and therefore of sufficient age to draw a pension (her husband, Stephen, had died in 1972). He made her bare her head, an ignominious act, to see if her hair were grey. It was not grey, and because many whites believe that blacks are old only when their hair has turned color, she did not receive the pension.

She has strong opinions about the European-style schools that spread through southern Africa from the mid-nineteenth century. She creates a fictional situation to urge her point: 'I'm quite old,' one of her characters announces during a debate regarding the establishment of such a school in the area, 'and I've never heard of this school nonsense before. At home, *amasi* [curdled milk, an important symbol in Xhosa traditions and rituals] was poured out into a spoon, and we drank it. At home, all that we discussed was in regard to what ought to be done concerning our homes. If there happened to be a misunderstanding between my aunt and my father, the people were called together and the case was judged in the court. Nothing was written down. Now I wonder. You want things for writing. Is it because things will work out better then? Perhaps, unknowingly, you're misleading yourselves with all this writing business.' The speaker concludes, 'We live according to the laws of the Xhosa and of nature and tradition. Keep in mind that Xhosa custom is traditional, of ancient provenance, and it requires traditional responses.' In the end, Mrs Zenani does not eschew the present in favor of the past, but urges the people not to forsake African tradition so readily. (Mrs Zenani also had withering views as to the way the policy-makers in Pretoria used such arguments for sustaining the African past as cornerstones of their apartheid system.)

The conflict between the two traditions finds another reflection in the autobiography, in the friction between the generations. She reveals the risks to deeply-felt ties between a daughter and her father when traditions clash. This discord is the emotional focus of this work.

As the account of her life story comes to an end, Mrs Zenani makes the decision to become a doctor, again precipitating a clash, this time between the wife and her husband. 'There are various ways of becoming a doctor,' she told me, 'but they all come together at one point. A doctor is a person who has become troubled by certain pains; she is troubled by pains, and is treated in every possible way for them. But there is no relief.' She may also be 'a person who has no pain but who unaccountably leaves her home. When she returns, she is very uncomfortable with things at her home. That is the way it begins,' she explained. 'A person develops a kind of nervousness which causes her to become excitable. This nervousness is accompanied by chest pains, it narrows the mind's scope. She loses her appetite, she becomes incompatible with all that is evil. The nervousness causes her body to tremble when she sees a person who is somehow bad.'

Mrs Zenani argued that, 'The institution of medicine originates from a talent bestowed on a person by his ancestors. That ancestor is one of the first people, an original person who died long ago . . .

And it is said of him, "He has gone to heaven. He returns to you as a spirit, in your sleep. He tells you what you must do. When you have done that, things turn out as you envision in your sleep." We Xhosa say, "It is the ancestor." We say, "It is God," because God was the first being, he created the human. After that, the human himself named it; he said, "There is such a thing as Ancestor".' Mrs Zenani spoke of the 'various areas in which a doctor may specialize. He may become an examining doctor—he only examines, he does not prescribe medicines for healing the patient. Another doctor specializes in both examining patients and in divination . . . There is another kind of doctor who, after he has examined the patient, practises *ukuqubula*. This is done with the mouth. The doctor draws out the thing that is inside the patient, the thing that is hurting the patient. He draws it out with his mouth. This is the single competence of that kind of doctor. He is an *unobumba* who practices *ukuqubula*. Another doctor, who cannot examine a patient and does not practice *ukuqubula*, who does not divine, who does none of the things performed by those others, has one specialty—to cure. He is called an *itola*. And there is the doctor who, when he has finished divining, becomes an *umbululi*. Among sick people are those who have been stricken by practitioners of evil things, destroyers of the flesh. A person might be sick because a spell has been cast on him by holders of arcane knowledge. A doctor who practices *ukumbulula* exorcises that spell. He is distinct from the others.'

Mrs Zenani suffered fear of such persecution. She was afraid of being *thakatha*-ed, bewitched, and destroyed by *amagqwira*, infamous persons who rode on baboons and bore sticks that were death-dealing and life-giving. Was she superstitious? Well, yes, she said with some reluctance, in a way, perhaps. She believed that a person could *think* another person to death. What a person wills to happen will happen. She prided herself on her tough-minded, realistic appraisal of life's vagaries, but she became uncertain when it came to the *amagqwira*.

There was also uncertainty regarding Qamata and Thixo. She was convinced of the hypocrisy of the *amagqoboka*, the Christian converts. She worried about the *abashumayeli*, the Christian missionaries, and was unsure about Christianity, about Thixo, the Christian god, and about her own destiny. She was critical of the smoking and drinking habits of the *abashumayeli*, and recalled that one once attempted to seduce her. She told other stories of Christian converts and their hypocrisy—how, in church, they would sneak *isixhaxha*, the nicotine deposit from a pipe stem, out of their pockets and eat it; then, they would wipe their teeth with sharp-smelling grasses to make their breath sweet when they went to greet the preacher's wife. Mrs Zenani wondered about the origins of humans, and seemed as sceptical of Qamata, the Xhosa god, as she was of Thixo.

Mrs Zenani is now eighty years old. Her home, in Nkanga, is about twelve miles from the Indian Ocean. Her *dompas* (from Afrikaans *dom*, 'stupid,' and English, 'pass'), the hated pass-book that all Africans must carry with them in South Africa, gives her name as Nongenile and her surname as Mqotso (her grandmother's name), but it says nothing about the magnificence of the woman—a great performer, a respected doctor and marriage counselor, her keen sense of irony, her bludgeoning wit, her humanity. This autobiography was taped on 3 August 1972, under a grove of lemon trees, near Mrs Zenani's home in Gatyana District, the Transkei. The audience consisted of five Xhosa women. The English translation is by Harold Scheub.

Nomatikiti is the name that was given to me at my home of birth. My mother, Nowekeni, was a member of the Tshawe royal clan; my father, a son of Gosani, was John Numa. My mother married him, and then I was born: I was the first-born child.

I was born, and grew up. I had a happy childhood, a healthy childhood, and ultimately the time for my weaning arrived. I was weaned, and then I went to the home of my mother's parents, to the mother of my mother. That was at the royal residence of the Tshawe, home of the chiefs. I was raised by my grandmother there, I awakened to life in the company of traditionalists who lived there at the royal residence among the Tshawe chiefs.

As I grew up, I took part in the activities of the traditionalists for the first time. With others of my age, I played the games of the traditionalists. I remember one of our earliest childhood games—it was I-am-coming. We played in dirty pools, we smeared our bodies with mud. We played, we did everything—we made clay models: cattle, human figures, dolls. We did all those things, and there were also the times when we would continue to play beyond the time when we were supposed to go home. Then the older people would have to come for us, and I would sometimes be scolded by my grandmother, the mother of my mother.

She would say, 'You'll become a vagabond! At this stage of your life, you mustn't remain so long away from home. You're a girl, not a boy? You're not supposed to be playing out here in the pastures. Act like a girl!'

Sometimes I would be beaten for staying out so long. Then I would cry, and be comforted—I was spoiled because I was the child of a daughter of this place.

And so I grew up.

School was not at all important to these people. Actually, nothing among my mother's parents' people required a school. It was not valued in any way. So I did not attend school.

Time went on, time passed for me, and at length I began to attend certain social gatherings—feasts, dances given when a girl arrives at young womanhood, when a girl is initiated. We went to these affairs, we played there, we 'made do': this was the time when the boys chose the girl who was the most beautiful, we were beginning to develop breasts then. The boys played this game of 'making do'. One of them would say, 'Do it, Girl!' and then one of the girls would play a flirtatious game with him. And I would do that too, I would 'make do' with a boy. And that is the one who became *the* boy for me, the one of whom it would be said, 'He's your *imetsha*[1], your special boyfriend!' And it was important to us that we see those boys regularly. A girl would put on airs, she would show off when she saw her boyfriend, and he would do the same thing.

Then the time came when the boy would make a vow. He would say, 'Let's get together!' When the boy had said that, we would take some knives. We were getting older now, and all of us in my age-set[2] knew how to use the knives. We would go off to pick *imifino* [grasses, herbs, and plants], a plant that is picked in the fields, an edible weed picked in the stubbly fields. We would go there, and I would eye my boyfriend, and the other girls also—they would be eyeing their boyfriends.

So it went, time passed. Time passed, and then our relationship had developed to the point that the boy said he would come by at dusk. And this is what would happen: when he arrived at dusk, he would sit outside, just beyond the confines of the homestead. We would come together, but when we did we would always be accompanied by other children, younger than we were—children I lived with here at my mother's parents' place, children of my uncles, children of my aunts who, like me, were being raised here. The things that we did were not observed by the older people. We hid our little evening walks from them. A girl would pretend that she was just a child going to the veld to relieve herself.

During those nights, we were sleeping in the house of an old woman, my grandmother. And my grandfather[3] was also there.

They were old people now, people who just slept with the children. As soon as they were asleep, we would creep out secretly, and go off. I was a little older than the others, so I would tell them, 'Go away! I'm older than you! You go and sleep in another homestead, and come back in the morning! when you return, I'll go out to meet you, and everybody else, all the other people will think that we're all just getting up together, that we all spent the night in the same house!'

But our grandmothers and our mothers—the wives of our uncles— would caution us: 'A girl does not sleep with any man, she does not sleep with any boy!'

'You must be careful now that you're getting older, you're already developing breasts!'

'If you sleep with a boy, don't let him go up, don't allow him to bring his penis from the thigh to the vagina. Don't let him bring his penis up, don't let him bring it here to your vagina.'

'The boy is allowed to insert his penis in the thighs, nowhere else!'

'Remember, you've still got to be inspected!'

'You're to be examined!'

'Your fronts [i.e. vaginas] must be inspected by the women!'

'And the girl who has been misbehaving will be exposed!'

This made me very anxious, and whenever I went to my boyfriend, I was always very careful. Whenever he seemed to be going up, I would say to him, 'You're too dangerous! I'll never come back to you if you go on like this!'

And the boy would say, 'I know that. I won't do such things!'

That was the understanding, then, among those of us who were growing up. The boy and the girl would agree not to do 'those things'.

So it went on, and in the end, we really did arrive at full womanhood. As I grew into womanhood, I began to experience something that was very new to me, I had never experienced it before. I saw now that '*Tyhini*! Why am I bleeding like this? What's making me *bleed*?'

I was alone when it happened, I was coming home from the stream. When I got home, I was crying. The bleeding frightened me, I didn't know who had *stabbed* me!

I arrived, and said, 'Grandmother, please come! Something strange has happened to me!'

My grandmother said, 'What is it, Child of my child?'

I said, 'Come here and see!' I had taken my long cotton skirts, and was holding them away from my body. I was bleeding, but did not feel anything painful; I just saw the blood. There it was, the blood was coming out of me! Why was it coming out? I had not been stabbed by my boyfriend in that area. How could I be bleeding? I asked this question of my grandmother, the mother of my mother.

She said, 'No, Child of my child, it's just that you're a *girl*. You have *arrived*. Don't ever speak of this matter again, it's something that is not mentioned. Don't show anyone! Hide it! Hide that thing!' So said my grandmother, and she took a cotton blanket and tore it. Then she sewed it, and strengthened it. She helped me to put it on—around the waist, then between my legs; she fastened it with a pin.

She said, 'Do you see, Child of my child? You'll have to be careful when you sit down. Don't spread your legs, because this thing is not shown to other people. From now on, you mustn't drink *amasi* [curdled milk], you mustn't drink milk from this day. And you must no longer go into the cattle kraal—a person in your state does not enter the kraal, she does not drink *amasi*. This condition of yours will have to pass before you can drink *amasi* again. Now you must take care of yourself. You must not go to a boy, Child of my child, when you're in this condition. You must remain here now, you must sleep here at home, because you don't know how to handle yourself when you're like this. When it's clear that this thing is at an end, then you can wash. And when you finish washing, don't drink *amasi* on that day—you mustn't drink *amasi* yet on the day that you wash. And don't go into the kraal on the day that you wash either. You can go on the next day. And on that following day, *amasi* will be poured out for you, and you can drink it. That's called *ukomulisa*,[4] because you've been refraining from drinking it during this period.'

Time passed for me, for three days I followed these instructions that had been given to me by my grandmother. Then the bleeding stopped, and I said, 'Grandmother, it's stopped now.'

She said, 'Oh? When did it stop?'

I said, 'Yesterday, it stopped yesterday already. And today it's not here either.

My grandmother said, 'Well, all right. Tomorrow, get up, go and wash in the river. You don't have to wash at home,[5] you can wash in the river.'

Well, morning came, and I went to wash in the river. I washed everything—my cotton skirts, my body. I remained there at the river, I spread the clothes out so that my skirts would dry. Finally, they were dry, I tied them around my waist and went home.

I ate food, but that day I did not drink any *amasi*. On the next day, *amasi* was poured out for me from a calabash.

Someone said, 'Drink it.'

But the *amasi* was sour.[6]

I said, 'I don't want any *amasi* that's sour!'

I was told, 'No, drink! This is the breaking of the fast, *ukomulisa*—you haven't been drinking *amasi* for a time.'

I drank the *amasi*, and finished it.

The next day it was all right for me to go to the cattle kraal. I could go to the kraal now, I could go anywhere. I could even drink *amasi* now.

I grew up, I continued in that way. And when I went through my next menstruation, I said nothing to my grandmother. I did not tell her that, 'There's that thing again, it's come out!'

I just sat there that next month, and did what my grandmother had told me to do.

When she saw that I did not come to eat the porridge of thick milk and corn, she said, 'What's happened to you, my child? Have you a problem[7]?'

I said, 'Yes, Grandmother.'

'Oh.'

Then she gave me some beans,[8] so that I should eat proper food. I cooked these beans for myself.

And I grew up in that way . . .

When I was fifteen years old, it seemed that—well, really. I'm a young woman now. I went to all the social gatherings—traveling with others to the boys' night dances. At these affairs, the boys would come together with girls from many areas. A certain homestead would be designated for the dance: it would be said, 'The party's at So-and-so's place!' All of us would go to that homestead then, we would go in the afternoon of the day of the party. The groups would continue to arrive, one at a time, one at a time, until dusk. Then everyone would be there, and the dancing would begin. The girls would sit and sing songs, and the boys would rest their heads on the girls' laps. And the boy who was going out with me, who played with me and *metsha*-ed with me, he too would come and put his head on my lap.

Then songs were sung, commanding us to get up. And we stood. The boys danced, stamping the ground. My *imetsha* also stood—he put his stick above me. Then the girls clapped their hands, and clutched those sticks.

I grew up in that way, things went on, and then it became evident to me that my boyfriend had another girlfriend. This angered me. When I saw him speaking with this girl, I wanted to hit her, to say, 'Why are you talking to my *imetsha*?' And we did fight, we hit one another, we attacked each other—striking each other with our hands, our fists! with our belts too, I tell you! It went on, and then finally it was stopped.

My boyfriend would not talk to this girl in my presence, then, he insisted that *I* was his *first* girlfriend!

So things went on, until we reached the stage at which we were older girls, going with boys who were also older now.

Circumcision time for the boys approached, and it was necessary that we adorn these boys with beads that we ourselves had fashioned. We made tobacco pouches, beads for the head, beads for the waist, for the throat, diamond-shaped beads, wide belts made of beads, a variety of beadwork—earrings, head ornaments, and we adorned the boys with these jewels.

I provided my boyfriend with these beads, and he reciprocated. He bought a pipe for me, and taught me how to smoke. He bought a kerchief for me, so that I could wear a lovely head covering. Other boys and girls were doing the same thing for each other.

One day, because the boys were about to be circumcised, my boyfriend tied up ten shillings for me in my kerchief.

But I did not agree to this: 'I'm afraid to take money,' I said.

He said, 'All the girls are given money!' He tied it up, and forced it on me. So I took it.

Then, because the circumcision ritual was approaching, I purchased other gifts for my boyfriend, gifts that are presented when a girl's boyfriend is being circumcised. I purchased a dish for him, a bucket, a billycan, a rope for tethering the cow when the initiates want to milk. I also bought paraffin, I bought salt. But I myself could not take these things to the boy, because he was an initiate now. I sent them with a small child. Even this child could not take the gifts to the circumcision lodge while the older men were present. He had to go secretly, walking in shaded places. He could be seen by the initiates and the wardens, but he could not go there while the older people were still present.

Our initiates used to dance during this ritual period. Wild palms were plucked, and the initiates were assisted in attaching these leaves to their waists. Someone would fetch ox hides, to be drummed while the initiates danced.

All of our things were transported to the initiates by this small child of our home. He took them over to the circumcision lodge, but he did not show the older people what he was carrying.

We made beads for the initiates. Various ornaments, decorations were made for them, beadwork for the calves, the ankles, the arms—all of the jewerly for the initiates. I made many things for the initiate whom I was still very close to.

That is the way I grew up.

Finally, the initiates came out, they graduated and were now fresh young men, youth entering manhood. Now I had to present my boyfriend with still other gifts, celebrating his admission to manhood after circumcision. So I gave gifts to this raw young man, the boy I had *metsha*-ed with. I gave him a bag and diamond fashioned white beads for his head—not the same kind of diamond-like beads as those made for uncircumcised boys, however. I also gave my young man a handkerchief and some tobacco to smoke.

Now these young men did not come directly to us girls, because it was said that a young man should not go to his girlfriend when he returns from the circumcision lodge. He had to 'wipe off'. Now, to 'wipe off' meant that he had first to sleep with someone else; he must not come and sleep at once with his girlfriend. If he did, it would be said that he had used *her* to 'wipe off', and the girl would then have a stigma, she would have misfortunes. So we fled from these young men, even though we had missed them very much, even though we really desired them. We ran, custom dictated that you must flee from him when he has not yet 'wiped off'. Those raw young men continued to keep their distance, but they missed us too.

When he has 'wiped off', in whatever way he is able to do so, the signal is the shaving of his head, the exhibiting of a newly-shaved head. And he must throw away the things that you have given to him, things that he has been wrapping about his body. He must throw them all away, including his garment; he must discard them and be given different garments, old ones, from his home. He must be given different handkerchiefs, old ones, also from his home. That is how one knows that he has 'wiped off'.

I saw my own young man when he had been 'wiped off', and I
went to him gleefully because I had missed him. He rejoiced too,
because he had missed me. We came together, we were *people*
now—I was with a circumcised man, we were circumcised men
dancing![9] No more of those children's dances for us! We went now
to the dances of the young men.

And this is how I came to leave my mother's parents' place and
the traditionalists. I lived as well as I possibly could while I was
there. But it soon became obvious that many suitors wanted to
marry me, to make me a wife. I began to wish, therefore, to go
home, to leave my mother's parents' place, because if I stayed here I
would be given in marriage in the traditional way, according to the
ancient customs of the traditionalists. Back at my home, there were
no traditional patterns to follow. At home, a girl is not just seen by
someone, then taken and abruptly married to him; at home, she
reaches an understanding with her suitor.

It became necessary now for me to go home, and that is how I
parted from the home of my mother's parents. I went home.

But I did not let the people at my mother's parents' place know
that I was going home permanently. I just said, 'I miss my Father.'
I said that I wanted something from my father, I wanted him to
give me a set of bracelets.

My uncle said, 'That won't do! We have bracelets here, you can't
go to your home merely because of that! Besides, your people are
school people,[10] they won't give you a set of bracelets!'

I said, 'No, Uncle, they *will* give it to me, because I'll insist that
my father do so. I'll wear the bracelets for a year, then I'll take them
off. So my father won't have to be too concerned about that.'

My uncle knew that I would soon be married to one of my
suitors; he had in fact already agreed to the marriage. So he said,
'Well, hurry!'

The day that I left my mother's parents' home was a Friday. My
uncle said, 'Sleep over on Friday and Saturday, then get up early
and come back on Sunday.'

But I knew, even as he was saying this, that plans had already
been made for me to be married on Monday. My uncle did not
know that I was aware of that. I had heard about it from this little
fellow with whom I used to send my things over there to the
initiates—the go-between. He told me that some men had come to
the homestead, 'And I heard them speaking. What'll you give me if
I tell you what they said?'

I said to this child, 'I'll give you four anklets.'

'Give them to me.'

I took the coils off, and gave them to him. The child took them, and put them on his calves.

He said, 'You see, Sisi—.' He used to call me Sisi, Sister. 'These men said that they want you. They're from Ngqaqini, it was said that you're to be taken there on Monday. I was there, I heard what they said!'

I was quiet, then I set off in the way my uncle and I had agreed upon. I was to return on Sunday.

When I got home, my father asked me fondly where I had come from.

I said, 'Father, I don't want even *one* traditional skirt! And these coils! they can be torn off my ankles, for all I care! I want a *dress* now! now! *now*!'

My father said, '*Tyhini*! What's the matter, my Child?'

I said, 'Remember, Father, I was sent there to be brought up. Now I'm coming home.'

My father said, 'But won't that cause tense relations between me and my in-laws, my Child? After all, I asked them to bring you up. Now, before I've even paid them the "beast of rearing", you suddenly come back!'

I said, 'Father, don't you see? Those are traditionalists over there. I'll never know the things of my own home if I go back! I'll grow up in the strange ways of the traditionalists, not knowing the things of my home, only hearing about them from others! And I'm already this old! At this rate, I'll never be able to distinguish between who's telling the truth and who's lying to me!'

My father said, '*Kwo*! Thank you, my Child, you speak well. Don't you want to go back at all? Do you want this to be the end?'

I said, 'Yes, Father. I want this to be the end of my life among the traditionalists. When they see me again, I should be saying that I want to go to *church*!'

My father and mother went to buy those dresses[11] then. It was clear to me that even though they were questioning me, they really approved of my actions. But they wanted to be certain that there would be no negative criticism from the in-laws. I could see that my parents were pleased that I had returned; they had actually been somewhat anxious about how they would bring me from my mother's parents' place.

At my home, I had a sister who came after me in birth, and a brother who came after that sister in birth—we were the only three children of my mother. My sister still went out with boys, although she was quite close to me in age. As for my brother, he was a boy, and the question of marriage was for him, therefore, more complex. My return made them happy too.

Dresses were made for me, and on the first Sunday that I was home I went to church. That was the way I grew up. I went to church and was trained, I was taught much. They began to teach me the Xhosa language so that I would be able to know a hymn, so that I would be able to see it to the extent that it spoke.[12] I was taught Xhosa night and day. Even when the people at home, including my family, were resting, *I* was being taught Xhosa. In the end, I had some ability to identify words. I became accustomed to words [i.e. to *read* words], and could identify a hymn. At length, I became a catechumen, educated for the purposes of the church, and I became a member of the church girls' guild. I followed the procedures as if I had been born in the tradition.

There were also young men in the church, some of whom did whatever they wished—things inappropriate to the church. They made amorous advances to girls. There were young men among them who wanted wives. Some of them wanted girls for sexual purposes, others for marriage. But I did not involve myself at all in these quests. I was still going out with my old boyfriend. Even though he was traditionalist, I loved him very much. But my love for him was a constant source of derision and criticism by my peers. How could I be going out with a traditionalist when I had left those people?

One thing I knew, one thing I learned in my life with the traditionalist people: a woman can have one man, and another, and another—and she is called a whore. One may enjoy men, but it is desirable that a woman be faithful to one person, that she have a mutual understanding with him. That precept remained with me, and I did not want to have another man. Nor did this young man of mine attempt to be seen with me in public. I had warned him: 'As you know, I'm a school person now. You must come to me at night, you mustn't be seen with me during the day. People here dress up, but *you* go around naked, *you* wear only blankets! That's not acceptable here!' He agreed, and was satisfied with our arrangement; we understood one another well.

But there were many suitors, so many suitors. The eighth one was from Nkanga. Now my father came to the conclusion that my refusal to get married was a bad thing. By this time, he had heard from my uncles at my mother's home that 'this child here is running away from a marriage that we had arranged for her!' My father concluded that I did not want him to profit from me.[13]

When I refused to marry, my father said, 'Nomatikiti!'

I said, 'Father?'

'What's the matter with you, Child? Why don't you want to get married?'

I said, 'No, Father, it's not that I don't want to get married. But I'm not impressed with the suitors I see here. Why, some of them already *have* wives! And I don't want to become involved in polygamy! As for the others, I'm related to them! And I don't want to marry someone who is a relative of mine!'

My father said, 'But there are so many suitors! Can't you find *one* among the eight who's suitable? Can it be that *all* of them are related to you? Can it be that *all* of them are polygamous?'

I said, 'No, Father, these others—really, I object to them because of their backgrounds, I *know* their backgrounds!'

Then my father said to me, 'From this day, take soap—and go and wash me at the sea [i.e. wash me out of your life]! This is the father you should have an understanding with, the father who will profit by you. I am giving up on you, my Child, if you are giving up on me, because you're my first child! You are my first-born child! Your decision not to get married is a bad example for this homestead! Others will emulate you, you're the first one to do it. Now the decision must be made on Tuesday. On that day, I want those eight suitors of yours to be here, at this home. I'll call all of them! And I want you to stand in front of them and swear solemnly, I want you to say, "I don't want even *one* of these!" Then you can depart on that Tuesday—with the soap!'

I said, 'Well, Father, we'll see what happens on the day that you have set. But I can't understand why you want me to marry among the traditionalists when I ran away from them! I thought I was doing something pleasing to you when I left them!'

My father was quiet, he did not speak.

A few days passed, and then it was Tuesday.

The suitors arrived that day, they began to gather in the morning. By the time for morning coffee, two of them were already there, one from Bhojini and one from Ciko. And after breakfast, they were *all* there. The one from Nkanga was there too.

I was summoned by my father. But I had been watching secretly, and had already seen all these people. I was called outside, to the court by the kraal.

When I got there, I said, 'Hello!'

They said, 'Yes!'

My father said, 'Shake the hands of these people.'

I shook the hands of all of them. They looked straight into my eyes, the eyes of a girl.

My father said, 'My daughter.'

And I said, 'Father.'

He said, 'Do you know these people?'

I said, 'I know them.'

He said, 'Do you know them all?'

I said, 'I know them all.'

He said, 'Have you spoken with them all?'

I said, 'I haven't spoken with that one.'

He said, 'Where is that one from?'

I said, 'He's from Nkanga, at Ngqaqini.'

He said, 'Then you know his home?'

I said, 'Yes, I know it. They're of the Ntlane clan. I know his home. I even know his name.'

He said, 'Who is he?'

I said, 'He is Steven.'

My father said, 'Where have you seen him?'

I said, 'I saw him at a boys' dance. I used to see him often—from a distance.'

He said, 'Has he ever said anything to you?'

I said, 'He has never spoken to me. He did speak to me once, when he was still a boy. But he merely spoke of the things of childhood.'

My father said, 'That's your suitor then. I choose him.'

I said, 'Father, do you mean this traditionalist?'

He said, 'He's *not* a traditionalist! His father and mother were Christian converts! In time, he'll come back to the church, perhaps soon after you've married him.'

I got up and left without answering. I went to my room, I lay on my bed and cried, my heart grieved. I was afraid, overwhelmed, because I would have to go against my father's wishes.

After a time, my father came in. My aunt was with him.

My father said to my aunt, 'Please speak to this daughter of yours!'

My aunt said, 'What's the matter, my Child? Why are you crying?'

I said, 'I'm not crying about anything.'

My father said, 'My Child, if you're crying because I've said that you must marry this man from Nkanga, then I'm not happy about this! I don't want you to bind yourself to someone if you don't want to. But I also want you to marry according to my desire. So you must think about this carefully. But it's nothing to cry about.'

I did not answer, I only cried more.

My father went out, saying, 'Calm her down, calm her down. I don't like it that this child's crying so much. It would be better that the question of her marriage be dropped.'

When my father had gone, my aunt said, 'Do you think that my brother would have such dreams for you if he didn't love you so much? Don't you realize that your father's affection for you surpasses that which he feels for any of the other children in this home? You can see that he's hurt now because of your weeping. Don't you understand that he's even considering dropping the whole matter? He doesn't want to drop it, but he'll do it—sorrowfully— because he's afraid that you might hang yourself, you might hurt yourself. And he doesn't want you to get hurt. No, my child, really! Stop this! You *can't* refuse to get married! For you to be born, your mother got married!'

I did not reply to my aunt. I was silent, I did not answer. I did not respond at length in any case when an older person spoke.

My aunt departed. I did not eat that evening, I did not want to eat. On the next day, Wednesday, early in the morning, my father called me. He called me below the kraal, and asked me what I wanted.

I said, 'What do you mean, what do I want?'

He said, 'It doesn't matter what you want.'

I said, 'Like what, Father? There's nothing, really, that I lack.'

He said, 'Isn't there something that you crave? Like a chicken?'

I said, 'A chicken's all right, if there is one.'

He said, 'Do you *want* a chicken?'

I said, 'It's all right. A chicken is all right.'

My father said, 'Boil some water, and catch yourself one of my chickens.'

I boiled the water, and my heart was grieved because of my father: I could see that he was pained because of all this. And I could see too that he did not want me to feel bad. I cooked the chicken, and when it was cooked took it out of the pot. I took it to him, and he was still sitting there in the same place. My father said that we should give some of the chicken to others, that we should not just eat it by ourselves. So I brought some other dishes, and he gave some of the chicken to other people.

He said, 'Come back here, then, and we'll eat together.'

I was not accustomed to eating with him, from the same dish. I was used to eating with the other children.

I came back and sat with him.

He said, 'Come and eat now.'

I said, 'Father, give me some food in my hand.'[14]

He continued to give me food, and I ate the chicken. I ate and ate, and during the meal nothing happened. My heart calmed down regarding this matter, and I continued to feel sorry for him.

Things went on in that way, but I was no longer told anything that was going on here. I saw materials, clothing, continually being brought into the middle house. And when I went into that house, I found many of the things of marriage. I knew that these goods must be mine! But I kept quiet, I did not say a thing. When everyone else was away, I would go and open that house and count those things. I counted them, I inventoried these goods. And I well knew that they all pertained to marriage. Nothing was lacking.

On Sunday, some suitors from Nkanga arrived. They were driving six cattle, all of them heifers. These cattle were being driven by my suitors—my fiance, his brother, and another brother (the middle one), they were three. I came out to take the yokes that were by the kraal, to bring them into the house. I brought them in one at a time.

The suitors were sitting outside, and they said, 'Why don't you come here, so that we can greet you?'

I was quiet, I said nothing at all. I did not answer, I walked into the house. I took the yokes inside.

Later, my father came out, accompanied by this boy of our family. My father greeted the suitors, then sat down in front of them. He called me, asking me to bring some water. I came with the water, but my father just held it, rather foolishly. He didn't really want the water. It was just part of his plan to get me to come out there in front of my suitor. I was surprised that he did nothing with the water, I wondered what he was going to do with it.

He just held the water, and said to me, 'Have you greeted these people?'

I said, 'Yes.'

They said, 'No, she has *not* greeted us!'

He said, 'Greet these people!'

I shook their hands. Then I realized that, Oh! my father wants me to come to these people, that's why he made me bring the water! He wants to see if I will greet them, he wants to hear what I might say to them. This water was just part of his plan to bring me together with the men.

I sat there, and finally he sent this little boy to call another youth, the son of my paternal uncle. He brought him. I did not know what they said, because I was over in the house. We were told to remove the beds in the young people's house. The guests were going to come in. We moved the beds away, we took them apart and spread mats. Then these fellows, the suitors, came into the young people's house. They stayed there, a goat was brought over to that house. I saw it as it was slaughtered outside, it was slaughtered for the suitors. It was taken there, and I saw a man carrying the meat into that house. But I was not told anything about it, I just saw what was happening without being told what it was all about, without being told why the goat was being slaughtered.

Time passed. Time passed, and at dusk I saw the people drinking from the bottles that had been brought by the suitors; the older people of home were drinking in the main house, the house in which we usually ate. A glass was poured and offered to this little boy of our home, and I too was given a glass.

But I said, 'No, *I* don't take white men's liquor!'

'No, drink it!'

I said, 'No!'

At that time, a child did not drink liquor. It was regarded as something that might choke a person, so we did not want it.

Time passed, and I was told to bring water to the house in which visitors were staying. I took the water in a jug, and arrived over there at that house.

I knocked.

'Come in.'

I entered, and stood there.

They said, 'Do you have anything to say, Girl?'

I said, 'I was told to bring water.'

The water was taken by my fiance. I put it down, he took it and put it somewhere else. Then I went out with the child, we went into the house and sat there. Soon a fellow came from that house of the suitors. He said that he had brought the meat, he was bringing the meat to my mother and father. The meat had now been cooked. My mother and father thanked him.

After a time, the meat was eaten. A piece was cut for me as well, and I ate it.

At dawn the next day, the suitors went home. I again looked in at those goods that were being stored in that house. There were a lot of them. Then I was called by my father.

He called me to the garden, and said to me, 'Now you must tell me certain things while we're alone here. You know the things of the traditionalists. What is usually done at a marriage among those people?'

I was quiet . . . quiet . . . quiet.

Then I said, 'Three pounds must be brought for the women, ten shillings for the beards. There must be ten shillings for the saying, "We know this homestead", one shilling for the pillar of the homestead, five shillings for the bar for the cattle kraal, five shillings for the urinating.[15] There must be ten shillings for the indirect approaches to the house, and there must be five shillings for a strap for tethering the legs of the milk cow, five shillings for entering the house. Five shillings will be needed for eating with the mother, one half-crown for holding the spoons. There will have to be money for kindling the fire—also five shillings. And ochre is usually put aside, called "The Ochre". How much all this should amount to is up to the person concerned.'

Then my father said, 'Oh, my Child, do tell me these things because I don't know them. Aren't beads also needed? Aren't beads desired among the traditionalists?'

I said, 'Yes, beads are needed.'

'What kinds of beads, my Child?'

I said, 'All kinds. But there's no one here who'll make the beaded things. All kinds of beadwork are needed, no kind of bead should be lacking. I'll make them myself. But I mustn't go to the shop, it's not proper that a new bride go to the shop. A new bride works at home, she does not go to the shop. A person who is no longer a new bride goes to the shop.'

My father said, 'All right. How about the mole-type bead, is that acceptable?'

I said, 'Yes, it's acceptable, because that one can be got from the shop ready-made, one just puts it around the neck.'

We parted then, but my father did not say that those beads were to be mine; he just sent some women of the village to get them. It happened that one of the women whom he sent was to be my escort into marriage. She was a traditionalist. He sent her to the shop, and she purchased all kinds of beads. She bundled them in her

kerchief, and they were put together, along with the mole-type
bead, the one put around the neck.

The following month, I suddenly saw some traditionalists coming
to our home. Among them were two men—an old man, and one
who was still young. And there were two women among them—
one of the women was old, the other was still young. There were
two girls as well, one of whom was my sister. She had been put
into this group.

Then I was clothed in traditional garments that had been made
and ochred. My father dressed me in these robes.

He said, 'Now, my Child, I am allowing you to leave this home,
according to Xhosa custom. This Xhosa custom has been in
existence since the beginning of things. We became converts [to
Christianity] at a later stage, but we were traditionalists before that,
in the time of our great-grandfathers. The original state for a
human being was that of the traditionalists. What I am doing is
correct and proper, as required by Xhosa custom. I am taking you
out through the door, not in a clandestine fashion. I am pleased
with the arrangement, I approve of your going and serving for me,
of your being steadfast in that homestead. Now don't be naughty,
my Child. I trust you, I know that you won't disappoint me.
Today, you must go. But before you go, my Child, go out to the
kraal.' Then he shouted, 'Anoint her with red ochre!'

I had been crying, but now my entire body was anointed with
red ochre. Even though I had just returned from washing, my
father insisted that I go and wash again. The young man who was
applying the ochre (he was one of the two men who belonged to
the bridal party) anointed all of our bodies with it. When he was
finished, we sat down.

All this time, a goat was being slaughtered outside, a goat that
would open the feasting for me, for the ritual of my departure from
home. They brought a foreleg of the goat inside, and cut off a slice
for me. It was roasted, then cut so that I could eat it.

I swallowed only one mouthful, then said I wanted no more.

It was said, 'It doesn't matter, she's done it. The requirements of
the ritual have been satisfied.'

The meat was then eaten by the rest of the people, and it was
finished.

It was said, 'Bring her out!' My father said that. He was outside.
He said, 'Bring her out!'

Everyone got up then, and they brought me out. I was crying

now, sobbing. And I was taken to the kraal where someone spread a mat out for me when I arrived, and I was made to sit on it. I had already been covered with a new cape that had been dipped in ochre.

When I got to the kraal, my father said, '*Heke! Heke!* my Child! It's good that you're going now to your house of marriage, it's good that you're being sent there by me, your father—with my approval, and with your agreement and submission to my word. Continue in that way, my Child, in the homestead of your marriage to which you journey today. Don't think that this is a happy thing for me, my Child; it's not at all enjoyable, the fact that you're leaving me, especially since I know that you're not anxious to do so. But that is in the nature of things. By custom, you cannot be a wife to me. You must be someone else's wife. You cannot remain here. It is natural and customary that you marry and go off with your husband, and leave your own home behind. Consider your mother—my wife. It was not pleasant for *her* father either, but it was proper: it was natural, customary. It is natural that one brings forth a child, and having given birth to her that she go and build herself a home somewhere else. She is establishing her own home, wherever it might be, for her parents! I therefore say to you, Go, my daughter! Here is the ox of the *impothulo*,[16] Selani. I give it to you. Drive this ox ahead of you, it should be the first thing that you will have in your new homestead. You will build on this ox, as you develop that new homestead. Go well, then!'

Another man got up, and said, '*Ewu!* Never have I heard a child spoken to so appropriately and eloquently by her parent! And you, my child, that *you* should humble yourself in this way—that's also splendid! It is clear that you have been raised in a royal house, where a person tends to be humble, where a person tends to submit to the authority of someone else. Go well, my Child. Go and serve for all of us, all of us here. When you're in that house of yours, we are your fathers! Anyone who comes there is your father. We shall then see the signs if you have not been performing well. When we pass by, and it is said that this woman is not from Gosani's household, we will know that you have disowned Gosani! We'll know if by your actions you have repudiated your past!'

That is the way I was sent off.

We set out. It was said, 'Let's go!'

We got up as one, and the goods were carried.

Along the way, there was an upsetting incident. In the evening, the ox of the *impothulo*, Selani, got lost. When we got to the Qwaninga River, we learned that the ox had not been lost at all, that it had actually outstripped us. It had run fast; it seemed to know the homestead of my marriage even though it had never seen it, even though that homestead was far away. But the ox had hurried along the way, and arrived at my homestead of marriage. An amazing thing! It got there, and lay down at the entrance.

When we arrived in the late evening, we sat above the homestead. The dogs were barking, and someone came to ask us where we had come from.

We said, 'We come from across the Mbashe, and we're going to the Nciba.'[17] We further told him that we were tired, that we were just asking for a place to spend the night. That is Xhosa custom, to do it that way.

The young man who had come to us said, 'I'll go and report this at the house.'

He left us there, then returned.

He said, 'Let's go.'

We got up. My head was covered with a blanket, as it had been for much of the journey. We went into the house. When we got there, a curtain was hung up, and we girls sat on the other side of the partition. The other four people—the two women and the two men—sat outside the curtain; the four of us girls were behind it. Then dishes of food were brought in: two dishes of stamped mealies, one for one side of the curtain, one for the other side. We ate.

Something unusual occurred at about that time: we learned about our ox. Someone knocked, and asked if something might have slipped out of our grasp during the journey, for they had found an ox that was unknown here. The ox, a big yellow one, had arrived at dusk, and it lay at the entrance to the house.

The people of the bridal party leapt up, and said, 'That's it!'

'That's the ox we've been trying to find!'

'We were going to try to track it down!'

'We thought that perhaps it had turned back, we lost it at the Qwaninga!'

That ox was slaughtered then, very early in the morning and according to custom. The ox was slaughtered, and a side of the beast belonged to the bridal party. The flesh of this ox was roasted the next day—this yellow ox which had been amazingly fat. Its fat filled the four-gallon tins! The children had runny stomachs because of that fat!

Then a gelding of a goat was slaughtered. Its ritual name was *umothula-ntabeni*, 'Take-down-from-the-mountain'. The bridal party was being ritually brought down from the mountain by means of this goat, a reference to the arrival of the bridal party to the groom's place, when the bridal party sat above the homestead. The slaughtering of the goat was carried out by the bridal party, which also apportioned the meat. It was a goat that had been given to them; they slaughtered it, and did the rest.

Later, it was said that the bridal party was needed outside. This, too, was according to Xhosa custom—the need for the bridal party to come outside, for the bride to come out of the house.

Among the Xhosa themselves, there are differing forms of marriage, but this one was the traditionalist form. Everyone there was anointed with ochre. We were naked, moving about in very brief things, our heads covered with black turbans. Then we were draped with capes. We put beaded boots on our feet, and we wore head ornaments. We wore seashells around our necks, and many strings of beads around our necks and the upper parts of our bodies.

The leader of our bridal party was that older man of the two men in the group. He was leading us now. Behind him in the procession was a young married woman, and after her came a girl. Another girl followed her, and then I came along. Yet another girl came after me, and she was followed by another young married woman. That was the composition of our procession, with the master of ceremonies in the front, carrying a stick. He walked along in front of us, clearing the way of bad things, kicking dried cowdung out of the way, clearing the path so that we would not stumble. We walked, looking at the ground.

So it was then, we walked until we came to the kraal. When we got to the kraal, a mat was spread out for us and we sat there in the same order that we had walked. Our heads were covered with blankets. Then the suitors came in, equal in number to the girls. They sat by the gateway to the kraal, and a mat was spread out for them too. They also wore beaded necklaces and shells and the head ornaments created from birds' feathers. Their heads were uncovered, and they were wearing capes.

We were now uncovered by the master of ceremonies. We knelt before the older men here in the kraal, and the women in the bridal party were then uncovered to the waist; the area above the waist was naked. This leader who was uncovering us was working rapidly, bending down, his buttocks moving rapidly in front of us.

And he was being mocked: 'You with those buttocks sticking out like that, we don't want *you!*'[18]

'We want our bride! Uncover!'

'Don't be so prissy, with your buttocks parted in our direction like that!'

'So stylishly!'

'We haven't seen our bride yet, we don't want *you* here!'

But the master of ceremonies did not laugh. The others laughed happily at these derisive comments which were being made not only by the men but by all the people who were present. They mocked him.

It was said, '*Tyhini!* Just look at this thing with the twisted neck!'

'This *ugly* thing!'

'What kind of repulsive thing *is* this?'

'The squashed face!'

'Dallying so long over this!'

'When will we *see* her?'

'*Kwi!* Never have we seen such a *fool!*'

'And he keeps company with *people!*'

Then the master of ceremonies became even more fastidious. Undaunted by these comments, he uncovered us with great delicacy, with elegant deliberateness, while the others were looking on.

It was said, '*Yu yu yu!* We loved her even before we saw her!'

The master of ceremonies opened my cape for a brief moment, then put it down again at once.[19]

'Why are you *covering* her?'

'Do it again, one more time!'

'We haven't *seen* her yet!'

'Has there ever been such a *fool?*'

'What *is* this?'

'Where is a really *respectable* man?'

'That anyone should ever think to bring a thing like *this!*'

And again he would open my garments briefly, then cover me again.

And it would go on like this, with all that laughter.

Then we got ready to leave the kraal. A shilling was left at the place where I—the person for whom the ceremony was taking place—had been sitting. Then we departed, moving precisely, our procession formed in the same order as before, the master of ceremonies again in the front. He walked ahead, clearing the way of dung, leading us now to the women in the courtyard.

And this same master of ceremonies would again be mocked, this time by all the women.

'*Yo yo yo!* This thing who seems to have a diseased and over-grown scrotum!'

'He has to walk with his legs *apart* like that!'

'When will this thing *get* here?'

'Just *look* at him! This *thing!*'

'Going and clearing the way of *dung!*'

'This *fool!*'

'*When* will he arrive?'

'*Kwo!* What an *ugly* person!'

'*Grimacing* all the time!'

And they would laugh—'*Yaa!*'

Finally, he got there, and the women spread out mats. We sat there in the same order as before. Again, a shilling was placed under me.

Then the master of ceremonies uncovered me again, and when he had done so, the women said, '*Yo yo yo,* Friends! Isn't she beautiful? Isn't she beautiful? *Yu yu yu yu,* Lovely one!' Then the master of ceremonies covered me again.

'Why are you covering her, you old *fool?*'

'*Kwo!* This thing deserves to be *beaten!*'

And again he uncovered me a little—just a little. He was teasing them in return for their abusive comments. Now he was enjoying himself at their expense. He did not care about their mocking statements, because it was customary that the master of ceremonies be made the butt of jokes at this ceremony. He got up then and covered me again, and we prepared to go to the house. Our heads and faces were covered, our blankets again dragged on the ground. We went to the same house that we had come from.

The women were saying, 'Legs! *Legs!*'

'We want to *see* her!'

'To be sure that you haven't brought us a *lame* person!'

'Are you sure she isn't a *cripple?*'

'Is the second leg missing?'

'Show the *legs!*'

And we stopped then, with our backs to them. We returned, our backs to the women, then revealed our legs.

'*Yu yu yu yu yu!*'

Then the master of ceremonies covered us, and he was again mocked. He stopped, and went to the house. When we got to that house, *awu*! the women of the homestead here had also arrived. They came, carrying pails and hoes and sickles.

They said, 'This is how we do things *here*!'

'At *this* homestead, water is dipped!'

'Fields are cultivated!'

'At *this* homestead, wood is gathered!'

The master of ceremonies came along, carrying a thong. He arrived, then knelt before them, making the sound of milking—*tyoyiyo*! *tyoyiyo*! *tyoyiyo*! *tyoyiyo*! He played at milking, then said, '*We* milk at *our* home! *And* we inspan oxen! We drive cattle! *Yek'*! *Maan*![20] And so on!'

The exchange went on like that, then the women of this homestead turned back. They departed, and the master of ceremonies went in and sat down.

Then it was said, 'The cattle are burning, master of ceremonies!'

The cattle were chased and brought together, then put into the kraal. One of these cattle, an ox, was slaughtered.

The killing of this ox is the point at which the marriage really takes place.

It begins with the procession, and ends with the slaughtering.

'They are burning, Master of ceremonies!'

They said that because they wanted the master of ceremonies to come out, to go over to the kraal. A bar was put across the entrance to the kraal, so that the master of ceremonies was obliged to remove it. But he did not remove the bar with his hands. He gave some money, he was carrying ten shillings with him. He put the shillings down, then members of the groom's homestead removed the bar so that he could go into the kraal to get the ox.

Then it was said to the master of ceremonies, 'The spear!'

The master of ceremonies now had to produce five shillings so that the ox could be slaughtered. After the man had produced the necessary money, the ox was killed, then its flesh was brought to the house. The master of ceremonies was told that he should take the meat that belonged to the bridal party. He brought the pieces of meat into the house, one piece at a time; he took it bit by bit to the house of the bridal party. Then the meat was taken to one side. The whole side of the ox's carcase was taken in, a piece at a time.

The viscera of the ox cost a shilling.

It was said, 'The backbone!'

And he had to produce a shilling.

'The leg!'

A shilling.
'The head!'
A shilling.
'The hoof!'
And we produced another shilling.

And so it went. Each time he took the meat to the house, he took with it its money.

Money had already been produced for the urinating of the children. When they had come to the house of the bridal party 'to urinate', they had been given five shillings.

Now a young married woman came in, and she said, 'The stick of the house!'

The meat was being eaten in a hurried way, in an inelegant and unpolished manner. There was no chance to relax and be happy; there was no time to eat the meat in a delicate way. The people ate as if they were under arrest.

And the young married woman said, 'The stick of the house!'

Then the stick of the house was produced—that was one shilling. She went away, then returned immediately: 'The recognition of the homestead.'

Someone said, 'Now just wait a little, we're still eating!'

The woman said, 'I have no time! I have no time! No time!'

She was told to get out, and she departed.

A little later, while the members of the bridal party were still eating, the woman again arrived.

'I want it now! Before, I wanted "The recognition of the homestead" and now I want "The approaches to the house"!'

She was given 'The approaches'.

'I want "The beards" immediately!'

'Oh, go on! We've heard you!'

She went off a little distance, and stood just outside the house. Then she returned, and was given the money.

'I want "The apron"!'

'*Awu*! What's that? We don't know that!'

'How could you not know that? Is there a homestead without an apron?'

There was quibbling over this. No matter what the object, there was always a little discussion about it—even though both sides well knew that the money for 'The apron' was there. And that 'apron' was eventually produced, because the money had been set aside for it by the bridal party.

The woman went away again for a brief time, then returned: 'I want "The beards"!'

She was given the money for 'The beards'.

After a very short time: 'I want "The thong"!'

'The thong' was produced. She left, then after a brief time: 'I want the money of the women!'

But it was said, 'No, we'll meet again tomorrow. We hear, we know, we understand. We'll deal with it in the morning. We don't deny your request, for we cannot really deny that.'

Then the young married woman went away. She had been delayed, because this 'money of the women' is tied to the production of the cattle of the *lobola*, to the final fulfillment of the stipulations of the marriage contract. Only then are the men satisfied.

After a long time, a man suddenly appeared. He said, 'How did you come to know this homestead?'

'Oh! After all this time, you're still asking us how we came to know this homestead? Don't you realize that we've been here for some days already?'

'Well, but we want to know how you come to know this homestead! I've been sent here by the old man, the father of the groom. He sent me to ask you this.'

A bottle was presented to the groom's people now. The young man who was the spokesman for the groom's party returned to the groom's house. He gave a taste of the liquor to two people, then after a time the young man returned with the bottle.

'I've come from that house over there.'

'What is it now?'

'Well, they're demanding "The seat! The seat!"'

'What kind of seat?'

'"The seat" that you're sitting on!'

A bottle was then produced by the bridal party, and the young man took it and went to the house of the groom's party. Then he returned from that house, to give a taste of the liquor to the older woman and older man of the bridal party. He again departed.

At dusk, the 'people of the meat'[21] were divided up for a young people's party, they were matched up. The people of the bridal party included these girls, and they were to sleep with the young men of the groom's party, the men who have accompanied the groom in the same way as the bride is surrounded by the girls who have accompanied her. A certain house is slept in.

At night, a woman of the groom's homestead came to the house of the bridal party, and knocked. 'Well, I've come to fetch those girls of the bridal party!'

Then the master of ceremonies went out with us, and we went to the house where the young men were sleeping. The master of ceremonies was carrying my mat, the mat of the bride. When he got there, he spread my mat out on my side of the house, and he spread the other mats in their places. One girl was to go to one of the men, another girl to another of the men, the other girl to the other man, and I went to my husband.

Time passed then, and early in the morning, before the red dawn, we were supposed to leave that house. If one of us were to oversleep, until the dawn had come and it was light, the master of ceremonies himself would have to come to us. He would knock, then inquire where the girls of the bridal party were. Then the groom's party would be fined for this oversleeping incident. That groom of mine was fined ten shillings because of this. And those who accompanied the groom were fined five shillings each. All that money, combined, goes into the pocket of the master of ceremonies, the member of the bridal party who takes the meat from here to there.

So it went on, until the bridal party's stay came to an end. At this time, the members of the bridal party insisted that they complete 'the eating of the *amasi* [curdled milk]' ritual. But the men of the groom's party did not agree to this, they raised objections.

The master of ceremonies from the grooms side said, 'It cannot be that the two rituals—the beast of the marriage and the *amasi* ceremony—should come so close together. One of them must not be confused with the other!'

A person who has experienced the ritual with goat's milk does not marry again. Such a person is married forever—such is the significance of this ritual. The really important part of the marriage ceremony is the ritual eating of the *amasi*, that is the part of the ceremony that really counts. If there is a law suit, in the office of the magistrate it is asked, 'Did she eat even a little *amasi*?' If it turns out that she did eat *amasi*, that is the clinching testimony, the evidence that she did indeed marry into that homestead. The stay of the bridal party at the groom's place is a matter of joy, an occasion for celebration. But in itself, it does not bind a marriage relationship. It cannot be leaned on as legal evidence of anything.

There was a great argument over this matter, and in the end the

people in my home of marriage were defeated. A goat with white
and black spots was brought out—it was my husband's goat. It
became the goat for the ritual of the *amasi*. For this part of the
marriage ceremony, the first thing that had to be done was to
slaughter the creature.

It was said, 'Today, we're marrying this woman for good! We
are fulfilling the ritual of the *amasi!*'

The goat was slaughtered, then a steak which had been cut in the
kraal was brought by my uncle, the younger brother of the groom's
father. My uncle himself roasted this piece of meat in the house of
the bridal party. He was carrying a pail of *amasi* and a thong for
milking. He soaked the milking thong, then dipped it briefly into
the *amasi*. He cut a piece of meat, and he soaked that in the *amasi*
also. He took the thong; the end that had been soaked in *amasi* he
put into my mouth. Then he put the piece of meat that had been
soaked in *amasi* into my mouth.

He said, 'You've done it now, Woman of our house! You're
married now!'

Then he went out, and all the meat was brought into the house.
That was now the meat of the marriage. The bridal party received
the meat as a gift; this time, no money was paid for it, as in the
other activities here at the groom's place. Now it was meat that was
given to the bridal party. Its members were repeatedly given
cooked meat.

When the bridal party was feasting on the meat of the ritual of
amasi, a dish for the groom was taken from the goods belonging to
the bridal party. A knife for the groom was also taken from those
goods. Then meat was placed on the groom's dish, and it was taken
to the groom in his house by the master of ceremonies. And when
the meat had been cooked, a knife and some of the meat were
presented to me as a gift.

Then came the beginning of the end of the ceremony. The
master of ceremonies went outside, and sought the men of this
groom's homestead.

He said, 'We're about to ask for leave to depart. Please give us
what belongs to us, let the business go forward.'

Two beasts were produced, in addition to the six beasts of *lobola*
that had been negotiated earlier.

It was said, 'Fulfill the obligations that you incurred in your
negotiations with the bride's father. It's not necessary that we go
over all those provisions again, you know the terms agreed to

between you and the old man when you were given the girl over there at her home. We just want to depart now with the things that were agreed by those prior arrangements.'

'Oh!'

As this was being said, the master of ceremonies turned to the groom to ask him what he knew about this.

He said, 'My older brothers know that business.'

Two beasts were produced then. The cattle that the members of the bridal party were going to depart with now amounted to ten—four of them being added to the *lobola* cattle during this last day of the ceremony.

When the women saw the men returning from the courtyard and the cattle being taken out and presented to the people of the bridal party, they said, 'What did we say yesterday?'

'Say about what, Women?'

'Weren't we here yesterday?'

'Weren't we saying that we wanted "The money of the women"?'

'Yes, you did say that.'

'Then what's the matter? Give us what is ours!'

The money, three pounds, was produced then, and given to the women—money that was called 'The money of the women'. Usually they distributed this 'money of the women' among themselves, according to their own wishes and terms.

The goods were all taken then, and it was time for me to be taken to our house. I was to be left there, and the bridal party was to return home.

I prepared to depart then. We girded our skirts, my black kerchief almost covered my eyes. The girls in my party also wore their turbans so that they partially covered their eyes. We were clothed in lighter garments now, we did not have our heavier capes on. When we came to the house, all the goods were put down, and we all sat.

We sat to one side, then it was said, 'What's your business, Sithathu clanspeople?'

'Well, we of the Sithathu clan are going home now. We're bringing your bride here to the house. Now this wife of yours has no blemish. There's only one thing that troubles her that might give you some difficulty. She's often bothered by chest pains. But when we take her to the doctors, they conclude that her chest pains are an indication that she has a vocation to be a doctor. She should be initiated into the profession of medicine by doctors. Now we agree with those doctors, so there's nothing about these pains really to be worried about. She does her work, and does it well. But when these chest pains begin to bother her, she tends not to want to talk. There's nothing else wrong with her, we've never had to take her to a doctor for anything else. Never. You'll not be troubled by her except for that affliction that we've mentioned. And we can now identify that problem without the help of a doctor. That's the only thing you have to watch out for.'

When that was said by the people of my home, the younger brother of the groom's father rose and thanked them. He said, 'Well, that's fine. That's nature. We know it, we'll see. There is nothing more to say. Actually, too many words can defeat our purpose, preaching's not a good thing. Too many words make it difficult for a person to sort out what's important. The words spoken at her home by her father before she was brought to us, when he told her how to behave—those are the important words! There's nothing to add to them. If the bride serves her home of *birth* properly, then she'll be doing well for us here at her home of *marriage*. There's nothing else that we can say, Household of the Sithathu clan. We thank you.'

After that, they produced five shillings—they said it was for the bride's entry into the house. They produced another five shillings for the bride's privilege of dining with her mother-in-law. Five shillings was presented for using the kitchen [literally, holding spoons], and two pounds ten shillings for the ochre of the young wife.

Then they got up to go. Two girls leapt up and accompanied the bridal party a part of the way. I too went along for a short distance, then turned back.

'Well, let's go back.'

When we turned, they said, 'Well, stay well, Daughter of our father!'

I kept quiet.

We went into the house. I remained there for a brief time, then took a pail and went with a little girl to the river. We got there, and dipped water. Then we returned. When we got back, I took a pot and washed it. Because it was already late in the day, I wondered in my heart what I would cook. I did not know where anything was, these were unfamiliar surroundings for me.

The wife of my older brother-in-law said, 'Give her some maize. Take that mortar and pestle, and put it in the house so that she can pound the grain.'

I was given some maize, and I pounded it, I pounded it. When I finished that, I winnowed the stamped mealies, then cooked them in that same house.

After the evening meal, we sat there. Then I was taken to another house, the house that the bridal party had stayed in.

This sister-in-law sat there with me, she had brought a mat along. She kindled a fire, then said, 'You'll sleep here.'

Then I saw my husband coming in, He sat down.

My sister-in-law got up, and said, 'Well, I'm going now. I'm going to go to bed now.'

I too got up, saying, 'I'm going too. My sister-in-law and I are going to sleep.'

She said, 'No, *you*'ll sleep here!'

So I remained.

Time passed, and things went well.

Early the next day, at dawn, I got up and went to the house to get a pail. I took it to the river, and dipped water. I also washed my body. When I got home, I put the pail of water down, then went to the younger people's house and anointed my body.

Even in the way that I walked, I showed deference. I went about that homestead very carefully, taking the long way around, being very submissive to my in-laws. I went by the side of the house, pretending to go to pick up firewood. Then I turned and walked below the homestead. This is the way I went to the other house, I went by the side. I followed the custom of the young wife— walking behind, keeping to the rear, taking care not to be too forward.

I continued to act like that until I began to sense that I was pregnant, that I would soon give birth to a child.

I did bear a child, I bore her right here in my home of marriage, without going to my home of birth.

Then, one day, I felt the need to 'repeat the way', to return home for the first time after my marriage. 'Repeating the way' refers to the return journey of a bride to her home of birth, the journey generally taken with her little child. So I went with my child, and when we got home, a beast was slaughtered as is generally done for a person who has 'repeated the way'. And all kinds of garments and blankets were brought for that child. Then, when I was about to return to my home of marriage, I was given a bag of maize, at a ceremony called 'I am given the seed' at my home of birth. And I brought all those things along with me, all the appropriate things— the bread and its sugar. This is called 'repeating the way'.

When that child of mine was just beginning to walk, it was 'anointed for'—that is the name given to the ritual in which a goat is slaughtered for the child. A white goat, with a spot on its forehead, was slaughtered ritually for the child. And I became a 'nursing mother' again—that is, I *acted* as I had when I was confined with my child, only now I was doing it *ritually*, as a part of this 'anointing' ritual. The baby was being anointed for, and I put white ochre on its face.

So that first stage of being a wife came to an end, this state of deference, and my husband boarded a train. Everything was well in our homestead when he left to seek work in the white man's land in Johannesburg. He remained there in Johannesburg—but he did not write to me directly, he wrote to the wife of his older brother. No letter was addressed to me because in that first generation of modern times, that first generation of those who went to work in the mines, this is how those who went off to Johannesburg showed respect. The letter was written to an older person, and the young wife would hear of her husband through that older person. Even when he was sending something, money for example, he sent it through the wife of the older brother.

Then this wife of the older brother would say, 'My brother-in-law says that I should give you this money. He's still well. I told him that you're all right too. Now, do you want me to ask for anything from my brother?'

And I would say, 'No, I don't want anything.'

I was content with this form of communication, it did not upset me. I appreciated that my husband should address himself to an older person, showing deference to an older person with whom I lived.

When he returned from the white man's country, he would go into the house of the older brother; he would go there, and I would only hear what was being said.

'Come! My younger brother is here!'

Then I would go in, and he was there. I would greet him, and sit down. He would remain there for several days before saying that his own house should be prepared. And our house did not yet have the status of being a house of marriage; it was still a young people's house. It had no independent status yet. Things occurred elsewhere. We would go to that house only at bedtime: we would use it as a bedroom, not yet as a full house. We were really living at the house of his older brother.

Things went on like that. And then I became pregnant again.

When I was in the eighth month of my pregnancy, the first child died. She had become very sick. My husband was there, and we went all over the country seeking medical help for the child, but there was no help—the baby left us. I was eight months pregnant, and I delivered the next child at that time. That second child grew up well, and she is here today, with children of her own.

After that child, I again became pregnant, and delivered the child that followed that one. It was a boy, and when that boy was at the stage of moving about for himself, he also became ill. And he died.

In time, I became pregnant again, and I again delivered a boy— and that boy also died.

Another child was born, and he died after the eclipse.

That was the last of my children.

Time passed, and we were happy. No problems.

Then difficulties arose. The subject regarding my vocation to be a doctor came up again, it became more persistent as my nervousness and chest troubles intensified. Now, whenever a person who had done something came into my sight—if this person had done something bad—my body would itch, I would become uncomfortable; I would become excitable, nervous, I would experience intense pains in my chest. I could not stay with a person who had done something bad.

This became more and more evident in me, and caused my husband considerable anxiety. He wanted to send me to more doctors then, to determine what was wrong with me. And he did take me to the doctors, he took me by night. We went to a doctor, and my husband had me examined there. The doctor explained that my body pores were those of 'white death'.[22] My blood was repelled by anything evil or dirty. I am therefore a 'white' person. The doctor advised that I be treated to insure my strength against the things that trouble the blood.

My husband said, 'Well, I give her to you, Doctor. Treat her, because this is painful to me too.'

The doctor then charged a fee for pounding herbs, but he did not charge for the diagnosis. I was to do the pounding.

My husband produced the money, a pound, and left me with the doctor, saying that he would come to visit me frequently, but that I would be under the care of this doctor.

I stayed with that doctor then, and time passed for me there. He treated me in every way, purging me, washing me, feeding me a medicine that pained my body. And my trouble ceased.

The pains in my chest ended, my anxieties were calmed. He

made me dance, also a part of the treatment—he did everything.

Then, during the year, as his place was visited by sick people who had come to be treated, this doctor told me to go and take care of a person who had come to be examined. I was sent to another house; I went and examined that person. I finished that, and the doctor asked me to prepare some medicine for this patient. I did that. I treated him, and he became well. The doctor then rewarded me with doctor's white beads, a string of beads that was tied to my head, on the cranium—the first string of beads, beads of initiation. These were tied on.

The second time I completed an examination, a set of doctor's beads was put around my neck. Then my husband came again, he arrived to find me wearing these sets of beads. During his presence, a sick person came; I went to examine him, and I finished the job while my husband was still there.

Time passed, we went on like that—until I was treating my own patients. I would diagnose some of their diseases, they would come to me and I would treat them, and they would get well. And some of them would also become doctors, those with symptoms similar to mine. Various kinds of people came to me—a person with one kind of ache, a person who was barren, a person burdened by some illness. There were all kinds of people, all sorts and conditions of diseases that I continually treated until finally, the doctor who was treating me said, 'Well, it's about time that she should go and set up her own practice, at her own house. She should treat her own people, because she's now got quite a clientele here.'

That was the decision of the doctor. I returned then, and remained at my own house.

There were some difficulties, which might have caused great confusion had they not changed in time: while I was establishing my practice, traveling all over the countryside treating people, my husband became very angry. Why did I not come home anymore? I seem to be going to so many homesteads to treat patients, and I don't return to my own home! I might be gone as long as a week, even *two* weeks. That bothered him, we were annoying each other now, and it began to seem like a bad situation for our marriage. Eventually, it became clear that I wanted my husband to return the *lobola*.[23] I could no longer be his wife, because I would not be able to treat people as a white doctor does—people come to European doctor's offices to be treated, but the Xhosa doctor goes to the people, and must thus travel throughout the area. We are fetched, and go all over the countryside. When a doctor is called, she must go to treat people wherever they happen to be. Now if my husband demands that I operate in a manner that is unnatural, in a way that is not the way I have been created, then it is better if I depart from him for a period of ten years.

I did leave him, then I returned. He was suffering because of my absence. He begged me, saying that he had done a childish thing, not realizing what he had been doing. He feared that his wife would be carried away from him by certain people.

So I did come back, and from that time there were no misunderstandings in our relationship . . . though another difficulty might have arisen.

Notes

1. *imetsha*—sexual activity in which the penis is not inserted into the vagina, but only between the thighs. Albert Kropf calls it 'unconsummated sexual intercourse' in *A Kafir-English Dictionary* (Lovedale, 1915) p. 234.
2. age-set—a group of people of the same age.
3. 'my grandfather'—literally 'my grandmother who is a man'.
4. *ukomulisa*—causitive form of *ukomula*. 'To break fast; to resume drinking milk after abstaining from it during the menses, of after the death of a husband, or after the winter during which milk is scarce . . . ' Kropf, p. 315.
5. 'You don't have to wash at home'—where, perhaps, she has been washing only her face to this time, suggested Mrs Zenani.
6. 'the *amasi* was sour'—It was purposely soured, kept longer. It was made sour for this ritual occasion.
7. 'Have you a problem?'—'problem' is a euphemism here for the menses.
8. 'she gave me beans'—because there are plentiful proteins in beans.
9. 'we were circumcised men dancing'—The youth's circumcision gives both him and his woman friend access to the social activities of young adults.
10. 'school people'—contrasted with traditionalists. 'School people' were those had accepted western education and religion.
11. 'dresses'—that is, as contrasted to traditional clothing.

12. 'to see it to the extent that it spoke'—i.e., to read it.
13. 'to profit from me'—i.e., enter *lobola* negotiations.
14. 'to give me some food in my own hand'—I won't take it in my own hand from your dish, out of reverence.
15. She is speaking of the distribution of gifts at the marriage ceremony.
16. *impothulo*—the ox the bride takes with her to her homestead of marriage.
17. 'from across the Mbashe . . . to the Neiba'—the Mbashe and the Neiba (Great Kei) are rivers in the Transkei. This is an obvious exaggeration, but this kind of story-telling is expected on this occasion. They will not inform their in-laws that they are members of the bridal party, but will make up some incredible story.
18. The taunting and mocking of the master of ceremonies is a part of the ceremony, as are his fastidious and teasing antics.
19. 'then put it down again at once'—to tantalize the people in the groom's party.
20. '*Yek'! Maan!*'—sounds made when driving cattle.
21. 'people of the meat'—this is the bridal party, the people for whom the slaughtering has taken place.
22. 'white death'—a trance, a sickness revealing a calling to the vocation of medicine. One is troubled by this sickness until she or he becomes a doctor: this is how the call to the vocation reveals itself.
23. *lobola*—This is the complex contractual arrangement made between the bride and groom and their families. Here, Mrs Zenani is referring to the *lobola* cattle, a symbolic part of the exchange.

Hajiya Ma'daki:
A Royal Hausa Woman[1]

BEVERLY B. MACK

Introduction

The Northern Nigerian towns of Kano, Katsina, and Sokoto have figured significantly in the major political and social transformations of the area since the beginning of the nineteenth century. Usman 'Dan Fodio's *jihad* (holy campaign of Islamic revivalism) began around Sokoto in 1804 and subsequently swept eastward across northern Nigeria. 'Dan Fodio's *jihad* marked a major social transformation of the region in which traditional Hausa and Fulani Islamic rulers were replaced by reformist Fulani *jihadists* who established their hegemony as both political and religious authorities known as emirs.[2] Almost precisely a century later Northern Nigeria underwent yet another major social reformation, as the British deposed emirs they found threatening. These were replaced with individuals who promised to co-operate with the British in a system of indirect rule, which lasted until Nigeria's independence in 1960. At that time a civilian government was established, although traditional leaders like emirs continued to share authority with civilian officials.

It is the rare individual who has experienced these transformations from a position at the heart of two major emirates. As a daughter of royalty in Kano, and a wife of royalty in Katsina, Hajiya Ma'daki has been privy to the events and figures central to the unfolding of Nigerian history since the turn of the century.[3] She is also affiliated with a wide range of social positions: the grand-daughter of a non-Muslim *Ha'be* slave, she is the daughter of a royal concubine, and became a royal wife to a devout Fulani emir. Complementing this background, Hajiya Ma'daki is personally familiar with figures central to the shaping of Britain's policy of indirect rule in Nigeria: she knew Captain (later Lord) Frederick Lugard and Flora Shaw, as well as British Governors and Residents

47

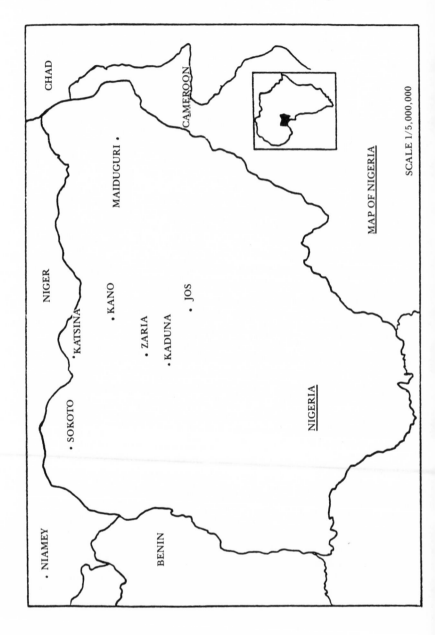

in the North, and impressed chronicler Dame Margery Perham with her active support of women's education in the North at a time when women's roles did not involve the need for literacy. She was confidante and advisor to her husband, the Emir of Katsina, Alhaji Muhammadu Dikko (1907–44). In addition, her senior brother, Alhaji Abdullahi Bayero, was the Emir of Kano from 1926 to 1953, during Nigeria's early formative years; Hajiya Ma'daki often conferred with him, and he respected her opinion.[4] To better appreciate Hajiya Ma'daki's unique position in and perspective on history requires an understanding of the circumstances of, and key actors in, both the *jihad* of 1804 and the British invasion of Northern Nigeria one hundred years later.

Historical and Political Background

Since the fifteenth century the walled city of Kano in Northern Nigeria has played a dual role as a major economic and cultural center for sub-Saharan Africa. As a terminus for trans-Saharan trade routes, it has long been influenced by North African culture and Islam. In 1807 the Fulani revivalist Usman 'Dan Fodio overthrew the North's Hausa rulers in a holy campaign that reached Kano by 1807. As a result of this *jihad* the ancient line of rulers was replaced by a Fulani elite. The role of emir was one of political and religious authority, and thereafter emirs of the region were answerable to the successors of Usman 'Dan Fodio, Commander of the Faithful and Caliph of Sokoto.[5] The north-western town of Sokoto, established in 1812 by 'Dan Fodio, became the recognized seat of the caliphate. It became customary for northern Emirs to be selected through the sanction of the Caliph, expressing their allegiance to him in Sokoto. Thus Kano, one of Northern Nigeria's most ancient and important cities, became linked both politically and socially with the new city of Sokoto in the early nineteenth century.

After the Fulani overthrow of Kano's Hausa dynasty, the city was ruled by a succession of emirs of the Fulani line, all of whom assumed their positions with the approval of the Caliph of Sokoto.[6] Kano's own civil war (1893–5), however, interrupted this process, as a power struggle unfolded over the process of succession within the Fulani dynasty. The principals were Kano's Muhammed Tukur, son of the former Kano Emir Muhammed Bello, and Tukur's rival, Yusufu. When Tukur was installed with the sanction of the Caliph of

Sokoto, Yusufu protested by retreating from Kano, accompanied by many devout followers. In the ensuing years of struggle, Tukur became known for what is alleged to have been inhuman treatment of prisoners captured from Yusufu's following. Thus a significant division among both Hausa and Fulani followers grew into rival Kano factions. When Yusufu died in August 1894, Aliyu Babba[7] took his place as claimant to the Kano throne. One month later Aliyu Babba invaded Kano, driving Tukur into Katsina, where Tukur was killed at Takalafiya in March 1895. He died as he was being carried back to Kano,[8] leaving Aliyu Babba as Emir of Kano from then until the British invaded Kano in 1903.

The Kano civil war not only left a legacy of conflict among Kano citizens, but also compounded long-standing rivalries among neighboring emirates who competed with Kano in slave-raiding. Aliyu then had to unify the Kano citizens as well as mobilize them to avert challenges to his legitimacy. Long-standing rivalries among northern emirates meant that Kano was occupied with attacks from Zinder in the north, as well as conflict from the northern-western emirate of Maradi. Such conflict among neighboring territories represented the continuation of a long history of local conflicts and slave-raiding.[9] At the end of the nineteenth century, despite—or perhaps as a result of—Islamic influence, slave-raiding of surrounding towns was still a common practice. Slaves represented an important agricultural labor force and were also significant in the urban growth necessary to the military strength of an emirate. Slavery was sanctioned by Islam, which reasoned that it created the opportunity to redeem *Hab'e* captives by converting them to Islam during their service as slaves.[10] This was the situation the British found when they extended control over the northern regions of Nigeria at the turn of the century: Fulani leaders struggling to maintain their own control of a Hausa populace and competing with one another for slaves captured in the rural areas. When the British forbade further slave trade and raiding in a decree on 1 January 1901 (effective 1 April 1901), the declaration was perceived as a direct threat to the indigenous economy.

In 1902, under Frederick Lugard, the British advanced northward along the Niger River, meeting resistance from the Fulani dynasties that sought to guard their hard-won control from yet another rival force, this time Christian foreigners with greater fire-power. When the British stormed the Kano walls and occupied the palace in January 1903, Emir Aliyu had already fled to Sokoto to confer with the newly installed Sultan Attahiru Ahmadu.[11] Aliyu received the news of Kano's occupation during his return journey to Kano. He then decided to launch his own flight eastward rather than submit to the British. In the process of this withdrawal he was caught and exiled to Lokoja. Lugard subsequently appointed Aliyu's younger brother, a royal title holder Wambai Muhammadu Abbas, to the Kano throne, ignoring other claims to the kingship. Muhammadu Abbas, who was Hajiya Ma'daki's father, was willing to co-operate with the colonists. Thus in 1903 the British added yet another element to the already disturbed society of Northern Nigeria: having in 1901 outlawed slavery in Nigeria, and imposing control in the North through their greater force of arms, they secured their influence by appointing emirs in Kano and other major northern emirates.

In Katsina, where the effects of slave-raiding and long-standing conflict with Kano had been signally disruptive, the British met little opposition.[12] Katsina had long enjoyed a reputation as an important center of learning and a bastion of Fulani control. Yet although its leader readily submitted to the British, he and his successor were deposed. In the end, Alhaji Muhammadu Dikko, a title holder but not a member of the ruling family, was installed by the British as the Emir of Katsina in 1906. He had ruled Katsina for several years when Hajiya Ma'daki was married to him.

Thus, British intervention in the selection of northern leaders facilitated amenable relations between colonizers and subjects. At the same time, British support of these leaders ostensibly helped to resolve the Hausa-Fulani conflict, exacerbated by the *jihad*. Although the Fulani had in 1804 replaced the Hausa hierarchy with their own candidates, they could not replace the characteristics of an entire culture. Over time the two groups assimilated many of one another's customs, creating the Hausa/Fulani society that today blends both cultures in one tradition. In many ways colonization provoked a similar process; as the British introduced Western technology and culture on a scale never before experienced in Northern Nigeria, they were assimilated within a sophisticated cultural context, not simply adopted wholesale.

Royalty and the Role of Women

The nineteenth century *jihad* and the invasion of the British in the twentieth century influenced the role of royal Hausa/Fulani women in significant ways. For instance, Hausa tradition once included women as political leaders, while Islamic orthodoxy excluded women from overt membership in political and religious groups.[13] Islam advocates separate social roles for men and women. It is a male-oriented religion; a wife is expected to be Muslim like her husband, and children assume their father's religion. Boys receive religious instruction outside the home from an early age, while girls rarely, and never publicly, attend mosque prayers, nor are they Muslim scholars. Since the formal establishment of Islam in Northern Nigeria, women's responsibilities have, therefore, been not religious, but cultural obligations to the family. The Muslim Hausa woman is guardian of the domestic domain, while the Muslim Hausa man's realm of influence is the public sphere; this is in stark contrast to the roles of Hausa women prior to the influence of the Fulani.[14]

Slave-raiding traditions of the area, however, gradually fostered the establishment of separate gender roles by offering certain women the chance to become a part of the elite royal class. Women captured and kept by an emir, or given to an emir as a gift, could become his concubines or, if captured with a daughter, act as his servant and offer the daughter as a concubine, through whose status the mother could free herself. Furthermore, a concubine might easily become wealthy and important should one of her sons become emir. From the Islamic perspective, then, slavery under a Muslim master was a means to conversion, and thus, to freedom. Once freed however, a Muslim woman's proper place was within the sanctuary of her husband's home. The Fulani establishment of Islam in Northern Nigeria thus meant that a woman's respectability was thereafter diminished by activity in the public domain. Fulani Islam promoted the seclusion of wives of free men, and their relegation to the domestic scene.

Thus the ancient traditions that women held political office, had titles, and were significant political figures—although not forgotten by women—were ignored by *jihadists* who gave new importance to slavery and concubinage as mechanisms for cultural assimilation and the integration of conquered peoples, especially women.[15] Through slavery and concubinage conquered women were relegated to the domestic scene and prevented from participation in leadership roles that might threaten the Muslim men who initiated the *jihad*.

The arrival of the British and Westernization further complicated matters. As early as 1909 Western education for the sons of Fulani royalty was promoted in the North.[16] Comparable schools for girls were not begun until the Kano Girls' Training Center was established in 1930. Western education for either gender, however, was not at first accepted by the Fulani clerics, whose resistance was echoed among the aristocracy. Gradually emirs realized that their successors would have no choice but to function in the English language to deal with the British, so they began to accept the need to send their sons to Western schools. In Kano, Abbas even authorized annual contributions to Vischer's school.[17] For girls in the north it was a different matter, however. It took a great deal of persuasion to convince northern emirs that their daughters should have the option of attending Western schools. It was against such resistance that Ma'daki was important to the establishment of girls' education in Katsina.[18]

In the thirties, literacy was becoming an important political issue outside the realm of royalty. In 1933 the Northern Literacy Bureau was established, and it soon began producing a Hausa language newspaper (*Gaskiya Ta Fi Kwabo*). Just as they had resisted Western education, Fulani aristocracy and clerics initially refused to support this news medium; *Gaskiya* and many other indigenous newspapers gained the support of the populace, however. The proliferation of newspapers, along with access to literacy, had the potential for profound impact on women's roles. Education and newspapers meant that even the most strictly secluded Hausa/Fulani woman had access through the media to public events. Although girls' education has still not reached universal levels in Northern Nigeria, the potential for literacy substantively altered women's opportunities to be aware of current events while upholding cultural obligations to remain secluded. In Northern Nigeria the transition first from traditional Hausa customs to stricter Muslim practices, and then to the accommodation of Western technology was accomplished in the brief span of several generations.

Hajiya Ma'daki's life has spanned these significant historical, political, and social spheres of influence since her birth, which almost coincided with the arrival of the British in Northern Nigeria. A daughter of Kano royalty, she soon became a royal wife in the nearby emirate of Katsina, thus in her lifetime representing officially each of two historically rival emirates. During her formative years as a young wife in Katsina, Hajiya Ma'daki witnessed her husband Dikko's concerted efforts to co-operate with the British colonists as they sought to control Northern Nigeria through indirect rule. Although colonial records are silent on the matter,

Ma'daki is known to have been a trusted confidante of both Nigerian and British officials who welcomed her advice on various topics. It is clear that her husband, the Emir of Katsina Alhaji Muhammadu Dikko, valued her perspective on events as well as her company, taking her with him during his travels.

During Hajiya Ma'daki's adolescence British influence had not yet permeated the Hausa/Fulani traditions in which she was raised. Thus Hajiya Ma'daki herself represents a period of important historical transition in Northern Nigeria's relations with the West, and the resultant revision of Hausa/Fulani customs. Her life parallels the experience of many royal northern women during the early twentieth century. Despite enjoying the privileges of royalty, Ma'daki faced the same restrictions as most Hausa/Fulani women of the period.[19] Her support of women's education is, perhaps, her only acknowledged public role, and even in this endeavor, she maintained a conservative profile, especially while her husband was alive. This is an account of a royal Hausa/Fulani woman who experienced a new era of Nigerian history first hand; making the transition to a new historical era while retaining her own cultural and personal integrity.

Childhood and Marriage

Ma'daki was born in the Kano palace around 1907, after Emir Abbas had replaced Aliyu as Emir of Kano. As the daughter of a concubine, Ma'daki enjoyed the privileges of royal life. She grew up in an environment that was both economically and politically secure, at least for the women of the secluded *harem*. Kano Emir Abdullahi (1855–83) was her grandfather along both paternal and maternal lines: he captured her concubine mother's parents in a slave-raid, and he was also the father of her father, Kano Emir Abbas.[20] Thus Ma'daki, royal daughter, traces her slave ancestry:

> Our grandfather, the father of [Kano Emir] Aliyu, brought my grandparents from the outside.[21] My mother was not married, but was secluded [as a royal concubine]. They brought her father here from Adamawa; he was a slave. They caught him during a war and they caught her mother in Filatin Borno. From the time they grew up, they set a good example, with her inside [the palace] while he worked outside, behind the Emir's palace. When they reached the right age they married and they lived together in

Gidan Sallama, near the North Gate [of the Kano palace]. They were given a house among the rifle guards. They married and had children. And then they secluded my mother . . . If a slave of the Emir gives birth you send word to the Emir. The Emir will give you a ram and all the things for the naming ceremony, and send them to the new father. If the child is a girl, when she is between seven and ten years old she will be sent . . . It was the custom to take a daughter and give her to the Emir as his slave. He said they should bring her here. Thus they secluded my mother. Emir Aliyu [did]. And then when he got up to leave . . . they all traveled to Sokoto. From there to Nasarawa where [the British] captured him and took him to Lokoja. When [others] returned with [the rest of the entourage] my father secluded her. And not long after he secluded her, she was pregnant.[22]

By bearing a child for an emir, a royal concubine enjoys both enhanced status and the option of freedom upon her master's death. Upon an emir's death, however, she is not obligated to leave the palace. In fact it is unlikely that she would relinquish the respected and secure status that being a royal concubine confers. Considering that a woman could, through concubinage, move from slave status to an esteemed position through the accession of a son to the throne, the benefits of royal slave status among the Hausa/Fulani are obvious. As Ma'daki points out, British intervention in this matter caused certain problems:

When the Europeans outlawed slavery, the male slaves of the Emir married the children of men from out there, from the bush, and of the town, and they brought them here. So it was that we could not seclude very many because there were no second-generation slaves.

When slave men marry free women, their children are free, and therefore ineligible for concubinage and eventual royal status. To be eligible for seclusion as a concubine now, a woman must be able to trace her ancestry to slaves in the maternal line.

Girlhood in the palace afforded Ma'daki uncommon security and status. Despite the Hausa/Fulani tradition of distance between parent and child, she experienced a warm and open relationship with her father, Kano Emir Abbas. Such an open relationship between father and child was surely a function of her age: respectful distance is kept as one passes into adolescence; Ma'daki left the Kano palace for her marriage home prior to such time. The freedom she enjoyed within the confines of the Kano palace women's quarters continued in Katsina; it is difficult to speak of her childhood without discussing both the Kano and Katsina palaces.

In keeping with tradition, Ma'daki was sent to her marriage home early, at the age of seven according to her own testimony.[23] This marriage, however, did not mark the end of childhood pleasures. There were plenty of children to play with before she was ready to become a wife; their toys reflect the rapid rate of Westernization in the North.

> There were children to play with there [in Katsina], the children of the concubines. And those like Nagogo, [Dikko's successor] who used to come and play the gramophone for me. It was something that you would set going round and round, and then you'd put a record on top. Long ago there were none of these. Long ago there was no radio—there was an engine with a wire. He would come and make it go for me and his younger brothers and the other children of the Emir with whom we played. We'd play this way, they'd get up and wrestle with him and the others. He was here, he would play the gramophone for me . . . And there was one who laughed all the time—*kel! kel! kel!* As for me, if he was laughing, and if I laughed too, then Nagogo would say, 'Well this must be the place for lizards. If you keep laughing the lizards will come and enter your mouth and they will not come out again.' That's what we did. I would laugh and laugh. And the children of the concubines would come and we'd dance. And then when we got the chance we'd run around in the open spaces of the palace.

The palace provided the children with an unusually large play area, but they understood they were not to wander beyond the boundaries of the secluded women's quarters.

> In the field area, there was enough space to satisfy you. I had my goats and sheep there grazing and we'd go catch them and play with them. And we ran about, however we had the chance . . . but if they know you have gone out, most certainly they will beat you . . .

The match was a good one: as a daughter of the Emir of Kano, her marriage to the Emir of Katsina represented an alliance between two emirates led by men with different rights to their positions: while Dikko represented a new line of rulers, Abbas was linked to a royal line with authentic claims to the throne. Nevertheless, both Kano and Katsina were ruled by leaders installed by the British, so their attitudes toward colonial innovations were relatively sympathetic.

> Her marriage celebration was greater than any other that had taken place at the palace, a celebration befitting the important status of her husband. He was famous everywhere in the country for having co-operated with the British when they first arrived in Katsina. At that time [i.e. during the arrival of the British] Muhammadu Dikko was not yet Emir, but was known as a counselor [*Durbi*]. Because of his success with the British colonial officers he was made Emir of Katsina. He saw to it that Ma'daki reached Katsina accompanied by her slaves, her dowry, and her parents' gifts of grains and other foods—corn, millet, rice, wheat, palm oil, groundnut oil, butter, etc.—for her new in-laws. Everything was loaded on horses and camels because at that time there were no cars. After she reached Katsina another wedding celebration was held and this one was even bigger than the one held in Kano. Some years after the wedding the Emir decided to take Ma'daki around the countryside to show her his domain. After that he decided to take her everywhere he went.[24]

Women's Titles and Slavery

Traditionally women in many Hausa states held important titles and offices prior to the nineteenth century *jihad*. A small legacy of this tradition exists in concubines' titles in Kano and royal wives' titles in Katsina.[25] Ma'daki is a royal title used only in Katsina and reserved for the daughter of an Emir who marries an Emir of Katsina. People know Princess Salamatu Binin Abbas, daughter of the eighth Emir of Kano, Muhammadu Abbas, by her title, Ma'daki, better than by any other name. To confer this royal title, an elaborate celebration was held shortly after her marriage to Emir Dikko. She was given extravagant robes and a turban, the symbol of her status.[26] People were invited from everywhere for the celebration and Ma'daki distributed bolts of cloth as gifts to those who attended.

One has a celebration for the convocation of the title; my father
sent both men and women. They went to the palace where the
turbanning ceremony was taking place. Everyone was gathered
there, town and country folk alike. The drumming for the
turbanning was done then, with the royal drums, the *tambari* just
as for the Emir of Katsina—the drumming for him and for his
Ma'daki is the same. During the time of war or victory, if a slave
was brought to the Emir, he would also be brought to see the
Ma'daki. She had a town, and in ancient times she was like a
regular village head.

The title 'Ma'daki' is one of the few ancient traditional women's
titles to survive to the present. Traditional reverence of the
Ma'daki, and the Mai Babban 'Daki, an emir's mother, are mere
vestiges of women's more public social roles prior to the *jihad*.

Before the Fulani came, I have no knowledge of that time. But in
Dabo's [Dabo was the first of the current Fulani line of emirs in
Kano] time there was Shekara [his wife] . . . when Dabo died
her children said she was to be Mai Babban Daki. They took her
and put her in her son's house. Long ago it was Maje Ringim's
house [Maje Ringim, i.e. 'the one who died at Ringim, or
Usuman, who was] . . . the son of Kano Emir Abdullahi Maje
Karofi [i.e. the one who died at Karofi].[27] When Dabo died Maje
Ringim took his mother [Shekara] and put her in his house that
was built for him when he married . . . When Maje Ringim was
born he was weaned early because Shekara was pregnant with
Abdullahi Maje Karofi. Then she got pregnant again and had
Muhammadu Bello. Then she weaned Bello and had two more
children, twins, a boy and a girl. [The boy] was given the title
Sarkin Shanu. As for [the daughter], she was taken to Sokoto
where she was married. She raised me. Yes. The boy was given a
titled position and she was married in Sokoto where she had her
children and her grandchildren. Then when their mother, Mai
Babban Daki Shekara died, the Emir of Kano Abdullahi, after his
older brother [Usman] died, they made Abdullahi Emir. So he
sent to Sokoto for Hussaina and put her there [in Babban Daki]
instead of his mother. He said she was taking the place of their
mother. When he died it was Bello [who succeeded], and as for
her, when she died, they brought her here and buried her next to
her father and mother. Yes. Mai Babban Daki was Hussaina. So

that's the reason that now, when a man succeeds to the throne, he puts his mother there to be Mai Babban Daki.

In keeping with the customary avoidance required between mother and first-born child, Ma'daki's mother was not the one who raised her; instead, Hussaina, described above, cared for Ma'daki in her early years.[28] It was for situations like this that slaves were crucial in royal households.

> If you cried she would go and find the guardian to take you to the mother to be nursed. If she finished and the child was full, she'd put him back and she'd go out . . . the mother and child don't go to the same sleeping places until the night, after one has finished all there is to do, then she'll come and fix the bed and put the child on the sheet in front of you. But during the day it is not your business, only if the child aggravates you with its crying does someone call you to nurse it, then you go out and leave it. Yes, the one who carried me was a slave, the child of a slave, she was born in the Nassarawa farm community. Someone caught her and gave her [to the people] here and then they told her to take care of me.

England and Mecca

Following the wedding festivities, Ma'daki and the rest of the royal household in Katsina spent several years living quietly with the British and enjoying life in the palace. In 1921 the Emir decided to make the pilgrimage to Mecca, thus setting a precedent among northern emirs. He sent a letter to Sir Hugh Clifford, colonial governor in Lagos, requesting permission to travel. This request was passed on to King George V in England and arrangements were made for someone to take the Emir's place during his absence. King George not only agreed to the pilgrimage, but also invited the Emir to visit him in England on the way to Mecca.

The Emir agreed to travel to Mecca via England, a decision that established his reputation as the first Muslim leader in Nigeria to make such a trip.[29] It also, of course, demonstrated his commitment to co-operative relations with the British. Before and long after the trip his advice was sought by other travelers. His praises were sung throughout the North:

You were the first to go to Mecca, Dikko,
You were the first to go to England.
You are upright and honest, Nikatau, son of Durbi,
Sarki, you have set us an example.

Katsina Emir Dikko's biography, *Sarkin Katsina Alhaji Muhammadu Dikko* mentions Ma'daki only briefly in regard to this momentous trip to Mecca. The import of her accompanying him may be lost on those unfamiliar with the Hausa/Fulani practice of wife seclusion; allowing one's wife to move about in public places is failing a religious responsibility to protect the woman's welfare. Nevertheless, in an unprecedented decision, the Emir chose to take Ma'daki along with him. It is certain that Alhaji Dikko had no intention of challenging his religious obligations; Ma'daki spent much of her travel time secluded in curtained ship cabins and enclosed cars. But her traveling companions were good friends, and they enjoyed the adventure together. Accompanying them were also the Emir's son Nagogo (who was to become the next Emir of Katsina), and Kankiya Nuhu, Dikko's brother, as well as Nuhu's wife, other servants, and concubines of both the Emir and Nuhu. From Katsina they traveled to Kaduna by train and then to Lagos where they boarded a ship for England. For a secluded Hausa/Fulani woman, this was an unforgettable experience.

> After I had spent five years in Katsina, we went on the first Hadj to Mecca. Seven years old, and then five more years; I was twelve, eh? I was twelve when we went on the Hajd the first time. We went, me, and the Emir, and his younger brother the Hakimi, Kankiya, [and] Nagogo [Dikko's son], who at this time had been married for the first time at the age of seventeen. So we took to the road. We made the pilgrimage and we returned. That is the reason for going to England the first time.
>
> When we were going, the King of England said he had never seen an African man. For this reason, when you get permission to go to Mecca, you must pass through England. So you see the reason for our going to England—so that they could see an African , whom they'd never seen before. So we took to the road, and we went in a boat.
>
> We went by train to Lagos. It was the first time I had been on a train. At Kano at this time there was a train to Kaduna and in Kaduna at that time there was no electricity, only the lantern

light. The station had no power. We took to the road to Lagos. The Governor of Lagos said we should stop for a while. We stayed four nights in Lagos, in a house right next to Governor Lugard's house. Then we got back on the road. They put us in a boat. I was shaking with fear. Had I ever seen water? Not even a river, much less this ocean. I was scared. They told us to go on board, and we got into a canoe, an electric one, to go to the big ship. I was shaking with fright. I grabbed my husband's robe and held on. Were we on our way to paradise? The water rose and rose. We went on. Nagogo said, 'Oh it's nothing.' And then someone said they were going to put us into a basket.

We reached the big ship. I said, 'That's it, they're going to toss us in the water and we're going to die.' Nagogo came and sat down next to me. He grabbed my wrapper and held on to me. And there *I* was, holding on to my husband's gown. But then we got up and went. My husband's younger brother's wife didn't worry. She was older [than I]. She hadn't already done this, but she was mature. By then she knew better than to worry. So we went on to the ship.

We spent seventeen nights on this ship called the *Apama*.[30] We reached Sierra Leone, Dakar, and in Spain we went on land—it wasn't England but there were Europeans on it. I forget the exact name of the place, its been such a long time. You could throw money in the water and they would catch the money. I said this water is very salty. How is it that if one falls into it, one does not drown? They had practised [swimming], you see.

Arriving in England after three months' travel, the entourage rested briefly, toured British cities, and visited London where Emir Dikko met with King George V.

Well, we were on this ship, we were traveling and traveling until we reached Liverpool. Then we disembarked and they removed us to a thing with an engine just like the engine on the boat, and we went in this. Then we got out and someone told us to sit down and wait for the European who was going to accompany us, the Resident of Sokoto, Mr Webster.

So we took to the road and went. We spent three days in Liverpool. And then they put us in a car and we went on to Manchester. We went to a place where they made soap, and one where they made cigars, and one where they made biscuits. We went to see how they made them and they gave us a box of biscuits as a gift.

We stayed three nights there, or was it six? Then they took us to London in a car . . . tiiiiiiiii. And so we saw London. In the city one could see black people; I had never before seen them [outside of Nigeria]. Someone told us we could not see the king until seven days later, so we settled down to wait.

Then one day someone came and left quickly. The Governor of Kaduna was our guide, Mr Brown. His wife came and took me shopping with her. We went everywhere and spent lots of money. She would buy and I would say I had no money. Where had I ever seen English money? Who would ever have given me money? . . . So Mr Brown's wife said, 'This is not good, Sarki, you should give Ma'daki some money so she can buy things.' Then I said, 'If there is a store that is easy to shop in, then take me there.' So they took me to Woolworth's, the store where everything is only about five cents. They took me there and I bought lots of small things. I bought soaps to take home.

Then we got up after about ten days in London and they said it was time for us to go on to Mecca. So we left. They took us back to Liverpool, and found us a boat. We went on . . . What was the name of the place? Between France and Spain, we went there . . .

After seven months of traveling the party returned to Katsina, but before long the Emir grew anxious to make the pilgrimage again:

After the first time, when we went through England, we returned to Mecca after twelve years and we went by road. We went in the car. Out there in the bush near Chad I found some baby ostriches. I asked someone to catch them for me and I put them in my cloak. They slept with me, and I fed them, I gave them meat. Before we got to Khartoum their feathers were all falling out all over things. At that point I said, 'Well what am I going to do with these? If they hear my voice they will follow me.' We were about to reach Mecca; what was I going to do with them when it was time to make the pilgrimage? I said, 'For my sake find a place for me to put them so I can have a rest.' Someone said, 'In Khartoum there is a zoo.' They took them to the zoo in Khartoum. Then we went on.

Then we entered a boat. There were lots of boxes. They said

the Emir of Katsina has lots of money. So he paid them, each
one, twenty gold pieces . . . When they got on this old ship to
take us to Mecca they said it was like Noah's ark, not the kind
that runs by motor. They took us in this old boat to the middle
of the water. Then after we had already got on, and they had
already taken us out to the middle, then they demanded more
money, and said if we didn't give it to them we would tip over.
The Emir said in that case everyone would die. Then he sat
down. I was holding his satchel with reading materials in it. I
said, 'For God's sake, and in the name of the Prophet, give them
this money so they won't kill us before we get to Mecca.' He said
we were going to paradise, and what could they do about it?
Meanwhile the boat was moving, and it had not tipped over as
they said it would. Heavens, this man was stubborn! He said I
should give him the bag. I gave it to him and he opened it and
took out the papers. He just read and read. Eventually we
reached some place where they put down anchor and there we
were near a big boat. Then someone paid what they had asked
initially, but didn't increase it as they had asked later. And we
didn't die, we didn't go to paradise, and the boat did not get
weighed down and kill us. I said, 'Ay, the religious man is a
frightening thing.'

Then we went on to Jidda. So that's why we did not return by
the same route. Instead we went via the Sudan and here we split
up our party. This traveling . . .

In 1939 the Emir decided to go on Hadj again. This time was sure
to be easier since he had already made the trip. The Emir, Ma'daki
and Nagogo prepared for this trip, intending to pass through Kano
so that Ma'daki could visit her family. After two nights in Kano
they left for London via Lagos, Liverpool and Manchester. In
London they were greeted warmly and a dinner party was held in
their honor. King George VI gave the Emir a commemorative
medal, and other Englishmen—Johnson and Walton—gave him a
medal which he passed on to Ma'daki.

Even today Ma'daki's extensive international travel would be
highly unusual for a woman of her position. Because Emir Dikko
worked so closely with the British it is likely that he was impressed
that they often traveled in the company of their wives. This may
have influenced his decision to take Ma'daki with him. In addition,
being involved with the British on a daily basis, both the Emir and

Ma'daki were interested in seeing the homeland of their colonizers. Such international experience broadened Ma'daki's horizons immeasurably.

Education

One of few infringements on Ma'daki's childhood schedule was education; like most children, she attended Qur'anic classes from an early age until she decided that she really preferred to play:

> I was born in a round clay thatched house. We were living here [in the Kano palace] and when I reached school age there was born a younger brother, although he was not borne by my own mother. So it was that there were three younger siblings and one who was brought here from Fanisau. Our father brought him here so he wouldn't grow up in a bush. He suffered for his difference from town children. He was brought to our quarters so we would take care of him. At dawn I would say, 'Okay brother, let's go to school,' and he would say 'You are the girl, you are also the oldest—you go and get the porridge. Run and bring it back so that we may all have some together.'
>
> Then I would run and bring back a bowl of porridge and we would sit together and drink it, my younger brother and the others . . . Then we would go to [Qur'anic] school. They would go to the North Gate, where the boys' teacher was. And I would come here, where the girls would be taught in this very room [inside the women's quarters in the heart of the palace].
>
> So I learned to read [Arabic]. But one day I no longer liked learning to read because I preferred to sit down behind the house and play. [But] they didn't agree with this. If the Emir was told about someone not going to school, he would normally beat them. But my father never beat me. When they told him I wasn't going to school he just said, 'One day she will . . .'
>
> Then I discovered the way to the concubines' quarters. Someone gave me a container so I could go get water for her. She gave me a container for water, and I would do the [women's] work, but I refused to go to school.

Ma'daki's childhood loss of interest in education is understandable, but this experience probably influenced her later attitudes. Initially she was skeptical about the Emir of Katsina's efforts to establish a women's school. Early on, her doubts were shared by other emirs who could reach no consensus when the British offered to build a facility. For some emirs the issue was irrelevant because their sons already were in schools in southern Nigeria. For others, such close affiliation with the British was unsatisfactory on principle. The Emir of Katsina, however, was eager to comply with the offer to establish a girls' school, thereby upholding Katsina's reputation as a center of learning in Northern Nigeria. He relied on Ma'daki to support him through her influence. Even in conservative Kano, a Western school for boys had been established in 1909, and a girls' school opened in 1930. Ma'daki's support of a comparable girls' school would carry weight with leaders of lesser emirates. The debate went on for several years. Colonial Governors Gowers and Brown failed to convince local emirs of the benefits of Western education. Then finally a district officer new to the area—Mr Patterson—invited Ma'daki and her husband's son Nagogo to visit him and his wife. Somehow they were able to convince her to support the school, for she returned to the palace and told Emir Dikko, 'If you go to give advice to the other emirs tell them I said I agree. I have agreed for them to start a school.'[31]

Thereafter Ma'daki made up for her initial hesitation by throwing herself into preparations for the school. She oversaw the procurement of a British woman teacher for the girls, arranged the teacher's accommodation, and did whatever she could to assure local leaders that this was indeed a safe and legitimate school for their daughters. She told her husband:

> Someone should connect the pump to the river . . . And you should remove your concubines. Put four people in the kitchen. Put two people to work as police, and give them hats and the uniforms of policemen—and whips. If you don't do that, the children will not fear them. And select four people to give to me to teach them how to teach the children. And with that, we shall have a school.

Ma'daki worked in both the Katsina girls' school and, after her husband's death, the girls' secondary school in Kano. She explains the differences between the Qur'anic school in Kano and the girls' Western school in Katsina:

> This school [in Kano] was a Qur'anic school. Not Western education; *that* one we received during the year that they said they would build Lugard Hall in Kaduna. They were always

calling the Emir of Katsina so we'd have to go to Kaduna, and we'd stay for three or four months down there . . . Mr Gowers was Governor of Kaduna, and Mr Brown's wife was Mr Gowers' younger sister . . . Nearly every day I was in their house. They would send a car to come and get me. Then they said, 'We want to give you a school. There in the south they agreed to have schools, and they can speak English . . . we pay Mallams to come in the afternoon and teach us Hausa. We speak Hausa and you speak English.' So we said we should call together all the emirs [to see if] they agree to start a school in the north.

But agreeing to the establishment of a school for girls and support-ing it actively are quite different matters. When local leaders hesi-tated to send their daughters as students, Ma'daki recommended that they be encouraged. She said to her husband:

Well, I told you how this would be, and now you see they will not bring their children. If you hold audience, when the D.O. comes to greet you, and the titled men and the policemen and the guards and the prison keepers and those who work in the clinic, tell them that those with two children should bring one to the school, and those with three should bring two, keeping one at home with them . . . Tell them that if you see a mistake, if they are not bringing their children here . . .

Thus the British vision of a 'miracle of progress' was achieved through establishment of a girls' school in Katsina.

In 1932, on Wednesday, 28 January, Margery Perham visited the girls' school in the Katsina palace; seeing secluded women of the Katsina palace and their school had a profound impact on her heretofore negative perceptions of wife seclusion. She wrote:

After the usual compliments [the Emir of Katsina] led me through to the women's courtyard, all his male attendants of course falling away since only he could enter here. We found a wide, high-walled space and on a cheerful veranda found the duplicate of that miracle of progress I had already seen at Kano, a girls' school. Duplicate is not the word; this school had its own atmosphere. Here was a Froebel teacher, Miss Robinson, half submerged by waves of little girls. The Emir has provided them with a uniform, which they had put on in my honor, homespun cream tunics with pink collars and gay little turbans of white silk striped with pink and yellow. They looked free and happy, crawling about or squatting as they sewed little mats with coloured threads or played with instructive kindergarten toys. Some of the Emir's wives were helping with them, notably Maidaki [sic], the Emir's chief and favourite wife, sister of the Emir of Kano (i.e. a very good match). These two women have, for Northern Nigeria, unusual distinction; they are almost 'pals'. The Maidaki came to him at the age of five and is now twenty-seven and, even though she is childless, she has not lost favour. He took her with him to Mecca and to England. She is an extremely fine-looking woman, with grave, courteous, yet independent manners.[32]

The Emir was hanging around me all the time so I had little time to talk to the teacher . . . I took a group of him with Miss Robinson, Maidaki and the children, and it was rather charming to see him helping to marshal the tots and their evident confidence in him. I certainly was given a new and happier picture of a Nigerian royal harem than I had expected to find.[33]

When Ma'daki's husband died in 1944 she returned to her birthplace, the Kano palace, where her senior brother reigned.[34] Kano Emir Abdullahi Bayero is said to have conferred with her regularly; they were, after all, siblings, and Ma'daki had learned a great deal traveling with her husband and being involved behind the scenes in Katsina politics. So well known was her interest in and support of girls' education that the colonial government wrote to her from Kaduna, requesting her assistance as a matron in a secondary school for girls in Kano. The Emir of Kano, with school-aged children of his own, was glad to give his permission and support, and Ma'daki embarked on an unanticipated career in education.

A former student gives an account of Ma'daki's duties as matron of the Kano girls' school:

She moved into the school where they gave her a house of her own. She lived in the house, but was with the students each morning when they awoke until they retired in the evenings. Her work involved many duties. In the morning when the girls got up they washed and said their morning prayers. Then they swept inside and outside their rooms. They also washed their rooms and the latrines. Then everyone would straighten up the lockers where they kept their things. They also had to fix their bed linens and put them in the big metal washer when they became dirty. After cleaning, the girls would open their locker doors and line up in front of their beds for inspection. Ma'daki would come into the room and look in each locker. If someone failed to straighten her things well, Ma'daki would tell her how to do it properly. Then if she returned the following day and the work remained unfinished, she would give a punishment like sweeping the compound or weeding out the grass. In this way Ma'daki inspected all four dormitories, each with fifty girls in it. There was also another dormitory for the oldest class which was separate from the other four. Then they would ring the bell and we would line up to go to the dining hall. Before we could go in, Ma'daki would come along and stop in front of our lines, checking to see which one was best arranged and quietest. If we were in proper lines she would give us the order to enter the dining hall. After going in we sat and waited for the rest to come in, and when everyone had entered Ma'daki told us to give thanks. So we began the meal with a prayer—*Bismillahi Rahamani Rahim*—'In the name of God, the Compassionate, the Merciful'. Those who did not follow our Muslim faith said their own prayers.[35] We began to eat and Ma'daki went around to each table giving us advice, saying we should practise eating slowly and that we should be drinking lots of water—just as the English headmistress had instructed her to do. Throughout the meal she kept on telling us the proper way to behave at the table. When we left for classes, she left for her own house to rest. In the afternoon she returned at about four o'clock to see that everyone rested on their beds. Also, she saw to it that we said our second prayers between two and three o'clock and our third prayers between four o'clock and sunset. If anyone neglected to say her prayers they would bring that person to Ma'daki to complain. Then Ma'daki would pull the culprit's ears and scold her. At five o'clock we would go out and play for a while. That lasted until six o'clock when we returned to wash. Then we ate the evening meal. At eight thirty they rang the bell for sleep and before nine everyone was to be in her bed. Ma'daki would go to each dormitory with each of the house mothers for a final bed check. If everyone was in bed, then that was it, she was finished for the day and she could go to her house to sleep.

This, in brief, was Ma'daki's daily work, though she did many other things. Whenever a girl or group of girls went out she would accompany them, for instance to go to the hospital or to go visiting. She also went to the headmistress's office if she was called, or if she had to attend a meeting. Although she could not speak English and therefore did not participate in these meetings she was invited to them because of her important status at the school.

Ma'daki received her first formal invitation to such a meeting on 19 January 1949 and she was proud to attend. This was a meeting to discuss the plan for the new girls school—how it should be run, who should teach the girls, the task of finding a qualified Arabic teacher, as well as teachers for Hausa and English.[36]

Historic Personages

Ma'daki's opportunity to act as an unofficial diplomat came with her position; as a princess and the wife of an emir, she was surrounded by prominent Nigerians and Europeans. But her efficacy in the role was due to her own fine character; intelligent, discreet and untiring, she acquired a reputation as a trustworthy and respected figure.

In the early years of her marriage, Ma'daki met regularly for tea with Flora Shaw [later Lady Lugard] when they were both accompanying their husbands in Kaduna. Through an interpreter, they would discuss a wide range of things. One of the most constant topics was the establishment of Western schools in Northern Nigeria.

> Lugard's wife we visited there in Kaduna. I often went there to have tea. [We talked of] what one would do to start a school. [She said] 'People in schools all know how to write, even the people of Okene . . . They take their children there to learn how to make the school. Here in the North you wouldn't even accept a school. If you don't accept the school, we will [stop trying to help you].' . . . Then I said to my husband [that we should], collect all the emirs and consult with them. It would be better for everyone to meet together and for someone to talk with [the emirs] all at once, to find out whether they agree or not.

Later on, when she was living in Kano again, Ma'daki entertained Churchill's wife, acting as spokesperson for the other women of the Kano palace. Throughout her life, Ma'daki conferred with the wives of Europeans who were busy making policy in Nigeria, acting as an unofficial liaison. The thoughtful advice she offered the Emir after her conversations with these European women was not ignored. Her sadness at their deaths testifies to the depth of the friendships they had formed:

> Even when the Prime Minister of England [Churchill] died, I cried and cried, because I had come to know them.

Ma'daki had met Princess Elizabeth on one of her trips to England, so when Elizabeth was crowned, Ma'daki sent her the traditional symbols of Hausa/Fulani royalty, ostrich feather shoes and fans. Ma'daki sent the following letter to Kano Resident Weatherhead, asking him to deliver these gifts:

> Sir:
> I shall be very grateful if you will be able to forward this, my humble present, to Her Majesty the Queen Elizabeth II. This present is to commemorate to Her Majesty my everlasting loyalty and delight in her accession to the throne as the Queen of England and Head of the Commonwealth.
> Attached is my latest communication with Her Majesty, when she was Princess Elizabeth II.
> The present consists of:
> 1. one pair of ostrich feather shoes, the type worn by her humble servant's princess of this province, and
> 2. two ostrich feather fans.
>
> Yours faithfully
>
> Binta Ma'daki

In 1953 the new Queen wrote back to Ma'daki expressing her thanks and enclosing a coronation medal for her. When the Queen was scheduled to visit Nigeria in 1956, Ma'daki had a new role. She was chosen guardian for the children representing Kano state in festivities to welcome the monarch. Traveling to Kaduna, Ma'daki discovered that she had been named Head Matron to oversee all the children's groups who were to welcome the Queen.

> In 1956 the Queen visited Nigeria. Because of this visit a letter was written and sent to our school, where they chose Ma'daki as

the guardian of the children from Kano State who were to take part in ceremonies for the Queen's reception. Ma'daki was to go with them to Kaduna where they would dance and do various other things to welcome the Queen. But when they reached Kaduna they found out that Ma'daki was actually Head Matron of all the groups from different areas of Nigeria. They all left Kano for Kaduna by train, mothers, daughters, and other young women from various places. As for us, we were left in Kano with the rest of the children, where for two weeks we practised on the airstrip, preparing to welcome the Queen when she came. After a time she reached Kano from Kaduna. We met her on the airfield in Kano. As she got out of the airplane we all kneeled down to greet her, saying, 'May God give you a long life!' Then she smiled, answering with a wave of her hand. Then we got up and stood in a straight line. She came and reviewed the parade we had made for her, asking some children about their names, their towns, their ages and classes in school and which subjects were being taught to them. After that the Queen got up and left the Kano airport. After staying two nights, Ma'daki and those with her returned from Kaduna. As the girls from the school told me, they were very happy and hoped that God would bring her back again another time.[37]

Conclusion

Like most histories of the period, accounts of Kano and Katsina at the turn of the century rarely mention women's influence on significant social or political issues.[38] Yet attention to the lives of individuals like Ma'daki indicates that their invisibility is by no means indicative of a lack of influence. As Schildkrout's study in this book indicates, Hausa/Fulani women rarely obtain independent social status, regardless of their degree of economic independence, which may be considerable. But Ma'daki's own perception of her contribution to the events of her time is testimony to her intellectual involvement and activity. She has been part of two important families during a significant historic period.

Ma'daki's father and husband were the first leaders of major Northern Nigerian emirates who were obliged to make strategic political decisions in dealing with colonial rulers. In the process of accommodating Westernization, however, these emirs maintained their cultural heritage. They assimilated aspects of the West within the framework of their own ethnic and religious traditions. Similarly,

Ma'daki maintained her own integrity during her country's transition period. A devout Muslim woman, she fulfilled her religious
obligations by attending to her husband's family, praying, fasting,
giving alms, making the pilgrimage to Mecca, behaving with
respect and deference toward her husband, and conducting herself
in an appropriate manner. None of these obligations, however,
precluded communication with her husband and an informed interest in the political events of her time. She understood that the Qur'-
an identifies a woman's role as different from a man's role, not
inferior to it. Indeed, Ma'daki's young womanhood was less than a
century after *jihad* leader Usman 'Dan Fodio's daughter, Nana
Asmau', had become famous for her scholarly religious activities.

Although Ma'daki, a traditional royal Hausa/Fulani woman, is
not a major figure in colonial reports of the period, she was directly
involved with decisions about schools for girls. She was a prime
actor in establishing these facilities, and during her widowhood she
actively maintained such institutions.

As a companion to the wives of international figures, central to
relations between Northern Nigeria and the West, Ma'daki became
a behind-the-scenes ambassador. Politically, Ma'daki's background
was valuable to her husband; as an insider in two historically
important emirates of the area, she had a clear perception of
political machinations. Ma'daki's keen perceptive nature, combined with her flexibility in foreign situations, could only have
enhanced Emir Dikko's regard for her. It is widely known that he
respected her and held her in high esteem. Ma'daki's influence on
Dikko's decisions is not measured or recorded as are men's roles in
history. But it is likely that her opinion, like those of many other
women of the period, was a more significant factor in the development of Northern Nigeria during the colonial period than has been
acknowledged.

Notes

1. For this and subsequent translations from the Hausa refer to
   Abraham, R.C., *Dictionary of the Hausa Language*, (London: 1968).

This study results from both formal and informal discussions with Hajiya Ma'daki during my three year period of residence in Kano between 1979–83. In addition I have cited commentary by Hajiya Abba Bayero, wife of Kano Emir Alhaji Ado Bayero and daughter of Katsina royalty. Where direct quotations appear without citations, they are culled from my taped interviews with Ma'daki, which I transcribed and translated from the Hausa; time for such transcription and writing was provided by the National Endowment for the Humanities. I am grateful to His Royal Highness Alhaji Ado Bayero, Emir of Kano, who welcomed me into the Kano royal household, and to the women of the Kano palace, especially Hajiya Abba and Hajiya Ma'daki, whose kindness and patience are inexhaustible. I also wish to thank the following for reading and commenting on earlier drafts of this paper: Alhaji Ado Bayero, Emir of Kano; Allan Christelow; A. Neil Skinner; M.G. Smith; and Connie Stephens. I take full responsibility, however, for any misquotation or misrepresentation.

2. Emir is the Arabic term (now used in English) by which these rulers were known; the Hausa term, used prior to the *jihad* and in continued use today, is *sarki*.

3. Hajiya Ma'daki, whose proper full name is Salamatu Binin Abbas, is the daughter of Kano Emir Muhammadu Abbas (1903–19), and was born around 1907 in Kano. Note that 'Mai'daki' is a title conferred upon a senior or favorite wife in the Katsina palace; it may be spelled 'ma'daki' or 'mai'daki', but in either case it should not be confused with the royal title 'madaki' which is conferred upon men. See Abraham, p. 629.

4. The late Abdullahi Bayero and Ma'daki were siblings, both children of Emir Abbas, who reigned from 1903–19.

5. Caliph refers to the leader of a theocracy; sultan, a term used later to described the Northern Nigerian religious leader, refers to the individual's secular authority. Thus the Sultan of Sokoto was a caliph (religious leader) until 1903 when, with the arrival of the British and their imposition of secular rule, he became known as the Sultan. (personal communication with M.G. Smith, 13 October 1985).

6. The first Fulani ruler of Kano, Suleiman b. Abahama, ruled 1806–19, but was not related to the lineage established in 1819 by Ibrahim Dabo, whose descendants still rule. See Fika, Adamu, *The Kano Civil War and British Over-rule 1882–1940*, (Ibadan: Oxford University Press, 1978), pp. 17–18 and Appendix 1. A council of king-makers chooses the new emir.

7. Yusufu felt that because Aliyu Babba was maternal grandson to Muhammed Bello, Kano's former ruler, his accession to the

throne could more easily be approved by the Sultan of Sokoto. For a more complete account of the civil war see Fika, *The Kano Civil War*, chapter III.

8. Fika, pp. 73–74. The exact date of Tukur's death is moot; Dokaji Alhaji Abubakar, in his *Kano Ta Dabo Ci Gari* cites it as occurring in December 1894, p. 57. M.G. Smith cites March 1894 (personal communication, 13 October 1985).

9. Such conflict long pre-dates Islamic control of the region. See also Dunbar, Ann, 'Slavery and the Evolution of Nineteenth-Century Damagaram (Zinder, Niger)', in Miers and Kopytoff (ed.), *Slavery in Africa*, (Madison: University of Wisconsin Press, 1977), pp. 155–80; Fika, *The Kano Civil War*. (Ibadan: Oxford University Press, 1978); Mary Smith, *Baba of Koro: A Woman of the Muslim Hausa* (New Haven: Oxford Univ. Press, 1981); M.G. Smith, *Government in Zazzau* (London: Oxford University Press, 1960); M.G. Smith, *The Affairs of Daura* (Berkeley: University of California Press, 1978).

10. A devout Muslim was obliged to educate his slaves in Islamic knowledge and to free them upon conversion. The extent to which slaves were freed in this way, however, remains moot. See Christelow, Allan, 'Slavery in Kano 1913–14—Evidence from the Judicial Records' in *Journal of African Economic History,* (forthcoming) 1986.

11. Attahiru subsequently was killed by the British at the Battle of Burmi, a conflict between colonial forces and Muslims who actively resisted European control.

12. See also Hull, R.W., *The Development of Administration in Katsina Emirate Northern Nigeria 1887–1944*, Ph.D. dissertation, Columbia University, 1968; and Perham, Margery, *Lugard, the Years of Authority*, (London: Collins, 1960).

13. Women in Northern Nigeria often note that prior to the nineteenth century many more women's titles—denoting women's political positions—were in use. Although very few such titles are used today, the fact of their having recently fallen into disuse is not forgotten by women of the region. See Smith, M.G., *The Affairs of Daura*, chapter 3 for a discussion of women's influential roles and titles prior to the *jihad*.

14. Until the Fulani established the custom of secluding wives, northern women were active in farming, marketing (several with titles controlled daily market grain prices), had the power to depose a leader, prohibit rulings and had ritual influence over the ruler of the pre-Muslim court.

15. The Kano Chronicle notes the leadership of Queen Amina, and the capability of one of her warriors, a woman named Zaria, during the early fifteenth century, in the area just south of Kano. Women

in Kano today often cite Amina and Zaria as pre-Islamic women leaders.

16. In 1909 Hans Vischer opened a government school for boys in Kano.

17. Smith, M.G., *The History of Kano*, (unpublished ms) chapter 7, p. 67.

18. The degree to which girls' education has been resisted is evident in the north even today. As Enid Schildkrout's study demonstrates, many conservative Hausa men even now remain reluctant to educate their daughters. As late as 1950, the Emir of Zaria forbade literacy classes for any Zaria women but the *karuwanci*, or prostitutes. (M.G. Smith, personal communication, 13 October 1985.) Speaking of girl's education in Kano in the thirties, Fika comments, 'At the city girls' school, the source of pupils was diversified in 1933. Hitherto all the pupils had come from the households of important nobility, who do not seem to have seen the benefit to be derived from girls' education and had only agreed to send girls from their households more or less at British insistence', *The Kano Civil War*, pp. 240–241.

19. Colonial accounts include—with rare exception—only the activities and perspectives of men, perhaps because Hausa/Fulani women were secluded, but more probably because women were considered to be guardians of the domestic scene, while men were responsible for public affairs and policy decisions.

20. Ma'daki's lineage is given below:

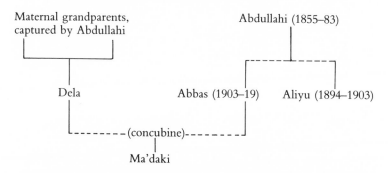

21. This acknowledges Ma'daki's complete assimilation into the palace family through the paternal line of descent.

22. This and all subsequent quotations from Ma'daki and Hajiya Abba Bayero, were recorded during interviews with them in 1982 and 1983 in Kano, Nigeria. I am responsible for transcription and translation.

23. The customary age for sending girls to their marriage home remains about twelve or thirteen; such a generalization, of course, is not accurate for those who remain in school well beyond adolescence. In other cases girls might be promised at such a young age, but they will not move to their home of marriage until much later. See Smith, *Baba of Karo*, for a more complete description of traditional marriage ages.

24. Commentary by Hajiya Abba Bayero, in Kano, 1982.

25. In Kano, titled concubines include the following: *'Uwar Soro, 'Uwar Waje*, and *Mai Soron Baki*; an emir's mother holds the right to the title *Mai Babban Daki*. Kano royal wives have no titles. In Katsina it is the emir's wives, not the concubines, who have titles; they are: *Ma'daki, Mai Lalle, Mai Wurare*, and *Mai Masharia*.

26. The conferring of a turban is the manner of conferring a title among the Hausa; usually it is only men who are titled, and therefore 'turbanned'. For this reason, the turbanning of Hajiya Ma'daki is unusual.

27. Usuman Maje Ringim and Abdullahi Maje Karofi are emirs who are identified by the name of the places where they died, having also been buried there, as is customary. Also, it is customary to avoid using the full name of a deceased emir; thus, the descriptive phrases are preferred.

28. See also Smith, M.G., *Baba of Kano*, 2nd ed. (New Haven: Yale University Press, 1981) in which is described the life-long taboos that exist between parents and first-born children among the Hausa/Fulani. Real status transmissions were upon marriage and becoming a parent.

29. Kagara, Muhammad Bello, *Sarkin Katsina Alhaji Muhammadu Dikko, CBE*, (Zaria: Gaskiya Corporation, 1981), p. 25.

30. *Apama* is the name Hajiya Mad'aki gives the boat; in Alhaji Dikko's biography it is referred to as *Appam* (p. 27); A. Neil Skinner comments that it was more likely *Apapa* (personal communication 22 September 1985).

31. Hull, p. 197, note 72. 'Katsina Division—Native Chiefs Confidential Reports, KPO, n.d., no file number. Entry by G.L. Monk, 22 January 1924. n.p. District Officer Monk added: "The Magatakarda and Waziri probably have more influence with the Emir than anyone except the Magajiya his wife and Haruna's sister and his concubine Malka . . ." ' Dikko's willingness to consider his women's perspectives on issues is evident here.

32. Perham, Margery, *West African Passage*, (London: Peter Owen, 1983), p. 107.

33. *Ibid.*, p. 108.

34. At this time Ma'daki was in her mid-thirties, an age by which Hausa women are considered matrons—mature, respected, well

into or past their child-bearing days, and more at liberty to confer with men and travel, than at an earlier age. Ma'daki might have gone to live with her foster children (she had none of her own), as is the custom, but she chose instead to return to her childhood home.

35. The school served a number of girls from the Christian minority in the north; such tolerance of Christianity is noteworthy for a school of Muslim girls in the predominantly Muslim north.

36. Commentary by Hajiya Abba Bayero, Kano, 1982.

37. Hajiya Abba, 1982.

38. See Last, Murray, *The Sokoto Caliphate*, (Ibadan: Longman, 1977) for explication on Asmau, the daughter of Usman Dan Fodio, and her role as a scholar and teacher in the nineteenth century.

Hajiya Husaina

Notes on the Life History of a Hausa Woman[1]

ENID SCHILDKROUT

Introduction

Within the relative ethnic, religious and ideological homogeneity of the old city of Kano, traditional status distinctions, merged with divisions based on economic class, create a society which is far more heterogeneous than it first appears. While Hajiya Mad'aki, the royal Hausa woman described by Beverly Mack earlier in this book, and Husaina Ibrahim share a common culture, the differences in their class positions are such that their day-to-day lives are very different. They probably differ no more than do upper-class and working-class women in our own society. Yet, in focusing our attention on other societies, the obvious cultural contrast between ourselves and others often causes us to ignore the significance of socio-economic variation. A comparison of the biographies of these two women conveys the contrast in their lives and illustrates vividly the effects of socio-economic class on Hausa women.

The fact that Hajiya Mad'aki was part of the Fulani aristocracy whereas Husaina Ibrahim was a commoner, of Kanuri origin, is not in itself of great significance. As Mack shows, Hajiya Mad'aki had ancestral ties in slave, commoner and aristocratic Fulani groups. While there are still some cultural differences between Fulani aristocrats and Hausa commoners, these do not hamper communication, nor even provide serious barriers to marriage. In comparing the lifestyles of those people who claim aristocratic Fulani ancestry with those of Muslim Hausa commoners in Kano, there are variations in certain marriage and childbearing practices;[2] there are differences in the practice of first child avoidance, and in the knowledge and use of certain herbal medicines. People note these, follow the traditions of their own family, but still regard themselves as united by their common identity as Hausa Muslims.

Much more important than these cultural differences are the

differences in socio-economic status between the two women. The social structure of Kano has been described by Tahir (1975) as consisting of thirteen classes: six in the aristocracy and seven in the commoner classes. In Tahir's scheme the aristocracy consists of six categories ranked as follows: the emir, specific title holders, the free nobility, the slave nobility, the court *'ulama'* (Muslim learned men), and the king's men. Commoners include the Hausa *'ulama'*, merchants, traders, craftsmen, farmers, musicians and entertainers, and butchers.[3] In this scheme Hajiya Mad'aki would fall into the highest class, whereas Husaina Ibrahim would fall into the fourth commoner class. In each case the woman's status was associated with that of her husband, Hajiya's being an emir and Husaina's a tailor. Were we to attempt to evaluate their status independently of that of their husbands', different categories would have to be used,[4] but Hajiya would still belong to the upper class and Husaina to the lower, whether judged by income, lifestyle, or parental socio-economic status. While women in Kano do work and often have independent incomes, they rarely can be said to attain an independent social status. When they do, it is most often by virtue of being unmarried, and then by attaining the dubious status of *karuwa* or prostitute.[5]

For most of her life Husaina has lived in a Kano neighborhood or ward inhabited by traders and butchers, whereas Hajiya Mad'aki lived in the palace in Kano or Katsina. Many of Husaina's closest neighbors were butchers, while the wealthiest people in her neighborhood were traders. A minority of the local enterprises were of sufficient scale to allow us to consider them merchants, as opposed to traders, following Tahir's schema.[6]

Another obvious difference between these two women is the fact that Hajiya Mad'aki never had children, whereas Husaina's life was largely devoted to bearing and raising children.[7] While this may not have been seen as a tragedy in Hajiya Mad'aki's life, because of her exceptional social status, it would be seen as such by most ordinary Hausa women. Hajiya Mad'aki was able to maintain her marriage for reasons other than maternity and she also had many other outlets for her energies. But in these ways she was clearly exceptional, and Husaina's story is more typical. Most Hausa women regard maternity as beneficial and essential and barrenness as an aberrant affliction. If their husbands cannot afford another wife who is fertile, women are often divorced because of infertility. Moreover, many women depend on their children for help in their daily activities—their household tasks as well as their income earning occupations. Elderly widows, that is widows past child-bearing age who are unlikely to remarry, also rely on sons for support.[8]

Hajiya Husaina's Early Years

Husaina was born in 1937 in Koki, a ward of Kano city. After she married Ibrahim, who was also from Koki, they moved to a house in a neighboring ward. Husaina was married at the age of twelve, and remained married to the same man for the rest of her life. After they were married, Husaina and Ibrahim moved into their house and lived rent free,[9] since the house owner, a woman, was a relative of Ibrahim's mother. There were other people living there at the time, all tenants. When the owner decided to sell the house Ibrahim bought it for just over 100.[10]

The house is a simple two-story structure with an entrance room, three living/sleeping rooms, a detached cooking room, and another detached room in which the older boys sleep. After he bought the house, Ibrahim added the staircase and upper room, which was used as his sleeping room.[11] The whole house is made of mud, plastered over with a thin layer of cement. The ceiling and roof are made of wood beams and straw matting. The cooking room, across the courtyard from the living quarters, has turned black from smoke from the wood fire which Husaina used to cook food for her family and for sale. A sheet of tin served as a door to the cooking room and was used to keep the young children and Husaina's seven sheep away from the fire. The small entrance room separates the courtyard from the street. Until 1981 when the eldest son graduated from Bayero University and took a job with a government ministry, the house had no electricity or running water. It was about this time that Ibrahim died. The eldest son married shortly thereafter and brought his new wife to live in the house. He then added a water tap and electricity and by 1982 there was a television set and an electric fan in Husaina's room.

Husaina's own room was a tiny space, about six feet by seven feet. It opened into a slightly larger room—what we would refer to as the 'living room', in which most of the household activity occurred. The only furniture in Husaina's room and this living room was a mattress on the cement floor, three wooden stools, and an assortment of straw mats. Clothing, tin cans, food supplies such as sugar, salt, Maggi (bouillon) cubes, enamel storage bowls and calabashes were stacked on the floor alongside the walls.

In the course of two years of fieldwork between 1976 and 1978, and a six week visit with Carol Gelber in 1982, I spent many hours in Husaina's home. In the course of these visits, I taped many conversations with Husaina in which we discussed the neighborhood children, and various aspects of marriage, child bearing and child raising. While I did not intend to write a biography of Husaina, in the course of these interviews many facts about her life emerged. From the conversations it is apparent that she was something of an expert on traditional women's medicine although her occupation was cooking food for sale. Husaina was an extremely hard-working, gracious, sweet and humble woman with tremendous patience and common sense. She was adored by her children and neighbors, asked for nothing and gave generously of herself.

Throughout her life Husaina remained in Kano, living in only two different wards. At the time of our interviews, she had never visited the commercial center of Kano, or seen the central mosque (which women may not enter), the emir's palace, or any government offices or hospitals. She very occasionally went on trips outside the city to villages where she sought medical advice or medicines. Occasionally a *biki*—a naming ceremony or wedding—would draw her to a nearby village. After her husband's death she realized the goal of all Muslims, the opportunity to perform the *Hadj*, or pilgrimage, to Mecca.

Her husband was considerably older than herself. For their first marriages it is common for young Hausa girls to marry men fifteen to twenty years their senior. While I rarely saw them together, their relationship seemed to be characterized by patience and respect. Ibrahim worked hard but he never really earned enough to provide more than basic support for his family, and at times not all of that. Husaina accepted this without complaint and saw it as her duty to work to make ends meet. Ideally, a Hausa husband should be able to provide for all of his family's basic needs—including shelter, food and clothing, whereas a woman's income should be hers to spend on luxury items and on her children's marriage expenses. Husaina's life had little luxury in it, and a good part of her income went towards feeding her family.

Husaina described part of her early history as follows:

My [maternal] grandfather was not staying here in the city. I did not know either my [maternal] grandfather or my grandmother. My parents came here on their own. My mother came here from Daura, in Kaduna State. My [paternal] grandfather died when I was young, I was a child. That was my father's father. I stayed with my grandmother from my father's side, my father's mother, here in Kano city. She was a Kanuri, and she brought me up.

My mother was not living here when I was married. When she left my father's house, that is when she was divorced by my father, she went to Jos where she married again. She even had a daughter, Gambo [this is always the name given to a child who follows twins]. At my father's house she had born twins, Hasana and I.[12] She then delivered another one at Jos after she was divorced. She had only three children, Hasana, Gambo and I.

After many years, when Husaina's mother's husband died, she returned to Kano from Jos. In 1977 she came to live with Husaina, but after two weeks they decided that the house was too crowded. Husaina's husband had another house in which most rooms were rented to tenants. She moved into a room in that house (rent free) and lived there until shortly after Ibrahim died, when she again moved in with Husaina.[13]

Childhood and Work: Earning For One's Marriage

As a child, Husaina did *talla*, or street hawking, just as her daughters were to do later on. She spoke often about how the significance of doing *talla* changed from the time she was a girl to the present. The developments are related to changes in the expected quantity of marriage prestations and dowry, for most of the profits a young girl makes from street trading go towards her trousseau and dowry.[14]

My grandmother was selling *fura da nono* [millet balls and sour milk made into a porridge] and she also did *tuwon dawa* [thick porridge made of guinea corn] in the evening which I used to take to sell. She also made *burabusko* [a Kanuri fried wheat cake] in the morning.[15]

When I was a girl I did *talla*, but not that sort which Memuna [her daughter] does. I only took things to sell and sat in one place. I was not going from one place to another. In the evening, before the sun had set, my grandmother would divide the food into bowls for me, and I would take it to a street near the house in Koki. I would sit outside the house, in front of the food. Then anybody who wanted some would come and buy. After it had finished I would then collect my belongings and go home. That was all for the evening, but in the morning I was not taking the *burabusko* out, it always was all sold at home.

When I was young most of the children were doing a lot of *talla*. This was because if one's children did not do *talla* they would be walking about doing nothing. So every woman tried to keep her children busy, especially by engaging them in *talla* through the day. There were many types of *talla*, for example, *tallen kosai, waina, funkaso* [fried bean cakes, wheat cakes, boiled wheat cakes]. So this indicates that most of the women had occupations, *sana'a* [business]. Walking about doing nothing was also done a lot, but now children don't do that because they see the rooms of others, their friends and relatives who did *talla*, filled with sophisticated things and well furnished. [She is referring to the rooms of young married women, in which are displayed all of their marriage goods, collectively called *kayan daki*, things of the room.] Girls now understand that by doing a lot of *talla* and not being lazy they can have their rooms well decorated and furnished. Now they are working extremely hard. In the past the children did *talla* but not as much as now. This is because the children before did not bother whether they had their rooms well decorated and furnished. The decoration and the furnishing of the room—such as bed, cushions, chairs, pillows and mattress, table, clock, standing mirror, and other furniture—are bought with the money the girl gets from *talla*, the profit she gets out of it. So every girl is now working to get such things in her room. But even before, when they did not value *kayan daki*, if one didn't have any, her friends would mock her. If she was ambitious she would engage herself in work to get *kayan daki*, and the work was pounding grain. The amount of *talla* that children do now started to set in when some of the innovations in marriage started.

We spoke a lot about the type of dowry, or *kayan daki* girls had in the old days, since Husaina's adult life was very much taken up with helping her daughters collect their own *kayan daki*. Husaina discussed the different types of bowls which women collected in the 1970s and in the past. This was an issue of major concern for Husaina and for her daughters, as it is for most Kano women:

> The type of *kayan daki* I had at that time was only *tasoshi* [singular *tasa*, a metal bowl or basin], and also *kwanukan shan ruwa* [metal bowls for drinking water]. There was no *langa* at the time [a small bucket-shaped vessel made of brass].[16] The drinking bowls were the same then as the ones we have now, but the eating bowls at the time had a pattern of flowers inside and the back of it was polished white. They were wider than the ones we have now. We used to cover it with *faifai* [a mat made by nomadic Fulani] made in Gombe. The bowls even then were being brought from outside countries, I don't know from which country. All I know is that they were sold in the market in dozens.
>
> *Kayan daki* was not as important and essential as now. Before, only those who came from well-to-do houses or rich families would have their rooms full of *kayan daki*. Those whose parents could afford it would do as much as they could, according to their means. The activities of the past are not the same as now, because before people did not value luxury. They were living a simple life. Even if one's parents did not buy any *kayan daki* for one, because they could not afford to—there was nothing wrong with that. After the marriage ceremony one would try and buy it for oneself, gradually. In the past, *kayan daki* was known only for the rich and wealthy families. It was not regarded as important as today.
>
> In the past we used *atamfa, sakake, karammuski da kante* [different types of cloth] in our marriages. *Sakake* was brought from Lagos, and not all people could afford to buy it, and only the rich could buy the good ones. The *lefe* of today is also different from that of before. Before, there was *karammuski da leshi*, [cut velvet], but it was different in material and quality. Their prices were very high, and only the rich could afford to buy them and put them in their *lefe* [the collection of cloths brought by a bride to her marriage]. We were calling *leshi*, that is lace, *ka fi zaman tabarma*. That is, the person who wore lace was said to be far from sitting on a common mat, and moreover only the rich, who were not sitting on mats as the poor, could afford it.[17]
>
> The sort of *kayan zance* [gifts given by the groom to the bride

before the marriage] we had then were totally different from now. The sort of *kayan zance* they do now would be enough to marry about twenty wives in the past. The sort we had were a bottle of perfume, sometimes two bottles, which each could not be worth 50k [kobo][18] and even that was considered to be too much—no pommade, only some kola nuts in a head tie.[19] Before, when a girl was going for *zance* she would do her makeup, and would put on the best of her dresses and then she and her escort would go out for the visit. The boyfriend would give her a hundred kola nuts and two bottles of perfume. The sort of *zance* we did was different then, because in the past the girl would first be asked to go and see the person who had called for her during the daytime. She would be told that somebody wanted to see her. She went to him with her escort and he would give her 50k. She would take it home, and that showed that he loved her, that he would like to marry her. At home they would exclaim, 'He loves her and he has given her 50k. He loves her and has given her 50k.' But if he had given her one Naira they would exclaim *'wai wai wannan mai yi ne'* that is, the person really loves her and really wants to marry her. The girl's parents would be proud of it because their daughter was given one Naira due to her charm and beauty. On Friday she would also ask to go for *zance*. On the day of *zance* her parents would prepare her after she had a bath and did her makeup, and she would be accompanied by someone to the boyfriend's house. At the boy's house they had prepared everything—fifty or a hundred kola nuts and two bottles of perfume. If he was rich he would tie a one Naira note at the tip of a *dan kwali* [head tie] and the rest of the gifts would be put in it with another 20k. This was then given to the escort of the girl and she would take it home. The *kayan zance* was not taken to the girl's house as it is now, rather she and the escort would go and collect it. When they reached home, it would be untied to see the items it contained. When it was surveyed they would consider whether the boy sent big bottles of perfume or not. At that time, there were no such perfume bottles with cup-like lids, but there were tall ones and others of many sorts. Some people would put in one bottle of perfume and others two, some put 20k and others put 40k. When the *kayan zance* was brought home the girl's parents and other relatives would be happy about it. It would then be taken and shown to many people, to different houses—relatives, neighbors, friends. The people taking it places would announce, '*Wance ta yi zance*', which means that she has got a marriage proposal.

It would be taken to different places, as they do now. People would say that the man was kind, exclaiming that he had put in one Naira. And they would add, '*madallah*', thanking him. Then the people it had been shown to would give out some money also, some 1k, some 2k, some more. The money was collected and taken home. Some people did *zance* twice and others even three times. Always this *zance* was on Friday. Then the aspects of marriage would be talked about. If the girl loved the man who had proposed to her, then that is all, as they loved each other. The girl is asked [how she feels about the proposal] by her parents, or anybody she is staying with [her guardian]. Then the parents of both would talk about the marriage and its arrangements.

In this particular conversation Husaina was then asked, 'How long ago do you think this sort of marriage disappeared? That is, the sort of marriage where the approval of the partners is asked'. She answered:

Ah, from the time I was married things started to change. I am going to say what I know. About two years after I got married one of my friends got a sophisticated *kayan zance*: a white washbasin (*kwanan wanka*) with, I think, two bottles of pommade, two big perfume bottles and one face powder, and some kola nuts. These were all in a big white basin. I was told that my friend had a sophisticated *kayan zance* and that a luxurious way of doing *kayan zance* had appeared. The people talked about it and described the items, and even added that the groom had put in one Naira. That was when things started to change and they have continued changing. Before, a bride who was recently married could stay with her husband for as long as three years without visiting her parents or without seeing her home. But if a bride delivered within a short time, say one or two years, she might, with some persuasion and a plausible reason, be allowed to see her parents at home.

Marriage and Maternity

Husaina was twelve years old when she was married. In those days, and still today, twelve was considered to be a normal age for marriage.[20] She married Ibrahim, a tailor, who was a Kanuri, like her paternal grandmother.

> I was grown by then. One of my breasts was out and the other one was not. But since it was the olden days I was not worried. And my husband did not have sex with me as soon as I reached his house. He allowed me to stay for some time before he started. But now husbands do not have that patience.

Husaina had her first child when she was thirteen or fourteen. She had three children, all of whom died, before the birth of Kabiru, her oldest surviving child. He was twenty-three in 1977, when Husaina was forty. At the time of our conversations, she had eight children, six of whom were living at home, one of whom (Kabiru) was attending Bayero University and living on campus. One daughter was married and living with her husband; she had one son whom Husaina had just weaned.[21] The child had stayed for two weeks, and might have stayed longer, except that children from his house kept visiting to see him. Finally, Husaina got annoyed with all the commotion and sent the child back. Her other children living at home at the time of the interviews were two boys, aged sixteen and ten, and four girls, aged fourteen, nine, six and four. All of the boys were attending primary school, but none of the girls were. Husaina said that her husband would not allow the daughters to go to school. As soon as the girls were old enough to participate in housework and Husaina's business, they began helping her sell cooked food.

Husaina's experiences with childbirth are typical of those of women who still followed traditional ways, eschewing modern medical care in hospitals and clinics:

> I have never given birth to a child at the hospital. I gave birth to all my children at home. I don't have difficult pregnancies. I have never been to the hospital. Nor did I ever take hospital medicine during childbirth. I don't go there. My first child was stillborn. I spent almost a day—from *'lassar*, evening, up to dawn, *asuba*, in labor but then the child was born dead. Since then I have not

experienced any hardship while giving birth. The reason for my hardship then was due to my immaturity. Then, when I was given medicines against *zak'i*, I refused to take it. It was this *zak'i* [amniotic fluid] that gave me the trouble. This, therefore, served as a lesson to me so that afterwards I started taking medicine against *zak'i*[22] in my seventh month of pregnancy. That is it. So now when I am about to give birth to a child, I start losing *zak'i* for up to about . . .With this one [pointing to her youngest daughter], I lost *zak'i* for up to two days. It came pouring out as if I was giving birth to a child. It ran out either when I was standing or when I was sitting. It finally forced me to leave whatever work I was doing during these two days because one can't stand children gazing at one. Immediately after, the childbirth followed, and this was done quite easily.

I have given birth thirteen times. Yes, none were miscarriages. Five of the children died when they were small. Two of them were two years old, one boy and one girl. They were weaned and were walking everywhere. They died after weaning. The other three died at infancy. The first one was stillborn. The second one was forty-three days old.

I had finished bathing. Even if you deliver a stillbirth you must bathe forty days. If the child dies before the forty days are over, you must still finish the bathing. The third child that died was thirty-three days old, not yet forty.

I was young at that time. I was inexperienced. When the midwife cut the umbilical cord, I was shy at the time and I didn't know anything. When the umbilical cord is cut, you will lay the child face down so that the blood can pass out. So when she cut it, she gave me the child on its back. She was to tell me to straighten my legs. She will then put the child on top, on its stomach, until she finishes sweeping and washing the place. As she does it, the blood will pass out little by little from the child. The midwife will take away the placenta, dig a hole and put it inside. They will boil water for the mother. The midwife will sit down and take the child from the mother. They will put water in a big calabash and bring it to her. The mother will then go and take her bath while the midwife bathes the child. By this means, all the blood will pass out. The midwife was very old and she was very slow. So when she cut the cord, she gave me the child in the wrong position. All the blood that is supposed to come out went inside his abdomen and it led to his death. The navel did not heal, it was septic. He died after thirty-three days.

Why, we asked her, did parents give their children out to be married when they were too young to have children:[23]

> Lack of sense. If they had thought it over and allowed the girl to grow up and become physically strong enough to bear children there would be no cause to fear. No cause for alarm. The parents would have peace of mind. But in taking a small girl to a husband—the parents definitely will not have peace of mind. They will always fear the outcome because the husband will be impatient and will start to make love to the girl right away . . . This is why we don't give out our daughters easily. But some do marry them off to be able to say that they have luck with men or that they are attractive to men. But, in time, when the girl gets pregnant, it becomes a problem for the parents. But if you allow your girls to be physically fit before you give them in marriage, then you will have nothing to fear. Now you see, I will only allow my daughters to marry when they are about twelve to fourteen years old. Because by then they will be physically fit to bear a child.

After the death of the first three children things started to improve for Husaina, perhaps because of her greater maturity, better health, or other factors. She herself attributed her improved fortune to her greater experience, to the will of Allah, and to her growing knowledge and use of herbal and Islamic medicine.

> All of my pregnancies were nine months. When my children were dying they started doing medicine for me so that they may live. I drank *rubutu*.[24] I was pregnant again after some time. I was still taking the medicine, then I got Kabiru. He was very healthy when he was born and he passed all the stages in health. After him I was pregnant again, with his junior sister, Hawa. She was born healthy too. From then, they lived. I got pregnant again, with Amadu. After him, his junior sister, Memuna, was born. She was weaned but died after two years. She died after weaning; she was weaned and then she suffered from dysentery, *kashin yaye*. Then the diarrhea became so serious that the anus came out. We bought one medicine that was used for a poultice, but she died. She died. Then I was pregnant again. After nine months, Memuna [the name is repeated for the surviving child] was born.[25] After her I had her brother. He died too. He suffered the same disease as his sister, dysentery. He was two years old.

You see . . . five of them [died]. Then later there was Salisu, Rabi, then Amina and after her A'i. After her, we said goodbye.[26]

Some people do not get pregnant until after they have weaned their children, but that is not the case with me. I always get pregnant before I wean my child. The pregnancy usually comes a year after the last delivery. I envy those who wean their children before they get pregnant again. In the beginning, when the pregnancy is about three months old, there is milk, but gradually it stops coming. After my children have had the milk for those three months they are weaned.[27]

Earning A Living

Like many Hausa women, Husaina has had a variety of occupations from within the confines of purdah. She views purdah as a sign of a woman's respect for her husband and for herself and she observes the rules of seclusion strictly. She does not leave the compound except to attend naming or marriage ceremonies or to seek medical care from malams or from those who prepare herbal cures. Given this limited mobility, she has had to alter her business activities depending upon the availability of children to help her.

It is not necessary for women with very young children to trade, but older women like myself have to trade just to feed our children adequately. You can feed one or two children with the money you get from your husband, but more . . . Even with richer husbands the mother must show off during the marriage ceremony of her children . . . by showering money on praise singers at the wedding and by giving money to the groom. So she must trade even if her husband has wealth. There are other expenses for *biki* [naming ceremonies], for *bikin kawaye* [gift exchange relationships between women],[28] and for gifts to relatives, *zumanci*. All of these things cost money.

Husaina's first occupation after her marriage was making a food called *'dan wake*, steamed bean cake. Her oldest son did the *talla*. The *'dan wake* was not profitable and she decided that she needed to raise capital. She sold some of the bowls from her dowry and began making a drink called *kunun zaki*, a sweet gruel which her son sold. This venture was profitable and she bought *kayan daki* with the proceeds. She did this for two years with the help of her son who was then six years old. Later, her next child, Memuna, helped her. While selling gruel, Memuna noticed that people were buying large amounts of rice, just where she was selling *kunu*. Husaina accepted her daughter's suggestion to sell rice and she continued this occupation for the rest of her life. Over the years she elaborated on the basic rice and meat sauce dish by adding a lettuce and tomato salad which was sold as a garnish on the stew.

At the time of her interviews she was assisted by two daughters, Memuna, aged fourteen and Rabi, aged nine. Both were engaged in *talla*, mainly selling the rice at one spot just as Memuna had originally suggested. These two daughters, as well as her son, Balarabe, aged 16, would do the shopping for perishable ingredients each morning. Sometimes the next son, Salisu, aged 10, would also help with shopping. Every day purchases would have to be made of meat, lettuce, tomatoes, and peppers while oil, salt, firewood and rice would have to be purchased weekly or monthly. Husaina's six year old daughter, Amina, was also beginning to help her by washing, sorting and cutting up lettuce. Even four-year old A'i was beginning to help with washing and sorting lettuce. The youngest two girls would also be asked to help deliver bowls of cooked food to customers who had dropped off their bowls in the house or to neighbors.

When Husaina sold some of her *kayan daki* to raise capital, she did not have to sell very much, for a bowl of uncooked rice was much cheaper then. The price of cooking ingredients, meat for example, went up six-fold since she started the rice business. The ingredients she needed to start this business were daily supplies of rice, oil, tomatoes, salt, pepper, meat and firewood. At first she lost money but slowly she began to make a profit. She could have made a greater profit, she says, except that she fed her family out of her cooking. 'The family ate the profit . . . But I was once advised by my husband's mother that whenever I start a trade, I must make it something edible so that I would be able to feed the children even if there's no profit.'

At the time of these interviews she cooked two-thirds more than she did when she started and she always sold it all. The daily profit varied by the type of sale: 'When you sell many small portions, the profit is less than when you sell larger portions.' She generally made about one Naira profit each day and put this into a rotating credit club (*adashi*).

In addition to feeding her own family, Husaina sent food to two other people: to an elderly women a few houses away, as a gift of alms (*sadaka*), and to her mother, who lived in the same ward. Husaina received food daily from her neighbor and closest friend, Rakiya. One of Husaina's children told me that when they get tired of eating their mother's food, they would ask her for money to buy food from Rakiya, who also cooked food for sale. Rakiya's children similarly would buy food from Husaina. But the daily food that Rakiya sent Husaina did not come from Rakiya's *sana'a*, or business, it came from the household cooking allowance given by her husband who, compared to Husaina's husband, was affluent.[29]

Husaina and her husband's combined income was still only enough to feed their children and meet their kinship and friendship obligations. They could not afford extra clothing or furniture. Ibrahim gave Husaina money every morning for some of the household expenses: for bean cakes and porridge for breakfast. He also bought sacks of guinea corn monthly, and got supplies of firewood from a village outside Kano; he bought soap powder for washing dishes and cloths. Husaina used the grain to cook *tuwo* for the whole family in the morning, but she bought the meat and soup ingredients from her own earnings. Unlike most husbands, who eat their evening meal at home, he worked late and bought food in the market in the afternoon and evening. Husaina fed her family in the afternoon and evening from her *sana'a* and from the food Rakiya sent. She gave the boys money for snacks at school from her earnings, but they also came home from school (as did many other children) to eat *tuwo* for breakfast. In addition to feeding her family and meeting social obligations Husaina used most of her income for her children's marriage expenses. At the time of these conversations she was collecting *kayan daki* for her daughter Memuna's marriage which was to take place three months hence. She started collecting the bowls eight months before. All of her own *kayan daki* were given to her first daughter when she married, in addition to other new ones. This was the second daughter to marry. Husaina's eldest son confirmed that, 'the first daughter always gets more because everyone, including other relatives, are so pleased to see her married. When my sister got married, just before the actual marriage, all the relatives started sending so many things we had nowhere to put them.'

Memuna did *talla* everyday to help with her expenses. She did not know the total of what she had already bought, but among it was two sets of three enamel bowls, for ₦54 per set; one set of three bowls (of another named type) for ₦50; six sets of three bowls at ₦24 each. She also had bought twelve plates at ₦2.50 each; three 'buckets' at ₦7 each; six plates at ₦3.50 each; another set of bowls for ₦14.50 The sub-total of all this was ₦304.50.

In addition her father would have to buy bed sheets, a mattress, and everything else to do with the bed (pillows, pillow cases). He had already bought a cupboard for ₦50, a bed for ₦70, and two chairs for ₦10 each.

There was also the contents of the cupboard to be purchased by Memuna and her mother: twenty-four cups and saucers at 80k each, five teapots (two of them gold, one with matching cups) at ₦6 each, an assortment of glass cats, glass elephants, sheep and other animals at ₦4 each; two glass vases at ₦3 each; six sugar bowls at ₦2 each; six glass pencil sharpeners in the form of animals, 40k each; eight small cups at 25k each; four glasses at 25k each; eight metal antimony containers (antimony is used for eye makeup) at 25k each; and another antimony container for ₦1. The total of these items was ₦ 94.20.

Then there is the *kayan zance*, consisting of soap and cosmetics, sent by the prospective husband. Memuna had already received one large basin full and one head tie full (the head tie or scarf is used as a container for assorted cosmetic items). Husaina explained that the husband must send at least two large basins and the head tie full of cosmetics. 'The head tie is compulsory and shows he bought so much it could not fit in the basins.' Memuna's husband had sent one basin so far. Memuna's brother noted that a prospective husband might have to spend ₦300 on cosmetics alone. Husaina added that:

> If a man gets engaged to a girl and does not want her to do *talla* he has to take the responsibility himself of feeding and clothing her after the engagement. If he allows her to do *talla* he has no responsibility to feed and cloth her until after the marriage.

In discussing her own work, Husaina explained how women's occupations had changed over the years. Not only do individual women change their careers as their families develop, but historically women have also adjusted their occupations as the context of women's work—the social and economic conditions of Northern Nigeria—has changed.

> Yes, the sort of work women used to do was different. In the past they used to sew caps as they do now, but not the type we

have now, because in the old days they did the one knit with wool, and they also knitted children's socks. Now women embroider men's caps. Old women who could work did the pounding of guinea corn or millet: they washed it, pounded it and ground it. Threshing—separating the grains of corn or millet from the stalks—was not done by people in the villages. You would be given only the grains. If the grain was two *mudu* [a large pan, containing perhaps ten pounds of grain which is used as a measure] you would be paid 2k. One kobo for each *mudu*. Three *mudu* for 3k. A woman would pound corn or millet to separate the husk from the grain, wash it, wait for it to get soft, pound it, spread it in the sun to dry, and then grind it. And all for 2k for two *mudu*. After the grinding you would do the winnowing—that is, you would separate the coarser grain from the finer grain, and keep them separate. But then there were some lazy women who did not want to work and so they always slept and were only dependent on their husbands; had less to spend. But those who did work got some money to spend and did other things. At that time a person could get satisfied [fed] for only 1k's worth of *tuwo da miya* [porridge and soup].

During my time women were not going to farms, but I heard from my mother-in-law that before the first rain had fallen, some women in our quarter used to go to the farms for sowing. But they only sowed, and this was the only farm activity that women here in Kano city used to do. Boys would be going to the farms with their fathers in the days before schools. Most of the people here, or nearly all, had farms at that time and farming was the main activity then.

Husaina's Last Years

There were major changes in the last few year's of Husaina's life. After her husband died she began to think about sending her younger daughters to school. Her son, who had moved into the house with his new wife, who soon had a baby, was supportive, if not totally enthusiastic, about this novel idea. Sending the girls to school would mean, however, that Husaina would have no one to help her in her business. Even though she was now a widow and not under the strict rules of seclusion, she felt she was too old to go out and hawk bowls of rice. In 1982 Husaina told me about these ideas, and said that what she really wanted to do was get a job, either in a factory or perhaps as a matron in a girls' school. She had a 'sister' who had taken a job in a biscuit factory and was earning ₦100 per month. Using the labor of her entire household—with the one exception of her oldest son and oldest married daughter—she was still only making ₦30 profit each month. Her son was not quite sure he could go along with such a radical idea, but in our last conversations Husaina told me she planned to pursue them. At the end of that year, after I returned to New York, I heard that Husaina had been diagnosed as having breast cancer. After several months of medical care she died, at forty-five years of age, in one of Northern Nigeria's hospitals. This was her only experience of a modern hospital.

Notes

1. The research on which this paper is based has been supported by the National Science Foundation (Grant No. BNS 76–11174), the Wenner Gren Foundation, the Social Science Research Council and the American Museum of Natural History. I am grateful to Carol Gelber who has provided invaluable research assistance over the years. In an effort to protect confidentiality, the names of people in this paper have been changed.

2. Husaina described, for example, how the Fulani use milk in performing the ritual washing of the bride, whereas the Hausa use henna.

3. See Tahir, Ibrahim A. *Sufis, Saints and Capitalists in Kano 1904–1974. The Pattern of Bourgeois Revolution in an Islamic Society*, Ph.D. dissertation, Cambridge University 1975.

4. This is because women do not have the range of occupational opportunities and extra-domestic roles that men have.

5. Unmarried women who are not prostitutes are referred to as *bazawara*, that is widows or divorcees, and still derive many aspects of social status from their husbands or fathers. See Schildkrout, Enid, 'Widows in Hausa Society: Ritual Phase or Social Status', in B. Potash (ed.), *Widows in Africa*, (Stanford University Press, 1986), pp. 131–52 on widows and Pittin, Renee, 'Houses of Women: A Focus on Alternative Life-Styles in Katsina City' in C. Oppong (ed.) *Female and Male in West Africa*, (London: George Allen and Unwin, 1983), pp. 291–302.

6. See Schildkrout, Enid, 'Women's Work and Children's Work: Variations among Moslems in Kano' in S. Wallman (ed.), *Social Anthropology of Work*, (London: Academic Press, 1979), pp. 109–139 for a discussion of the characteristics of this particular ward.

7. This also is a distinction between Husaina and Baba of Kara as described in Smith, Mary, *Baba of Karo: A Women of the Muslim Hausa*, (London: Faber and Faber, 1954).

8. See Schildkrout, Enid, 'Roles of Children in Urban Kano', in J.S. LaFontaine (ed.) *Sex and Age as Principles of Social Differentiation*, (New York: Academic Press, 1978), pp. 109–139; 'Women's Work'; 'The Employment of Children in Kano' in Gerry Rodgers and Guy Standing (ed.) *Child Work, Poverty and Underdevelopment*, (International Labour Office, 1981), pp. 81–112; 'Dependence and Autonomy: The Economic Activities of Secluded Hausa Women in Kano' in C. Oppong (ed.) *Female and Male in West Africa*, pp. 107–127; 'Widows in Hausa Society'.

9. At some point Ibrahim had another wife whom he divorced. She had four children with him, none of whom survived. I am not sure whether Husaina came to his house as a second wife or whether he married the other woman later.

10. As this occurred before Nigerian independence, the currency referred to was British.

11. Most Hausa men have their own rooms, which their wives visit. Women have their own sleeping quarters which they share with their children.

12. Husaina never spoke of her sister, except once in 1981 when she referred to a 'sister' who had a job (see below). However, it is likely that this was not her twin and that the twin died some years before.

13. It is common for widows to live with their married sons, but very unusual for a woman to live in her son-in-law's house.

14. See Schildkrout, 'The Employment of Children'. Dowry is perhaps not the best description of these marriage goods, since most of the property remains a girl's own.

15. *Fura da nono* is a Fulani dish of millet balls made into a porridge with sour milk; *tuwo* is a thick porridge made of corn, guinea corn, or rice, in this case of guinea corn (*dawa*), and *burabusko* is a Kanuri fried wheat cake.

16. These and other translations were done in Kano and are confirmed in Bargery, Rev. G.P., *A Hausa-English Dictionary and English-Hausa Vocabulary*, (London: Oxford University Press, 1934). I wish particularly to thank my research assistants in Kano, Bilkesu Aminu and Alfazazi Nanairege. I am also grateful to Beverly Mack

for reading an initial draft of this paper and assisting with some of the translations.

17. Cloth of many kinds is an important part of marriage presentations, both as gifts from the groom to the bride, and as part of the bride's dowry. Here Husaina speaks of the different kinds of cloth: *atamfa*, European imported trade cloth, generally used to refer to lost wax cloth used for women's wrappers; *kante*, a colored woven cloth made in Togoland or Ghana, commonly referred to as kente in English, ie; narrow strip weaving; *saka*, weaving, woven cloth; *lefe*, refers to the cloths brought by a bride to her marriage, from the word *lefe* which actually refers to the basket in which the cloths are placed; *leshi*, is a pidgeon term for imported lace; *karammuski* is velvet; *ka fi zaman tabarma* probably refers to a cloth woven of cornstalks, ie. a strip woven mat.

18. There are 100 kobo in a Naira(₦). The Naira fluctuated at around $1.50 in the late 1970s.

19. The kola nut tree (*cola pitida*) is common in the forest zones of West Africa and produces a nut which is chewed as a stimulant. The nuts are used as gifts on many ceremonial occasions throughout the region.

20. This is beginning to change with increasing female school attendance. See Schildkrout, Enid, 'School and Seclusion: Choices for Northern Nigerian Women', *Cultural Survival Quarterly*, (vol. 8, no. 2, 1984), pp. 46–48; and Callaway, Barbara and Schildkrout, Enid, 'Law, Education and Social Change: Implications for Hausa Muslim Women in Nigeria', in Lynne Iglitzen and Ruth Ross (ed.) *Women in the World: 1975–1985. The Women's Decade*, (Santa Barbara: ABC Clio Press, second, revised edition, 1986), pp. 181–205.

21. The relationship between a child and the person who weans him or her is significant. Most women take their children to their mother or to another close female relative. The child stays with this caretaker for about two weeks with no contact with the natural mother. The person 'who weans' a child is also often the person who later fosters the child at the age of six or seven. When people describe their life histories they always mention the person who weaned them, usually with a great deal of warmth.

22. Bargery, 'A Hausa English Dictionary' p. 1124, defines *Zaki* as 1. a pleasant flavour esp. of sugar or salt. 2. eagerness or keenness to obtain a thing 3. amniotic fluid. Women are cautioned to avoid eating sweet things during pregnancy in order to avoid miscarriage, following a premature rupturing of the amniotic sac.

23. One of the major reasons, discussed elsewhere, is fear that the daughter might lose her virginity before her first marriage. See Schildkrout, 'Roles of Children', and 'Widows in Hausa Society'.

24. A 'medicinal' drink consisting of the water in which verses from the Qur'an have been washed.
25. Her first son was also named after the male children who died before his birth, reflecting the belief that subsequent children replace those who have died.
26. This seems to imply that she ceased having sexual relations with her husband. He died, in his sixties, when the youngest child, A'i, was four years old.
27. Nevertheless, her youngest child who was four would still grab hold of her breast whenever she could.
28. See Smith, 'Baba of Karo'.
29. For more on the significance of women cooking food for sale see Schildkrout, 'Child Work, Poverty and Underdevelopment' and Raynaut, Claude, 'Aspects socio-economique de la preparation et la circulation de la nourriture dans un village Hausa (Niger)' in *Cahiers d'etudes africaines*, (vol. 17, no. 4, 1968), pp. 569-97.

Bitu

Facilitator of Women's Educational Opportunities

CHRISTINE OBBO

Introduction

> The Reformer is somebody who sees what should be done and has the ability to get it done . . . She is an educated [African] woman who sees need for a tremendous effort [in] the development of girls' education in her country. She sees the importance of good homes as an educational influence, and their [the girls] dependence on educated mothers. She sees the dangerous lack of balance in her society where men contribute most of the leadership even in the home . . . She is not fanatic, nor does she claim that women and men should be identical in social rights and duties. She imagines them both living full and useful complementary lives. This is her vision. Two main obstacles stand in her way: there are official obstacles and human ones. [The former concern official policies towards education and the curriculum. The latter involves the attitude of bureaucrats and teachers.][1]

Hodgkin's hypothetical case of 'a typical reformer in a changing society' sounds like Bitu, the woman around whom this chapter is fashioned.[2] Bitu (Beatrice), was a Muganda woman who in the 1940s and 50s championed girls' education in a novel manner. She was an educator who believed that education opened doors to bright futures. Bitu also realized that women would continue to be educationally backward in her society as long as girls got pregnant and schools expelled them because of their condition. She was determined to break the cycle of biology as women's destiny.

The girls with whom Bitu was involved attended a Christian school, where Victorian sexual mores on chastity were the guiding principles. When Bitu initially approached the school authorities,

MAP OF UGANDA

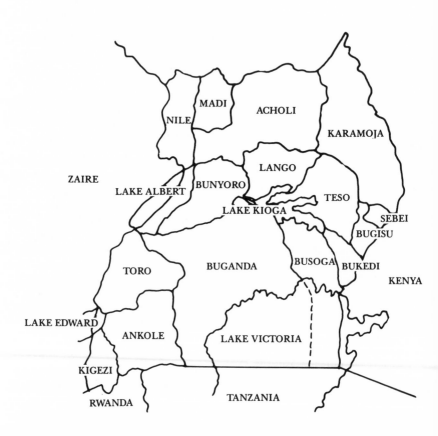

MAP 2

requesting that the pregnant girls be allowed to stay on, she was rebuffed. Her response was to turn her home into a refuge for pregnant girls, and a place for illegitimate children and orphans. While her actions were alien to the colonial mentality, they were in keeping with the Ganda society from which Bitu came—where children were fostered by relatives and strangers, and orphans adopted without questions. But tradition was no longer operative where the school girls were concerned: attending school meant that girls were not marrying at puberty or soon after. New marriage laws based on Western concepts had come into effect; and there were formal distinctions between legitimate children born in wedlock, and illegitimate or 'bush' children born without matrimonial blessing. Both of these changes had grave results among those young girls who came directly from traditional society into the Western culture they encountered in the schools.

In order to understand the society in which Bitu was operating, it is necessary to understand why school education was highly prized. Buganda, the southern province of present day Uganda, was a flourishing kingdom when the Europeans 'discovered' it in 1800. In 1894 Buganda was declared a British Protectorate. *Punch* magazine depicted Queen Victoria reluctantly receiving the orphan child of Buganda.

While it is true that Mutesa I, King of Buganda, welcomed and invited the British to stay and teach his people, the orphan cartoon in London was hypocritical because it masked the commercial ventures that necessitated *pax Brittanica* in the pacification of colonies under British rule. The British intended that Uganda was not to be a colony with European settlers like Kenya. The colonial mechanisms, however, operated in the same way as elsewhere in the British colonies.

The Africans were taught the dignity of labor through taxation. The head tax, the cattle tax, and the hut tax were designed to force Africans to go to work for Europeans, who defined their jobs and controlled the currency that made up the wages paid them. These initial changes contributed to a breakdown of the rural farming system. Men flocked to paying jobs. By 1904 more men were seeking jobs at Kismu port on Lake Victoria than could be employed. Many resorted to hawking industrial goods and did not return to their homes.[3] In addition, the task of collecting taxes was allocated to the local chiefs, who became the backbone of British rule—contributing further to the change in traditional society.

On 10 March 1900, the Uganda Agreement was signed between the British commissioners and the Buganda Regents on behalf of the King, who was then a minor. Among other things, the Agreement introduced the so-called freehold individualized system of land tenure. Under it the King received 350 square miles, the Regents and senior Chiefs received between 15–45 square miles and minor Chiefs received an average of two square miles. The majority of the population was excluded and their traditional holdings in common were jeopardized.[4]

A few years after the Agreement, cotton and coffee were introduced as cash crops. The people had money for taxes as well as industrial consumer goods from Britain. None of these new economic concepts benefited the common farmer. As Walter Rodney has pointed out, the Africans entered the colonial era with a hoe and came out with a hoe.[5] Mahmood Mamndani has reformulated Rodney's observation and states that the African cultivator entered colonialism with a home-made hoe and emerged with a factory-made hoe.[6] Perhaps we can take these concepts a step further and say that the African cultivators—man and women—entered the colonial era with domestically made hoes; the wife's was shorter and she was bent double due to the increase in her productive responsibilities. In fact, they had become peasants. The point at issue is that not only were local skills retarded but the division of labor between the sexes became distorted. By 1985, the 'he' in literature pertaining to African farmers was in reality 'she.' If she wanted an education, she had to abandon farming, most likely by leaving the rural area, where she lived within a defined system, and to go to the town where freedom offered temptations to which young women were not accustomed.

The handmaiden of colonialism was Christianity. Missionaries in Uganda preceded administrators and traders. Missionaries supervised the building of churches, followed by schools and hospitals. Then they preached the gospel, cured the ailing, and taught the three R's—Reading, (w)riting, and (a)rithmetic. This Christian education replaced the traditional methods of education as people were required to convert to Christianity and regard their dieties as devils; and those who believed in them as pagans. The Protestant and Catholic Churches would not have been so successful but for the practice of rewarding the Christians with education and privileges within the colonial structure. Furthermore, Christianity was soon spread by the zeal and dedication of the converted lay people who began to teach and proselytize the gospels. These African missionaries were men who had a vested interest in education because, according to an African catechist master, 'those who complete primary school education can read the Bible and understand it. They also read newspapers and letters.'

The catechist was a church appointed layman who drilled the scriptures, and expected proper (i.e. Western) behavior from those preparing to be baptized or confirmed into the Church. He was a witness or godfather to many baptisms and confirmations. Apart from memorizing the prayers and songs, trainee catechists were expected to build churches and then keep them in good repair. They also had to do the lowly work of bringing firewood and performing agricultural tasks for the teacher (usually European) who received no salary but prospered through the labor conscripted from the African catechist and other converts.

Bitu's father was a catechist. He performed all of these tasks, using whatever spare time he had to earn a living in order to support his wife, two daughters and a son.

His oldest daughter, Irene, became a midwife. Bitu and her brother, Mika, became teachers. Although small families were common, training girls for professions was uncommon. These women were representative of the transition from traditional life to Western training. The family enjoyed high prestige in the village because of the children's education and because their mother was an able cultivator, as well as successful hostess to various church-related gatherings. Villagers credit Bitu's mother with promoting community development as she demonstrated the proper way of making and serving tea, baking biscuits in tin 'ovens' (European oriented ways); as well as growing and preparing vegetables and fruits (traditional ways). Bitu and her siblings were thus a product of some traditional background, but their exposure to European culture, through both parents, influenced their attitudes toward careers.

Their village became Westernized apace. By the time Bitu graduated from the newly-constructed teachers' training college, a maternity school, secondary schools, and half a dozen primary schools had opened in the area. While she was in college Bitu became engaged to a teacher. She abandoned her plans for marriage, however, when her fiancee became deranged on return from a short visit to England. He threw aside his teaching and spent his days reading the Bible, singing hymns, or playing tennis (without a ball) at his parents' home. Perhaps this experience soured Bitu on marriage; or, perhaps no one else proposed. By the time she was twenty-eight, Bitu said, 'I was too old to marry' and with that she dismissed the subject. She also thought of herself as plain—she possessed neither large eyes nor the beauty gap between her upper front teeth. But, Bitu's mother, a small pretty woman, had often reminded her that she would marry because 'there are only ugly men but no ugly women in this world'. In other words, no woman was unmarriageable.

Aside from the failed romance Bitu tell us about her early life and aspirations:

> When I was growing up, nearly every girl and boy started school. Back in the early 1940s the youngest pupils starting school were at least ten, most of us were slightly older. By the time we had been in school for four years we were only four out of the ten of us who had been attending school. Some went to stay with distant relatives, others stayed at home but avoided us—their former school friends—and still others got married. In the top class there were three girls whom I admired greatly for having survived six years of schooling. After school I was always late in returning home because I was running errands, carrying messages or sweets from some of the teachers and boys to these girls, and had to take their replies back if I was to receive my reward of a sweet.[7]

Bitu survived the six years at primary school, including its romances. She went to teachers' training college for four years, taught for a few years in schools in other areas, and, in the early 1950s, was transferred back to the school she originally attended. Bitu's sister, Irene, also devoted herself to her professional career instead of marriage, and ran a maternity clinic for local women. Mika, her brother, married their best friend, Lusi, the daughter of a local chief. Marriage was not the end-all for Bitu. She discovered back at her old school—now a secondary school—that things had not changed for girls.

She had a plan. To put her plan into action Bitu bought occupier rights to two acres of land and built herself a big rambling house with a thatched roof. Malyamu, a poor, distant relative of her mother, came to work for her. Although she was in her early twenties, Malyamu already had two children and was divorced from the man who had been forced to marry her after making her pregnant. Malyamu cooked, cleaned the house, laundered clothes, and worked in the garden. She became Bitu's housekeeper—she could help carry out the plan while she received support for herself and her two children. Here again is a mix of traditional with Western ways.

Teachers had always been held in high esteem because they melded the old ways with the new. It was not long before Bitu realized that few girls completed seven years of schooling—not to mention high school. In those days girls married early (at twelve or thirteen), and girls who began classes at the age of eight were being pressured to quit and marry at puberty. Among those who stayed were a considerable number who became pregnant without benefit of marriage. Bitu worked hard to instill the notion of chastity in her students, but several factors militated against her counsel. One was the breakdown of society caused by colonial change; and another the traditional notion that children were a welcome addition to African families without emphasis on marriage. Bitu recognized that expelling unmarried pregnant girls hampered not only their futures, but that of their children. She prevailed on the school authorities to allow the pregnant women to continue with their classes without success, Victorian principles held over human concern.

Another problem was that of male influence over the youthful school girls. Women do not get pregnant without men. Bitu told me that:

My male colleagues found it convenient to have affairs with their female students who often found themselves pregnant. They either had abortions, thus losing many school days, or dropped out of school either to marry the man at the insistence of their fathers, or had a baby in secret and transferred to another school. I decided that the female students needed a lot of help if they were to compete effectively with the men. The first thing that needed to be done was for them to complete their education.[8]

This is when Bitu decided to institute her plan. Within a year of finishing her house, and with her cousin in residence as helper, Bitu persuaded two girls not to drop out of school but to come and stay with her. Although they were not allowed to attend classes during their pregnancy, the girls did not lag behind in school work because every night Bitu tutored them. Their babies were born within a six month interval. The girls returned to school but were expected to come home early and assist Malyamu with work there. On Saturday they washed and ironed their uniforms and worked in the garden for at least two hours each. In this way they helped produce the food that they consumed—and therefore contributed to their keep. They visited their parents regularly and Bitu convinced one to send her baby back home. Apparently the grandmother lactated the baby as well. This particular baby was brought up to believe that his mother was his sister.

As time went on, and as Bitu acquired additional pregnant girls, she found that sending the babies home represented the best solution all around.

> I know quite a number of professional women today who would not be where they are hadn't their mothers relieved them of responsibility of raising children, and who would not have married had it been known that they had been unmarried mothers.[9]

Indeed, the implications are that it would have been tragic for a Christian woman not to have been chaste before marriage! Without the help of Bitu and the girls' mothers it would have been impossible for these educated women to maintain the appearances of respectability.

In two years Bitu's reputation had spread to several counties. From near and far mothers with pregnant daughters requested space in her home until the babies were born. One man traveled eighty miles to deliver a cardboard box containing his emaciated baby boy. His wife of one year had divorced him soon after the baby was born. He had stopped her from taking the baby, believing that with the help of a sister he could look after it. His sister, however, was too busy with her own family and he was forced to seek other means of dealing with the little boy. He had heard of Bitu, who agreed to take in this little victim of custody claims.

Bitu's home acquired fame not only as a place where girls could seek refuge from gossiping neighbors and disapproving relatives, but as an orphanage for children whose mothers were 'unknown' or mothers who had died in childbirth. In many ways, what Bitu was doing in these cases was not novel, it was a variation on traditional practices. The key to understanding the fostering of children and acceptance of children's long absence from home lies in the clan system; and in settlement patterns which resulted from the development of the Buganda state (Map 2).

By the middle of the nineteeth century, the Kabaka (king) of Buganda ruled the kingdom by appointing county chiefs (*Saza*), sub-chiefs (*Gombolola*), and local chiefs (*Muluka* and *Mutongole*) to administer, collect tribute and ensure loyalty to the Kabaka. Previously, it had been common for provincial chiefs not attached to the Court to rebel against the king. Sometimes a chief would be so oppressive that people voted with their feet to escape his rule. The practice of escaping a cruel chief continued until at least the 1940s. At other times, when the Kabaka transferred a popular chief to a new area, many followed him, seeking occupier rights in land. The result was that members of any given clan were dispersed throughout Buganda. Members of clans recognized each other by names special to them because clan membership basically meant common observation of totem taboos and practices. Each clan had its roots (*Obuttaka*) in a specific area designated by a piece of land which was looked after by a clan leader (*Omuttaka*). Clan leadership was hereditary.

All this had an impact on social arrangements since clan members did not necessarily live together in the same village or county. People were, therefore, always in transit—by bicycle, buses, or on foot—reconnecting with members of their clan. Children were often sent to stay with grandparents, uncles or aunts. The rationale was that children raised by many families would be less self-centered (spoiled) and that they would learn the dignity of work and discipline. Likewise, grown-up children were sometimes sent to extended family members in the hope of increasing their opportunities for marriage. This practice was so widespread that people who wandered about staying with different relatives, and even sometimes friends, became a culturally accepted category (*Ba-Kirerese*). Traditionally these were often unmarried men who did not want to settle down by themselves, and had no female relatives nearby. However, by 1971, women came to dominate this category. As one informant put it:

Women who had failed to find husbands were assumed to be sloppy in appearance, housekeeping or the way they gardened; women who were poor cooks and had been divorced after short periods of marriage; women who were hot tempered or physically deformed; girls who might be pregnant and wanted a discreet way to have an abortion or to have a baby without everyone in their immediate neighborhood knowing. Married women often stayed with their mothers in the last months of pregnancy or sometimes women took respite from their marriages for long periods which enabled them to generate independent incomes through sales of beer or food crops. Lastly, in the case of illness when the diagnosis was sorcery or witchcraft—induced spirits as opposed to ancestral shades—the diviners often advised as a necessary step to the cure that the patient be temporarily moved away from their current residence. The home was then subjected to thorough cleansing for weeks or months.[10]

The cultural practice and acceptance of periodic absence from one's domicile accounts for why women from distant places found Bitu's home a convenient refuge. After delivery, girls would return to school with a simple explanation that they had been very ill, and been taken away to recover; or a girl might make the excuse that she had gone to look after a sick relative. This was common enough not to arouse suspicion. In some cases, there might be nasty rumors by skeptics, but otherwise girls would finish school without having to drop out, or worse, be expelled in disgrace.

Between 1955 and 1979, one hundred girls had been guests or sought refuge in Bitu's home. She had looked after one hundred and twenty-one children, and she had educated thirty—nineteen of whom were girls. This is an impressive record considering that she was a single woman earning thirty-five dollars a month. She was responsible for all the food and clothes and kerosine for lighting. Each child, however, had been expected to help with chores around the house and garden as had been the case with the two pioneer students.

Bitu solved problems of a medical nature through her sister, the midwife, and through help from her sympathetic mother. Her mother, Irene, was knowledgeable in treating with traditional herbs. She had medicines which cured or relieved stomach aches, fevers, diarrhea, measles, mumps, burns, rashes, or wounds. Irene also provided first aid on occasion, before Western professionals were called in, when illness or accidents demanded.

Bitu's own strong concern for education made her influence her brother and sister-in-law to open a day care center. They threw themselves into the project: hanging swings from large trees in their yards, and constructing a large playroom for the children. Because the essential concern was education, however, they bought slates and taught the children to count, to write and to recite the alphabet. Mika and his wife also sought to instill some elements of local tradition in these children and taught them to play traditional games. The children played at housekeeping, including making their own toys from seeds, fruits, clay, sticks, banana fiber and banana flowers. The 'school' could easily have accomodated at least twenty-five children but at any time ten children (half of them Bitu's wards) were all that Lusi could cope with, in addition to her own domestic responsibilities. The daughter of a traditional chief thus found herself helping the legitimate and illegitimate children to whom Bitu had committed herself.

Once the children started attending regular school, Bitu and Mika helped them with their homework. Bitu was proud of her record of thirty children having completed primary school education. Two of them continued on and obtained both BAs and MAs. Still others work as nurses, teachers, and bank clerks. This is impressive considering the alternatives. Bitu's intervention enabled illegitimate children to have a relatively fair start in life.[11]

It is important to note that the notion of 'outside' or illegitimate children was a by-product of Christian missionary work which forbade polygyny (the practice of marrying more than one wife). Before Christian teachings, a few men who could, married more than one woman. Their progeny was accepted by all in their community. In the case of illegitimacy, the mother would bring the child and introduced it to his paternal relatives. They either agreed to support the child by sending regular help, or insisted that the man's wife look after his child. If the child stayed with his mother, he was traditionally taken to his father at the age of ten years. This tendency was reflected in household compositions.

Out of the fifty-one Ganda households[12] I studied only one was polygynous—and also the most organic in that it consisted of a man, his eight children, and their two natural mothers. The rest of the households combined step-parenting and fostering. I found twenty-seven step-child situations resulting from husbands claiming their natural children. In seventeen households step-children lived with either a father or mother (in cases of very young children). Three households surveyed contained grandmothers raising either orphans or children whose mothers were continuing education elsewhere.

(The types of women Bitu pioneered among.) In one case a mother had made a good marriage but her child had been left behind. Over all, twenty-one households in the village had foster children of poor relatives, children of friends, or relatives, and children of total strangers.[13]

The point I am making is that traditional ways made it possible to incorporate children into households without much fuss about circumstances of origin. Most often it was (and still is) difficult to sort out members of households without lengthy discussions which involve unravelling personal genealogical charts.

With the advent of Western schooling, peasants increasingly struck up friendships with teachers and, of course, offered them their children to help with domestic work in return for the privilege of having these children in 'enlightened' homes. Although teachers have not been as highly paid as government workers, the ordinary people have always held them in high esteem. This is because education was the upward ladder which ultimately led to wealth, power, and prestige. The children were fostered to teachers because their homes were thought to be ideal educational environments. Indeed, in such homes teachers saw to it that the children had clean water and milk. They had a daily routine for their homework, and they could study at night with the help of kerosine lamps (instead of candles) with teacher as tutor. Often parents were unable to pay school fees or buy uniforms and books. Teachers then had to assume total responsibility for education, and economic and personal well-being of the children.

There were cases of abuse—overwork or corporal punishment. In most instances of this sort, the injured ran back home to their families. On the whole, it was widely held that children who stayed in their teachers' homes had a head start, did well in school, and succeeded later in life.

This scenario illustrates the cultural climate in which Bitu began and ran her home for girls, and later for various orphans. She was a teacher and she was fostering children in her home. One of the legacies of colonialism was to sensitize people to the fact that literacy was the key to social mobility. Nearly all of the colonial chiefs (models for their people) could read the alphabet and some, the Bible. A few even wrote books themselves.[14]

Bitu as a teacher was obviously most aware of education as a linchpin for social and economic advancement. Schooling, however, did tend to interfere with the traditional practice of girls marrying young, but if students started school at ten years of age, the chances of girls getting pregnant increased with each year they spent in school. Here were the conflicts between traditional ways and those transported from the West. Bitu, born into a mixture of these cultures, recognized that the practice of waiting until they were older complicated life for both the girls and their families. Most often girls never completed their education and were disgraced. Furthermore, mothers who released their daughters from work at home suffered hardships in increased labor, and often suffered disgrace through pregnant unmarried daughters.

Bitu represented the middle range of elite Buganda who worked for change as it pertained especially to women. The issues which concerned Bitu, however, are still prevalent and are topical in developmental circles. In the future, Bitu's ideas, as well as those who shared her vision, will be heeded if the vicious circle described here is to be broken.

Notes

1. Hodgkin, R. A., *Education and Change*, (London 1957), pp. 70–71.
2. This paper is based on numerous conversations with Bitu, her 'children', and their parents. I first met Bitu in September, 1972, while conducting research in a village near hers. We kept in touch until her death in 1985.
3. *Native Labour Commission, 1912–13* (Nairobi, 1913).
4. Mafeje, Archie, *Agrarian Revolution and the Land Question in Buganda*, (Denmark: Institute for Development Research, 1973).
5. Rodney, Walter, *How Europe Underdeveloped Africa*, (Howard University Press edition, 1982), p. 12.
6. See Mamndani, Mahmood, *Imperialism and Fascism in Uganda*, (Nairobi, 1983), p. 7.
7. Interview, 20 June 1974.
8. Interview, 20 June 1974.
9. Interview, September 1979.
10. Interview, 10 August 1972.
11. There are indications that at least by the 1940s some Asians employed underpaid child workers. Consequently, some of these boys became pickpockets and the girls prostitutes. Bitu's activities

on behalf of the children under her care spared them being thrown
to the unscrupulous traders. Low, M., *The Mind of Buganda*,
(London, 1971), p. 132.

12. In 1974 the two villages studied in Kyagwe county, thirty-three
households belonged to people of five other ethnic groups who
had migrated to the Buganda region.

13. The Buganda claim that a stranger is just a friend you have not
met. In fact, once people meet the relationship is often conceived
in a kinship idiom because kinship is created through sharing food
or associating with other people. There were ten Buganda children
fostered to non-Buganda teachers but there were no non-Buganda
children in Kiganda (singular) homes.

14. See for instance the books published by Sir Apolo Kagwa. These
include *Basekabaka Be Buganda* (Kampala, 1953), and *E Kitabo
Kyempisa Za Buganda* (Kampala, 1952).

She Who Blazed a Trail:

Akyaawa Yikwan of Asante [1]

IVOR WILKS

Preamble on Asante

The Asanteman or Asante nation is part of the present Republic of Ghana. Under the charismatic leadership of Osei Tutu the nation emerged as a unified monarchy in the last quarter of the seventeenth century. Symbolic of the new unity was the famous Golden Stool (*Sika Dwa*), which is said to have come down from the sky to rest on Osei Tutu's lap. The nation was ruled by a king or Asantehene, and queenmother or Asantehemaa. The latter was not commonly the mother or sister of the incumbent ruler, and might take over the government during *interregna* or when the king was absent from his capital.

By the middle of the eighteenth century Asante held sway over most of what is now Ghana and over some areas within the adjacent countries of the Ivory Coast to the west and Togo to the east. By the early nineteenth century Asante had reached its limits of expansion. The capital, Kumase, lay deep in the forest country, but the authority of the kings extended along the Gold Coast to the south and, to the north, far into the savannahs drained by the headwaters of the Volta River (see Map 3).

Along the Gold Coast British, Danish and Dutch merchants had established forts and lodges at which they sold imported manufactured goods for gold, slaves and other produce from inland. In the eighteenth century these merchants claimed no jurisdiction beyond their depots, and for the most part they had come to accept and even welcome the growth of Asante power in the hinterland. In that period the government in Kumase was dominated by an inner circle or junta of senior military commanders. They held strongly to the belief that the well-being of the nation was bound up with territorial conquest and the flow of tributes and taxes from periph-

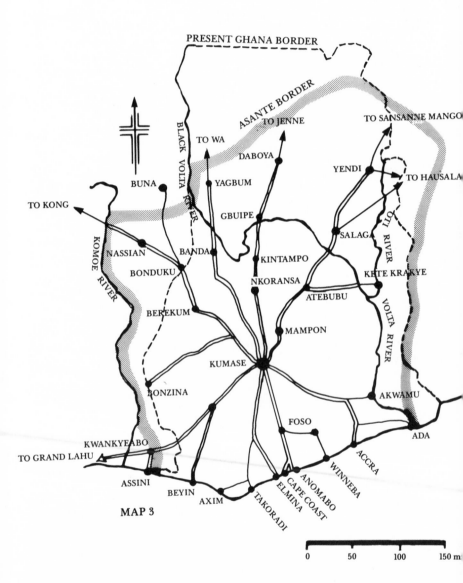

MAP 3

0   50   100   150 m

ery to center. By the nineteenth century a change had occurred. Asante politics were increasingly dominated by a new class of civil administrators to whose way of thinking economic prosperity depended on the expansion of external trade and close regulation of the markets.[2] From about 1820 onwards Asante found its interests threatened by the growing imperial ambitions of the British. The first major Anglo-Asante war occurred in 1824–6. The peace concluded in 1831 remained in force for more than three decades. During that time Asante accomplished a political transformation which enabled it effectively to respond to the new market forces unleashed by the development of industrial capitalism in western Europe.

Asante retained its independence until 1896, when it was finally incorporated into Britain's empire. Troops occupied the capital and the thirteenth king, with many of his senior councillors, was sent into exile. In 1900 Asante fought and lost a war of national liberation. The following year it was declared a Crown Colony by right of conquest and was placed under the jurisdiction of the Governor of the Gold Coast. In 1935 the British granted a measure of internal self-goverment to the Asante. In 1957, when the British conceded independence to the Gold Coast, Asante became part of the new nation soon to be renamed Ghana. To a remarkable extent, however, Asante retains its distinct social and cultural identity, and the fifteenth Asantehene, the London-trained lawyer Opoku Ware II, still commands the loyalty of the mass of the Asante people.

The Anglo-Asante peace treaty of 1831 significantly altered the trajectory of Asante history. Remarkably, the chief negotiator on the Asante side was a woman, Akyaawa. This chapter attempts to reconstruct her life history. Throughout the nineteenth century Asante remained an essentially pre-literate society, memorializing its past in the spoken rather than written word. The sources for Akyaawa's career are, therefore, of a far from conventional kind, and considerable reliance has to be placed on information transmitted by word of mouth over the generations.

Akyaawa, 'Royal' of Akorase and 'Princess' of the Golden Stool

Akyaawa's full name was Yaa Kyaa, of which 'Akyaawa' is an affectionate dimunitive. To the best of our knowledge she was born in the small village of Akorase which lies about six miles north-east of the capital. It is a village of some importance, for it belongs to the Asantehene and the Taa Dwemo shrine is located there. Akyaawa must have learned about the origins of her village as she grew up, for in Asante the past is an all-pervasive part of the present. The Asante child is not so much taught about the past as socialized into it.

The traditional history of Akorase starts in the time of Asantehene Osei Tutu.[3] The Taa Dwemo shrine was captured in the course of a war. It was brought to the place that became known as Akorase and Osei Tutu appointed one of his favorites, Kra Amponsem, to be its custodian (*bosomwura*). Kra Amponsem in turn deputed his sister, Tamra, to attend to the day-to-day affairs of the shrine, and she became its priestess. When Kra Amponsem died Tamra's son, Nantwi, became custodian of the shrine and also head, or *odekuro*, of Akorase village. He lived until 1807, and was succeeded in turn by his sister's son, Nkansa. It is not known when Tamra died, but it was during the reign of Asantehene Opoku Ware (*c*.1720–50). The family tree shows the pattern of succession more clearly:

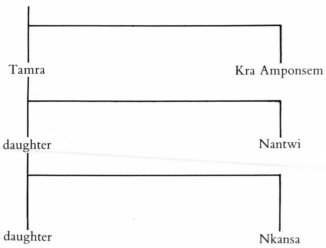

Figure 1: The 'royals' of Akorase

In Asante, primary descent is reckoned matrilineally, that is, from mothers through daughters to grand-daughters and so forth. This principle is well exemplified in the succession to office in Akorase. It will be seen, for example, that custody of the Taa Dwemo shrine passed from Kra Amponsem, not to one of his own sons, but to a son of his sister. Responsibility for the Taa Dwemo shrine at Akorase was, in other words, vested in the descendants of Tamra. In Asante these descendants, whether male or female, are referred to as *adehyee* of Akorase. This is often translated into English as 'royals' for want of a better word, but care is necessary. The status of 'royal' of Akorase carries with it rights to office in Akorase but not elsewhere. Each place in Asante has its own 'royals' and only the family from which the Asantehenes and Asantehemaas are chosen is royal in the more usual English meaning of the term.

Akyaawa's mother was named Ampomhemaa. She was certainly a 'royal' of Akorase, and probably a daughter of Tamra. Akyaawa was herself, then, a 'royal' of Akorase by virtue of her maternal ancestry. She had, however, a different status by paternity, that of 'princess' of the Golden Stool.

Akorase, founded as seat of the Taa Dwemo shrine by order of Asantehene Osei Tutu, became therefore a property of the Golden Stool. An incumbent Asantehene had the legal right to require the males of the village to serve him in the palace administration as *ahenkwaa*. He also had the right either to take the women as his wives or to present them to husbands of his choice. This custom was known as *ayete*, and a visitor to Kumase in Akyaawa's time made reference to it:

> The laws of Ashantee allow the King 3333 wives, which number is carefully kept up, to enable him to present women to those who distinguish themselves, but never exceeded, being in their eyes a mystical one . . . Many, probably, the King has never seen . . . The King has seldom more than six wives resident with him in the palace.[4]

In Asante women are the knowledgeable genealogists, doubtless because descent is reckoned through them. In 1965 I talked to the elderly Nana Yaa Kyaa of Akorase, a great-great-grand-daughter of Akyaawa. True to form, she was able to narrate the intricate ramifications of her family history.[5] Ampomhemaa of Akorase, she related, was one the true wives of Asantehene Osei Kwadwo (1764–77). Two daughters were born, the one Yaa Kyaa or Akyaawa and the other Akua Afiriye. Akyaawa, in addition to being a 'royal' of Akorase through her mother, was *oheneba* through her father. Often translated 'prince' or 'princess' in English, the title of *oheneba* literally means king's child. By virtue of the principle of matrilineality the *oheneba* had, of course, no claims on the offices of Asantehene or Asantehemaa. Nevertheless, an *oheneba* enjoyed high status within society, and many of Akyaawa's paternal half-brothers came to hold important positions in government.

For Asante there are no dated records of births, marriages and deaths for the eighteenth century. We can, therefore, only assign an approximate date to Akyaawa's birth. We are reasonably sure, first, that Osei Kwadwo only exercised his right to take a wife from Akorase after his accession, and second, that Akyaawa was not born posthumously (an event that would probably have been commemorated in her name). Her birth, then, may be placed between 1764 and 1777. Since, moreover, she was still very active in the early 1830s, she was probably born in the 1770s rather than 1760s. Tentatively, we assign her a birth date of 1774+/–3.

From Childhood to Middle Age

In the early 1870s a Frenchman, M. J. Bonnat, spent some four years in or near Kumase. He commented on the remarkably liberated position which women enjoyed in Asante. '. . . contrary to the situation in the other countries of Africa,' he wrote, 'the woman is considered not as a slave of the man, but as his equal.'[6] Gender, nevertheless, was a major determinant of the roles that Asante women assumed in society.

In the belief system of the Asante, blood (*mogya*) was the vital force which, transmitted from generation to generation, bound the living and the dead together in a web of kinship (*abusua*). The shedding of blood was seen as fundamentally inimical to the natural order, and even in its most natural form, menstruation, it was regarded as a potential source of pollution. The conduct of menstruating women was, accordingly, carefully regulated. Among the Seventy-seven Laws given the Asante nation by Okomfo Anokye were ones forbidding them from entering any dwelling, from swearing an oath, from addressing any servant of the king or any priest, and from having sexual intercourse. Female participation in government, and in affairs of state generally, was not encouraged, for the onset of menstruation might have untoward and unpredictable consequences for those in contact, even indirectly, with the woman. The king's wives still able to bear children were secluded in the harem. When they were allowed out, which was seldom according to a report of 1817,

> 'they are encircled and preceded by troops of small boys with thongs or whips of elephants hide, who lash everyone severely who does not quit their path for another, or jump into the bush with his hands before his eyes; and sometimes the offenders are heavily fined besides.'[7]

Between menarche and menopause, then, a woman's life in Asante tended to be restricted to the concerns of household and family.

For reasons that will now be apparent, very little is known of Akyaawa's life from childhood to middle age. Her routine involvement in household and family affairs is not the stuff of historical records. With the onset of puberty at the age of about fifteen, Akyaawa presumably went through the customary nubility rites.[8] These took place over a seven day period and required both her paternal and maternal kin to shower her with presents. It was an occasion on which the families vied with each other to demonstrate their wealth even if they thereby ran into debt. Akyaawa's father, Asantehene Osei Kwadwo, had been dead for a decade or more, but we may assume that his successor, Osei Kwame (1777–1803),[9] contributed generously to the rites of princess of the Golden Stool entering adulthood.

The ceremonies completed, a young woman was expected to marry as soon as possible thereafter. Her family may already have promised her, even as an infant, to a spouse of their choice. On attaining womanhood, however, she could reject such an arrangement, but considerable expenses would be incurred if she did so.[10] Be that as it may, in view of Akyaawa's status as titular 'wife' of the Asantehene it is not likely that she had any real choice in the matter. In point of fact Osei Kwame did not himself opt to marry her, but presumably he did select or at least approved the selection of her spouse. Unfortunately all attempts to identify him have failed.[11] It seems that, by virtue of matrilineality, his very existence has become genealogically irrelevant to Akyaawa's descendants. In 1965, however, Akyaawa's great-great-grand-daughter narrated without hesitation the names of Akyaawa's children by her unidentified husband: 'Nana Yaa Kyaa [i.e. Akyaawa] married someone, and there were two daughters, Nana Abena Konadu and Nana Bago, and one son, Kyeame Kofi Nti.'[12]

Akyaawa's three children must have been born in the 1790s. The two daughters attained womanhood in the early part of the reign of Asantehene Osei Tutu Kwame (1804–23), but he chose not to take either as wife. The elder daughter, Abena Konadu, was married to Kwaku Dua, a young royal of the Golden Stool, and the younger daughter, Bago, to Oti Panin, son of a wealthy counselor or *okyeame* of the Asantehene. The first son of Bago, Boakye Tenten, seems to have been born about 1812.[13] Akyaawa's son, Kofi Nti, was only to marry some two decades later, and his affairs will not concern us for the present.

It is useful to view matters from the perspective of Akyaawa say in 1820, when she was probably in her mid-forties and approaching, if not already past, the menopause. She had herself played no part in public affairs. She had, however, seen several of her paternal half-brothers achieve high positions in government and several marry into the royal family of Asante.[14] Akyaawa, then, might well have felt somewhat overshadowed by her half-brothers, yet she might also have felt reasonably sanguine about the future of her own children. Certainly her daughters had married well, and her son might expect in time to come to office in Akorase. What is sure is that in 1820, even in her wildest flights of imagination, Akyaawa did not forsee what the future in fact held in store for her and her children.

Taa Dwemo Goes to War

The river Tano runs through the western part of Asante. It is regarded as the abode of the god of the same name, one of the highest in the entire Asante pantheon.[15] Such gods were divisible. Water and soil from the Tano river might be removed to another location and, provided this was done with all due rituals and honors, access to the god could be gained at a new location. Such local offshoots, the *atano*, were regarded as 'children' of Tano and given a second name to distinguish each from the other, thus Taa (or Tano) Odomankoma, Taa Kora, Taa Kwadwo and Taa

Dwemo to name a few. An *atano* resided in a shrine, most commonly a brass pan, and this was housed in a temple (*abosomfie*) which was superintended by a custodian (*bosomwura*). The god was served by priests and priestesses and such other attendants as cooks, musicians and umbrella carriers, so that a temple might closely resemble the court of a chief.

Because Taa Dwemo belonged to the Asantehene, it enjoyed an especially privileged position. On special occasions it was brought into Kumase to greet the king and was accorded a place of honor beside him. He, too, would visit Akorase from time to time, to pay his respects to Taa Dwemo.[16] The god's help was sought in personal matters of, for example, sickness, and it was particularly important to have its support in times of war.[17] When the Asantehene himself took to the field with his armies, Taa Dwemo and its retinue of priests and attendants accompanied him. The god took part in the invasion of the Fante country in 1807, for example. Indeed, it was in the course of this campaign that Taa Dwemo's custodian, Nantwi, died, and as a result Taa Dwemo was given its own oath: *Meka Dwemo Fante*, 'I swear by Dwemo [at] Fante'.[18] It is unlikely that Akyaawa was among those from Akorase who accompanied Taa Dwemo to war on this occasion, for she would have been only in her thirties and therefore still subject to the restrictions on pre-menopausal women. In the 1820s, however, when Akyaawa was in her early fifties, we have evidence that she was present on Asantehene Osei Yaw's campaigns in the south.

Trade on the Gold Coast had languished during the two decades of the wars in Europe that came to a close in 1815. With peace came a revival of commerce. The British, Dutch and Danes vied with each other to gain access to the Asante market. The first, however, had the edge on all competitors, for changes in industrial production in Britain allowed many commodities, most notably cloth, to be offered at unprecedentedly low prices. In 1817 the British merchants concluded a treaty of 'perpetual peace and harmony' with the Asantehene. Conflicting British and Asante interpretations of its provisions, however, led to a deterioration in relations.[19] In 1820 the British government sent J. Dupuis to Kumase to re-negotiate the treaty, but under pressure from the merchant lobby in London the revised treaty was never ratified.[20]

In 1821 the British establishments on the Gold Coast became the responsibility of Governor Sir Charles MacCarthy who, from his headquarters in Sierra Leone, initiated an aggressive and indeed bellicose policy towards Asante. In the southern provinces of Asante one local ruler after another was induced by bribes or threats to transfer allegiance from the Golden Stool to the British Crown. Only Osei Tutu Kwame's strong commitment to peace deterred his generals from waging all-out war against the British, and when the king died late in 1823 there was nothing further to restrain them.

MacCarthy, in fact, moved before the Asante generals did, seeing in the *interregnum* an ideal opportunity to invade Asante's south-western territories.[21] On 21 January 1824, his forces were resoundingly defeated by Asante troops positioned only some thirty miles behind the Gold Coast. Meanwhile Osei Yaw (1824–34) took power in Asante. Circumventing the constitutional procedures for selecting a new king, he immediately proceeded to the war front with reinforcements. In June he laid seige to Cape Coast where the British headquarters was located.[22]

Cape Coast Castle was strongly defended by its cannonry. Smallpox broke out in the Asante ranks, provisions became scarce, and a number of the commanders threatened to withdraw from the field. In August 1824, Osei Yaw finally agreed to pull back his forces to a camp not far from Kumase. There he carried out an inquiry into the conduct of the campaign.

It is at this point in time that we have the first evidence of Akyaawa's participation in public affairs. The source is C. C. Reindorf, an Accra pastor of the Basle Mission, who published a *History of the Gold Coast and Asante* in 1895. Much of his information, however, had been collected from informants, two or three decades earlier. He also drew on lost literary sources, among them the writings of James and Charles Bannerman of Accra. The wife of the former, Yaa Hom, was a daughter of Asantehene Osei Yaw and an associate of Akyaawa. Reindorf's account of the proceedings at the camp reads as follows:

> . . . Osei Yaw, anxious to reach Kumase, hastened his retreat to Bereonaase, where he waited for the chiefs and generals of his army to impeach their conduct at the battle, and to punish them for cowardice. This brought on great disorder among the captains, some of whom determined to shake off the yoke of Asante. Even the royal family, among whom was one Akyiawa, a woman of masculine spirit, with several mothers whose sons had been lost in the campaign, did not approve of the inglorious

retreat, and many a scoffing song was heard when the king returned to his capital.[23]

Reindorf's tantalizingly brief reference to Akyaawa (Akyiawa) seems to imply that she accompanied Osei Yaw on his campaign and afterwards made quite apparent her opposition to his conduct of affairs. Her status of princess would scarcely justify such presumptuous conduct, though post-menstrual women in Asante often assume overtly aggressive and provocative attitudes towards males, as if in compensation for the earlier years of enforced domesticity. Be that as it may, it seems likely that in 1824 Akyaawa was serving Taa Dwemo in some capacity and that her criticisms of the king were religiously sanctioned. An episode from 1881 shows how a woman might intervene forcefully in public affairs. An Asante embassy, consisting of four male functionaries of the king and an old priestess, arrived at Cape Coast. The priestess, it was reported, 'threatened to utterly destroy both the English and the Fantis [their local allies] if they did not at once abandon any intention they might have of making war upon Ashanti.' Not surprisingly, it proved necessary to exclude the old lady from the subsequent delicate negotiations.[24]

Akyaawa Becomes a Prisoner

In 1825 Asantehene Osei Yaw devoted himself to preparations for a new offensive against the British and the so-called 'allied' chiefs, that is, those who had withdrawn allegiance from the Golden Stool. The plan was to march first upon Accra, re-establish the Asantehene's authority there, and then to attack Cape Coast once again. The omens, it is said, were not auspicious. Several gods were consulted, and they and the Muslims in Kumase all counselled prudence.[25] Osei Yaw nevertheless took the field and established camp some twenty miles north-east of Accra. On 7 August he engaged the British and their local levies, supported by the Danes, in battle at Katamanso, near Dodowa.

The Asante suffered a serious defeat. Casualties were heavy and the booty taken from them was computed to be worth about half-a-million pounds sterling.[26] At least two of Akyaawa's paternal half-brothers were slain and her son-in-law, Oti Panin, was captured and subsequently executed. She herself became a prisoner. She was among a group of women, including one of Osei Yaw's wives, Akua Pusuwa, and one of his daughters, Yaa Hom, who were seized when levies, recruited by the Danes, penetrated the Asante ranks to where the king was positioned.[27]

The Danish governor, Niels Broch, procured the women from their captors and ensconced them near his headquarters at Christiansborg. The British Governor, Sir Neil Campbell, informed London that the prisoners were being well treated. The Danes, he reported somewhat ruefully, reckoned that if there was peace with Asante they would use them to obtain preferential conditions of trade, but if there was war again, they would use them to conciliate the king.[28] In a rather garbled list of prisoners compiled by the British commandant there is a reference to 'the king of Ashantee's Crabah, a female dedicated to the sooman, fetish'.[29] 'Sooman' is the Asante *suman*, a term loosely used to describe a god.[30] 'Crabah' presumably refers to Akyaawa and the 'sooman' to Taa Dwemo.

The Colonial Secretary in London, Lord Bathurst, was not at all anxious to become embroiled in further wars with Asante, and with his approval Governor Campbell traveled from Sierra Leone to the Gold Coast to put out peace feelers.[31] This was in November 1826. It was, however, to be five years before peace was concluded. The delay was due to the opposition of the 'allied' chiefs of the Gold Coast who, having been cajoled, bribed and in some cases intimidated into taking up arms against the Golden Stool, now saw their new patrons, the British, intent upon establishing treaty relations with their erstwhile overlords, the Asante. These chiefs, however, controlled the routes between the British establishments on the coast and the Asante capital, and their co-operation was therefore essential if communications were to be opened.

Campbell's overtures for peace must have been debated in Kumase late in 1826. The Asantehene decided to open negotiations through two of his loyal Adanse chiefs, Fomenahene Kwante Barima and Akrokyerehene Brefo Akora, whose towns lay on or near the Cape Coast road. A son of the latter, Gyamera Kwabena, was chosen to carry out the actual mission.[32] In the first half of 1827 both sides were absorbed in matters of protocol, that is, not so much in making peace as in deciding how peace was to be made. Finally, on 23 October 1827, a party of senior negotiators from Kumase arrived at Cape Coast. They were led by a high functionary of the *nseniefo*, the Asantehene's corps of heralds. Campbell having died, Acting-Governor H. Lumley and his secretary, G. Maclean, arrived from Sierra Leone to represent British interests.

On 10 December, Lumley laid a draft peace treaty before the Gold Coast chiefs for their approval. He then passed it to the Asante negotiators who arrived in Kumase with it on 4 February 1828.[33] Over the next week the Asantehene and his councillors debated the British terms.

The draft treaty contained three major provisions. [34] First, and most far-reaching in its consequences, the Asantehene was to acknowledge the independence of the chiefs who had allied themselves to the British, renouncing for all time any rights to tribute from them. Second, he was to deposit 4,000 ounces of gold at Cape Coast as security against breaches of the peace. Third, as further security, two hostages were to be surrendered to the British for four years, namely, Osei Kwadwo and Opoku Ahoni, first and second heirs-apparent to the Golden Stool.

Asantehene Osei Yaw's response was contained in a letter of 13 February 1828. He expressed reservations about the amount of gold he was required to deposit and, while agreeing to surrender two hostages, made it clear that these would not be the heirs-apparent.[35] As a token of his goodwill, however, he released two prisoners held in Kumase from the time of MacCarthy. He suggested that the British might wish to reciprocate by releasing some of his family who had been captured at Katamanso, including 'Chang Wa, my daughter', that is, Akyaawa.

Had it been in Lumley's power, he might well have released the Asante women, but none were in British hands. Most remained in the households of the merchants of Danish Christiansborg, while Akyaawa herself had been sold to an Accra trader associated with the Dutch interest there.[36] As it turned out, however, the matter of the Asante captives became for the time irrelevant. Lumley and Maclean were ordered back to Sierra Leone and Captain J. Hingston assumed authority on the Gold Coast. In an ill-advised letter dated 1 May 1828, Hingston informed Kumase that under no circumstances would he modify the provisions of the draft treaty, and from this the Asantehene inferred that the British were no longer seriously interested in peace.[37]

Akyaawa Obtains Her Freedom

H. J. Ricketts, who had earlier served under Campbell, took over as Governor of the Gold Coast in June 1828. He immediately despatched a messenger to the Asantehene to reopen negotiations.

Reports from Kumase show that the king was still aggrieved by
what he saw as the British disinclination seriously to discuss the
terms of a treaty and even more so, by their failure to act upon his
request for the return of 'some of his families . . . at Accra.'[38]
Ricketts left the Gold Coast in September 1828, and another year
was to elapse before the peace talks were resumed. This time the
newly-constituted Council of Merchants at Cape Coast, under the
presidency of J. Jackson, first took steps to secure the full co-
operation of the Danes at Christiansborg.[39] It was, however, not
until George Maclean arrived back on the Gold Coast in February
1830, and took over the presidency of the Council, that real
progress was made. Having served as Lumley's private secretary
when the draft treaty of 1827 was drawn up, Maclean came with a
clear understanding of the situation.

Maclean's strategy was first, to secure a safe passage to the coast
for a new Asante embassy; second, to obtain the release of
Akyaawa; and third, to allow her to accompany the Asante emis-
saries back to Kumase and there use her good offices to obtain Osei
Yaw's agreement to a treaty. It seems that Akyaawa herself proposed this course of action to Maclean. She is, he wrote, 'a female
who is understood to have much influence with the king, and who
has declared that she will use every endeavour to bring about a
peace betwixt the British settlements and Ashantee, provided she
can be safely conveyed to Coomassie.'[40] We must assume that
Maclean had sensed something of Akyaawa's energy and vitality;
of what Reindorf ingenuously called her 'masculine spirit'.

The new embassy from Kumase arrived in Cape Coast in June or
early July, 1830. We can be reasonably sure that this was the
mission described by Reindorf, though incorrectly dated by him to
1827.[41] It was headed by 'Kwakwa', that is, Akuoko Nimpa Panin
who held a dual position as Domakwaehene of Kumase and
okyeame or counsellor to the Asantehene. His staff included two
afenasoafo or state sword-bearers, Amankwa Akuma and Kofi
Nkwantabisa, and the *nkonnwasoafohene* or head of the royal stool
carriers, Kankam Kyekyere.[42] The composition of the embassy
augured well for the peace talks, for in terms of Asante protocol its
members were drawn from the highest echelons of the diplomatic
service. The envoys reiterated the Asantehene's desire for peace and
Maclean outlined the terms of a treaty that left negotiable the
amount of the security to be deposited and the identity of the two
hostages. It remained only to obtain Akyaawa's freedom so that she
could return to Kumase with the envoys.

Late in July 1830, Maclean and the Asante ambassadors went by boat from Cape Coast to Accra. Maclean's report shows that Akyaawa's release was secured only with difficulty:

> . . . the princess Akianvah [Akyaawa] belonged to a native of Dutch Accra who had also paid a large sum for her redemption, and although he had given her up to the President [i.e. Maclean] (to his own great injury amongst the natives at that time), yet it was impossible that he should be asked to sustain so great a loss without compensation. The President, therefore, before leaving Accra, had pledged himself that the sum of £80 should be paid to him.[43]

The amount paid by Maclean testifies unambiguously to the importance he attached to Akyaawa's participation in the peace process.

Maclean arrived back in Cape Coast with the Asante envoys and Akyaawa in mid-August 1830. The problem was now to arrange a safe passage home for the Asantes. After lengthy negotiations Maclean obtained the co-operation of the Denkyira, Asen and other chiefs whose towns lay along the road. The Council of Merchants approved Maclean's actions, reiterating that every effort should be made 'by means of the woman Atianvah to induce the king to come into our arrangements for peace'.[44] In the event, Akyaawa seems to have arrived in the Asante capital in November or early December. She had been away for some four-and-a-half years.

It is unfortunate that no account of the discussions of the treaty by the Asantehene and council is on record. However, on 13 January 1831, messengers from Osei Yaw arrived in Cape Coast to announce that the broad terms were acceptable, that 600 ounces of gold and two hostages would be sent to the British as guarantees of Asante good faith, and that trade would be resumed. Maclean wrote to the Committee of Merchants in London to express his satisfaction that events had 'in a great measure justified the hopes we entertained from the alleged influence of the Princess "Atiawah" over the King of Ashantee.'[45]

Akyaawa Promotes a General Peace

When Maclean informed London of the satisfactory progress he was making, he was not to know the Asantehene was so impressed by Akyaawa's reports that he had chosen her to head the next mission to the Gold Coast. It was an appointment for which no precedent is known. The embassy that arrived in Cape Coast from Kumase on 8 April 1831, was indeed led by her, but otherwise seems to have been staffed by the members of the previous mission of mid-1830.[46] There was much excitement when the news spread that the ambassadors had indeed brought 600 ounces of gold to Cape Coast and that the two hostages they had with them were Owusu Ansa and Owusu Kwantabisa, sons of the late Asantehene Osei Tutu Kwame and of Asantehene Osei Yaw, respectively.

Talks between the Asante and British negotiators proceeded apparently without hitch. On 15 April Maclean informed London that Akyaawa had entered Cape Coast, 'in triumph with the Gold and the Hostages,' and that 'Peace with Ashantee is no longer doubtful'.[47] The expression 'in triumph' is curiously revealing, for the Asante negotiators did not see themselves as supplicating for peace so much as conceding it. The Asante commissioner resident in Elmina, Kwadwo Akyampon, sent spies to Cape Coast to report on the proceedings. In this he had the approval of the Dutch governor there, F. Last, who felt his interests vitally affected by the terms of the peace.

On 11 April 1831, Last was pleased to learn that Akyaawa's mission was empowered to treat with the Dutch as well as the British and Danes. Kwadwo Akyampon, he wrote,

> came to inform me that his boy had returned from Cape Cors [Cape Coast], that he had spoken there with Adjeoa [that is, Akyaawa] the King's Aunt herself, who had told him that among the Messengers there was one with a special Message for Elmina and who was only waiting for the Message intended for the British President to be delivered before he would come here. Adjeoa is the women who was fetched from Accra by the British President and was sent to the King with a message.[48]

Five days later the Asantehene's message was delivered to the Dutch in Elmina. The envoy assured them of the Asantehene's friendship and explained that the king had agreed to the terms of the treaty not because he was afraid of the British but 'as proof of his good intentions towards peace.'[49]

The peace treaty was formally ratified in Cape Coast Castle on 27 April 1831. It was signed by Maclean on behalf of the British Crown; by the marks of 'Akianvah, Princess of Ashantee', that is

Akyaawa, and of 'Quagua, Chief of Ashantee', that is, Akuoko
Nimpa Panin, on behalf of the Asantehene; and by the marks of
eleven of the chiefs described as 'in alliance with the King of Great
Britain.'[50] A salute of twenty-one guns was fired.[51]

Ratification of the treaty marked an important but not the final
stage in the settlement that both Akyaawa and Maclean sought.
The eleven 'allied' chiefs who had subscribed to the agreement all
held jurisdictions in the hinterland of the central Gold Coast.
Further east there were others who had similarly been persuaded by
MacCarthy to withdraw allegiance from the Golden Stool and who
had fought on the side of the British at Katamanso, but who had
not been involved in the peace negotiations. Many of them were
more closely associated with the Danes than the British. Accordingly Maclean and Akyaawa traveled to Accra in May 1831. After
lengthy talks with the Danish Governor, L. V. Hein, at Christiansborg, Maclean finally convinced him that all the 'allied' chiefs,
whether under Danish or British influence, should be included in
the one treaty.[52] Akyaawa, however, had other ideas, believing
Asante interests best served by a separate treaty with the Danes. On
8 August, Maclean had his treaty read out to a number of 'allied'
chiefs who had assembled at the British fort in Accra. It seems that
he already knew that Akyaawa had made her own arrangements
with the Danes, for he did not even bother to have the chiefs
append their marks to it. The next day Governor Hein, parading
his soldiers in new uniforms, received the Asantes in Christiansborg Castle.[53] A second treaty was signed by him on behalf of the
Danish Crown; once again by Akyaawa and Akuoko Nimpa Panin
on behalf of the Asantehene; and by various of the chiefs in
attendance.[54] The anxiety of the merchants to see trade resumed
was such that, with the exception of Yaa Hom who had married
one of them, they released the Asante prisoners without compensation.[55]

Maclean returned to Cape Coast by sea on 19 August. Akyaawa's party, including the freed prisoners, traveled overland with an
escort from Christiansborg.[56] They arrived at Cape Coast on 5
September. Contrary to Maclean's expectations, Akyaawa still did
not consider her mission complete. On 13 September, messengers
arrived at Elmina to inform Commander Last 'that the Aunt of the
King of Assantijn, named Akiawa, who held responsibility for the
peace negotiations at Cape Coast and Accra, was coming to pay a
visit to Elmina before her return to Comassie.' Last rapidly distrib-

uted two gallons of rum to the Elminans since, as he wrote, visits 'particularly from such high personages' required the generous distribution of drinks and of presents.[57]

Akyaawa and her colleagues spent three days in Elmina. The major business was transacted on 15 September, after Akyaawa had been presented with cloths and cases of rum and gin. Last informed her that he was about to send his own envoy to Kumase and wished her to know the contents of his message. He hoped that the Asante and the coastal peoples alike would experience 'order and prosperity' and that the Asantehene would be sure to send a portion of his trade to the Dutch in acknowledgement of the fact that they had 'withstood much for the sake of his alliance . . .' In response Akyaawa assured Last that the Asantehene was well aware that the Dutch treated him fairly, 'for which reason he was always their friend and would remain so'. Early the next morning Akyaawa returned to Cape Coast.[58]

Akyaawa's mission was ended. She was, however, required by the Asantehene to remain in Cape Coast for a time, 'on account of the Yam Custom taking place just now in Ashantee.' The reason for this will become apparent later. The decree was a cause of some dismay to Akyaawa. She knew that Last was sending a messenger to Kumase, but felt that she should be the first to give the Asantehene an account of her work. Maclean, too, feared that Last's messenger would be closely followed by Elmina traders intent on securing an immediate commercial advantage from the peace. Accordingly, by letters of 17 and 20 September Maclean advised Last that travelers from Elmina were likely to be stopped on the way to Kumase, and that all departures should therefore be delayed until Akyaawa had returned.[59] She finally arrived back in Kumase, so it seems, early in November 1831, having encountered some disturbances on the road.[60]

Akyaawa is Honored, and Retires

In the aftermath of a military campaign it was Asante practice to review the tactics and strategy and apportion praise and blame among the various commanders. The same procedure seems to have been followed after major diplomatic 'offensives'. The matter of the Anglo-Asante and Dano-Asante treaties was probably debated by the Asantemanhyiamu in Kumase in mid-September

1831. This body, the highest council of the nation, held its regular annual sessions at what Europeans called 'the Yam Custom', that is, the yearly Odwira festival when all the Asante dignitaries were required to assemble in the capital. If this supposition is correct, then it appears that Akyaawa was not permitted to leave Cape Coast on her journey home until the debate on her mission had been concluded *in absentia*.

No account of the proceedings is known to survive. There can be little doubt, however, that many members of the military establishment must have been strongly opposed to the treaties. Recognition of the 'independence' of chiefs who had once served the Golden Stool constituted a radical departure in Asante politics. The precise status of the old southern provinces of Asante was to bedevil relations with the British in later decades,[61] but there could be no doubt that in 1831 the Asante government had relinquished control over lands won in the course of the hard-fought campaigns of the eighteenth and early nineteenth centuries. More than any other single event, then, the decision to accept the treaties signalled the eclipse of the old military and imperial interests which had for so long dominated Asante politics, and the emergence to power of those who saw external trade as more critical than empire to the national well-being. The change was an ideological one, for there is no doubt that in 1831 Asante had the military capacity to force the British to abandon their depots on the Gold Coast.

Whatever the nature of the debate, the Asantehene and the majority of his councillors approved Akyaawa's conduct of the mission and ratified the treaties. Honors were distributed to those involved in the negotiations. Gyamera Kwabena, who had made contact with the British in late 1826, was rewarded with various paraphernalia of high office: a chair (*asipim*), a horse-tail switch (*aponkofe*), a hammock (*apakan*), a horn (*abentia*), and a staff (*poma*). Fomenahene Kwante Barima, who had initiated this contact, was given Akyaawa as 'wife'. The Asantehene, in other words, used his prerogative to take Akyaawa as *ayete* and award her (in a purely nominal way, since she was long post-menopausal) to the Fomenahene. The symbolism will be apparent: the man who opened the negotiations was 'married' to the woman who closed them. But the symbolism went even further. Kwante Barima is said to have been given his name on precisely this occasion, *kwan-te*, 'he who cleared a way',[62] while Akyaawa was awarded the name by which she is still remembered, *yikwan*, literally, 'she who made a new path', or, more idiomatically, 'she who blazed a trail'. In very typical Asante fashion, Akyaawa also made her own gesture to fame. It is one still remembered. She purchased a slave in Kumase and named him, *Nkranfo ye mmoa*: 'the Accra are fools'. She did so because only fools would have spared 'such a one as herself alive'![63]

After 1831, nearing her sixtieth year, Akyaawa Yikwan seems to have settled into retirement. The last known reports of her appear in the journal of J. Simons, an emissary of the Dutch who visited Kumase in early 1832. He travelled from Elmina by way of Cape Coast, where he met Maclean. 'His Excellency,' Simons wrote, 'requested me to forward his respectful compliments to Atjanwa, the King's cousin, and to tell her that he would send her some wine, etc. by the next opportunity . . .'[64]

On 13 February 1832, Simons was received in Kumase by the Asantehene and several hundred of his chiefs and functionaries. Among them was Akyaawa's son, Kofi Nti. After the reception, Akyaawa sent gifts to Simons: '30 eggs, 30 dried *patabia* fish, 5 papayas and one bunch of bananas'. The next day he reciprocated with gifts he judged to be to her tastes: 'a pure silk scarf, a white bottle of rum, and a half-pint of Eau de Cologne'. Seemingly not to be outdone, Akyaawa sent further presents two days later. 'From Atjanwa, cousin of the king', Simons noted, 'a ram, six bunches of bananas, ten yams, a box of white rice, a box of sweet potatoes, a box of oil nuts, a box of oranges.'[65]

Clearly Akyaawa did not intend Simons to feel unwelcome in Kumase, and on that happy note the record ends. It is not known how long Akyaawa lived to enjoy her retirement, but the absence of any references to her in the journals of those who visited Kumase in the late 1830s and early 1840s suggests that she was dead by then. Her influence, however, lived on. Throughout the greater part of the reign of Asantehene Kwaku Dua (1834-67) relations with the British continued to be regulated by reference to the treaty of 1831. Indeed, after Akyaawa's death Akuoko Nimpa Panin, who had served as her second-in-command, became the leading authority on matters relating to the treaty, for not all that had been agreed between Maclean and Akyaawa was embodied in its clauses. In 1844, for example, and again in 1863, Akuoko Nimpa Panin went to Cape Coast to explain his understanding of the implications of the treaty in such matters as jurisdiction over a escaped prisoners, runaway slaves and other refugees.[66]

Akyaawa as Ancestress

With the conclusion of the treaties of 1831 Akyaawa's public career was at an end. It had been a brief, arduous and quite extraordinary incursion into a sphere that was all but totally male-dominated. Akyaawa, by her powers of persuasion, negotiating skills and sheer force of personality had effectively changed the course of Asante history. In 1831 the policy of Kumase towards the Europeans swung from confrontation to accommodation. In a very real sense Akyaawa laid the foundations for the long, prosperous and peaceful reign of Asantehene Kwaku Dua Panin—her son-in-law—who was elected to the Golden Stool just three years after the treaties.

Notwithstanding Akyaawa's remarkable achievement in public life, one must not forget that the fundamental role of an Asante woman was to reproduce her lineage not only in a biological but also in a social and economic sense. She took major responsibility for ensuring her lineage's well-being, and not least by arranging the marriages of her offspring. We have seen that Akyaawa's two daughters were married in the 1810s. Sons, in contrast, tended to marry at a later age than daughters, preferably only after they had achieved some sort of standing in society. This was certainly the case with Akyaawa's son, Kofi Nti.[67]

Figure 2 shows the marriages of Akyaawa's three children. When Oti Panin succeeded his father in office as counsellor in or about 1815, he had already been married to Bago, or more fully, Birago for some five years, and had one son by her. Oti Panin was captured at Katamanso in 1826, and executed.[68] The little known Kofi Boakye took the counsellorship, but was soon removed from office for malpractice. The post then went to Kofi Nti, who was the incumbent in 1832.[69] In thus promoting him the Asantehene may have been further rewarding Akyaawa for her services. Indeed, Kofi Nti was also favored with a 'royal' of the Golden Stool as wife, namely, Afua Kobi.[70] She was a daughter of Asantehemaa Afua Sapon, whose brother was the Kwaku Dua married to Kofi Nti's other sister, Abena Konadu. Subsequently, after Kofi Nti's death, Afua Kobi remarried. Her second husband was Boakye Tenten, Kofi Nti's nephew and successor in office.

The fragment of the Asante royal genealogies shown in Figure 3 illustrates, from a different perspective, the closeness of the ties that linked Akyaawa's offspring with the Golden Stool.[71] It is of added interest to note that Asantehemaa Konadu Yaadom, with whom

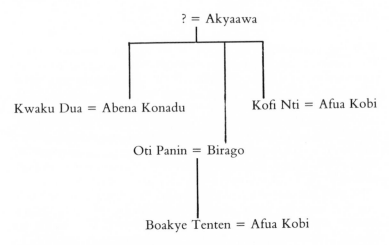

Figure 2:   Akyaawa's children and their spouses

the pedigree starts, was herself a daughter of Asantehemaa Aberefi
Yaa, and it was Aberefi Yaa's brother, Asantehene Osei Kwadwo,
who was Akyaawa's father. (No one, we should point out, has ever
suggested that Asante genealogies are simple!)

Akyaawa may have lived long enough to see her daughter's husband, Kwaku Dua, become Asantehene on the death of Osei Yaw
in 1834, but not to see her son's wife, Afua Kobi, become Asantehemaa in or about 1857. She must, however, have had a shrewd
idea of what lay in store for her grandchildren. Kwaku Dua and
Abena Konadu had a son, Kofi Boakye, and a daughter, Amma
Sewaa Anomade. The former became head of Akorase village, and
the latter was taken as wife (*ayete*) by Asantehene Mensa Bonsu. In
the next generation a daughter of Mensa Bonsu and Amma Sewaa
Anomade, Amma Sewaa Kobi, was taken as wife by Asantehene
Agyeman Prempe I (1888-1931). Akyaawa's descendants in this
line became, then, the wives of kings.

By way of contrast, Akyaawa's grandchildren through Kofi Nti
and his wife, Afua Kobi, were 'royals' of the Golden Stool. Two
became Asantehenes, Kofi Kakari (1867-74) and Mensa Bonsu
(1874-83), and one became Asantehemaa, Yaa Kyaa (1884-1917).
Of the three, Kofi Kakari appears to have been particularly closely
attached to his grandmother's memory. He called Taa Dwemo
'father' because the god had protected his mother during her

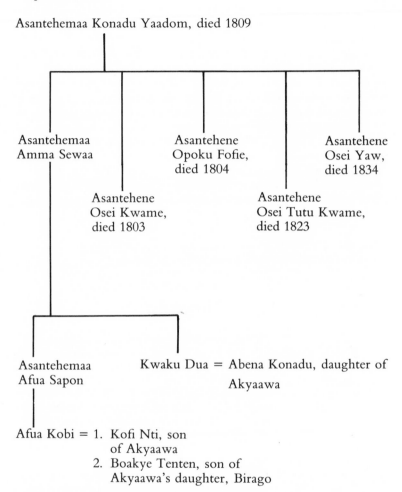

Asantehemaa Konadu Yaadom, died 1809

Asantehemaa
Amma Sewaa

Asantehene
Opoku Fofie,
died 1804

Asantehene
Osei Yaw,
died 1834

Asantehene
Osei Kwame,
died 1803

Asantehene
Osei Tutu Kwame,
died 1823

Asantehemaa
Afua Sapon

Kwaku Dua = Abena Konadu, daughter of
Akyaawa

Afua Kobi = 1. Kofi Nti, son
of Akyaawa
2. Boakye Tenten, son of
Akyaawa's daughter, Birago

Figure 3: 'royals' of the Golden Stool

pregnancy. When he became king he increased the shrine's prestige.[72] Later, in 1872, he held three Europeans captive. Although many of his generals insisted that a high ransom should be asked for them, the payments were waived because, so it was reported, 'the King's own grandmother [that is, Akyaawa] and other Princesses, who were taken prisoner in the Battle of Dodowa (1826), were sent back by the British without ransom.[73]

Finally, reference must be made to Boakye Tenten, who succeeded Kofi Nti, his maternal uncle, in office. His career was one of great achievement, as provincial administrator, diplomat and statesman.[74] It is particularly fitting that one of Akyaawa's grandsons displayed many of the same capabilities that had made her so successful a negotiator.[75]

Akyaawa Yikwan's children no doubt made all the necessary funeral customs to ensure her a place in the *Asaman*, that Asante Valhalla where the ancestors and ancestresses reside and keep watch over the affairs of the living. Akyaawa, we may like to think, from there followed the fortunes of her descendants with considerable pride and gratification.

Notes

1. This paper is partly based upon the career history of Akyaawa Yikwan published in *Asantesem: The Asante Collective Biography Project Bulletin*, 11 June 1979, pp. 30–37. I have drawn heavily upon the files of the Asante Collective Biography Project, and wish to acknowledge my debt to its co-director, Dr T. C. McCaskie, and to the many scholars who contributed to its progress. I am particularly grateful to Dr Larry Yarak, who has generously made his translations of Dutch materials, and his equally valuable advice, available to me, and to the Rev. Fr J. Agyeman-Duah of Kumase, who taught me much about Asante without in any way being responsible for my remaining misunderstandings.

2. Wilks, Ivor, *Asante in the Nineteenth Century. The Structure and Evolution of a Political Order*, (Cambridge: 1975), pp. 671–92.

3. The history of Akorase was recorded from Kwadwo Baa, seventh *odekuro* in succession to Nantwi, see Institute of African Studies, University of Ghana: IAS/159, Koraase Stool History recorded by J. Agyeman-Duah, 16 February 1966.

4. Bowdich, T. E., *Mission from Cape Coast Castle to Ashantee*, (London: 1819), pp. 289–90.

5. Africana Library, Northwestern University: I. Wilks, Field Notes, FN/39, interview with Nana Yaa Kyaa, Akorase, 5 August 1965.

6. Gros, J., *Voyages, Aventures et Captivité de J. Bonnat chez les Achantis*, (Paris: 1884), p. 206.

7. Bowdich, *Mission*, p. 290.

8. Sarpong, P., *Girls' Nubility Rites in Ashanti*, (Accra-Tema: 1977), passim.

9. Bowdich, *Mission*, p. 302-3.

10. For the most recent revisions of the chronology of the Asantehenes, used throughout this paper, see Yarak, L. and Wilks, I., 'The Chronology of the Asante Kings: a Further Revision', and 'A Further Note on the Death of Asantehene Osei Yaw Akoto and on the Enstoolment of Kwaku Dua Panin', in *Asantesem. Bulletin of the Asante Collective Biography Project*, 8 March 1978, pp. 39–40, and 9 June 1978, pp. 56–7; R. A. Kea, 'The Chronology of the Asante Kings: A Note on the Death of Osei Yaw Akoto', *ibid*, 9 June 1978, p. 55.

11. Compare Rattray, R. S., *Religion and Art in Ashanti*, (Oxford: 1927), pp. 325, 327, 333.

12. Wilks, FN/39, interview with Nana Yaa Kyaa.

13. Files of Asante Collective Biography Project, directed by I. Wilks and T. C. McCaskie, and see also *Asantesem. Bulletin of the Asante Collective Biography Project*, 1 March 1975–11 July 1979. ACBP/4, Boakye Tenten; ACBP/602, Oti Panin.

14. Wilks, *Asante*, pp. 136, 139.

15. See Bowdich, *Mission*, p. 262: 'the present favourite fetish of the Ashantee is that of the river Tando.'

16. Ramseyer, F. A. and Kühne, J., *Vier Jahre in Asante. Tagebucher der Missionare Ramseyer und Kühne*, ed H. Gundert, (Basel: 1875), p. 85.

17. Rattray, R. S., *Ashanti*, (Oxford: 1923), p. 149.

18. IAS/159, Koraase Stool History.

19. Bowdich, *Mission*, pp. 126–8. Wilks, *Asante*, pp. 166–7.

20. Dupuis, J., *Journal of a Residence in Ashantee*, (London: 1824), part II, cxx-cxxiii.

21. Public Record Office, London, CO.267/58: MacCarthy to Bathurst, 12 December 1823. Ricketts, H. J., *Narrative of the Ashantee War*, (London: 1831), pp. 40–1.

22. Wilks, *Asante*, pp. 179–80.

23. Reindorf, C. C., *History of the Gold Coast and Asante*, (Basel: 1895), p. 198.

24. Ellis, A. B., *The Land of Fetish*, (London: 1883), p. 232.

25. Reindorf, *History*, pp. 200–01.

26. Wilks, *Asante*, pp. 180–5, 438–9.

27. Reindorf, *History*, pp. 210–3, 261.

28. CO.267/74: Campbell to Bathurst, 5 November 1826.

29. Ricketts, *Narrative*, p. 125.

30. See Rattray, *Ashanti*, pp. 86–91. McLeod, M. D., *The Asante*, (London: 1981), pp. 57, 65–6.
31. CO.268/26: Bathurst to Campbell, 20 June 1826. CO.267/74: Campbell to Bathurst, 5 November 1826.
32. Manhyia Record Office, Kumase, 'History of Akrokerri', in file entitled 'History of the Immigrants from Takyiman', no date but c.1950, pp. 48–9. National Archives of Ghana, Kumase, D.2913, 'History of Adansi', by Kwabena Foli, July 1928.
33. Ricketts, *Narrative*, pp. 133–7, 146–8. CO.267/82: Ricketts to Campbell, 20 June 1827.
34. Metcalfe, G. E., *Great Britain and Ghana. Documents of Ghana History 1807–1957*, (London: 1964), pp. 114–5.
35. CO.267/95: Asantehene to Lumley, 13 February 1828. Ricketts, *Narrative*, pp. 149–51.
36. Public Record Office, London, CO.98/1A: Minutes of Council, 5 September 1831. Ricketts, *Narrative*, pp. 150–1.
37. CO.267/95: Hingston to Asantehene, 1 May 1828.
38. Ricketts, *Narrative*, pp. 162–9.
39. CO.98/1A: Minutes of Council, 23 September 1829.
40. CO.98/1A: Minutes of Council, 23 August 1830.
41. Reindorf, *History*, p. 258.
42. Asante Collective Biography Project, ACBP/623, Akuoko Nimpa Panin; ACBP/37, Amankwa Akuma; ACBP/ 624, Kofi Nkwantabisa; ACBP/625, Kankam Kyekyere.
43. CO.98/1A: Minutes of Council, 5 September 1831.
44. CO.98/1A: Minutes of Council, 23 August and 8 November 1830.
45. CO.267/112: Maclean to Committee of Merchants, 20 January 1831.
46. Reindorf, *History*, p. 258.
47. Co.267/112: Maclean to Forster, 15 April 1831.
48. Algemeen Rijksarchief, The Hague, Archief van der Nederlandsche Bezittingen ter Kuste van Guinea, NBKG/359: Elmina Journal, 9 and 11 April 1831. For Kwadwo Akyampon, see L. Yarak, 'Asante and the Dutch: a case study in the history of Asante Administration, 1744–1873', Ph.D., Northwestern University, 1983, chapter 1.
49. NBKG/359: Elmina Journal, 16 April 1831.
50. See text of treaty in Crooks, J. J., *Records relating to the Gold Coast Settlements*, (Dublin: 1923), pp. 262–4.
51. Reindorf, *History*, pp. 258–60.
52. CO.267/112: Maclean to Forster, 16 June 1831.
53. Reindorf, History, pp. 258–61.
54. Kwamena-Poh, M. A., *Government and Politics in the Akuapem State 1730–1850*, (London: 1973), p. 104, n. 2.
55. CO/98/1A: Minutes of Council, 5 September 1831.

56. Reindorf, *History*, pp. 261–2.
57. NBKG/360: Elmina Journal, 13 September 1831.
58. NBKG/360: Elmina Journal, 15, 16 September 1831.
59. NBKG/669: Maclean to Last, 17, 20 September 1831.
60. NBKG/669: Maclean to Last, 30 September and 3 October 1831. Reindorf, *History*, pp. 262–3.
61. Wilks, *Asante*, pp. 189–93.
62. Manhyia Record Office, 'History of Akrokerri', pp. 48–9. National Archives of Ghana, Kumase, D.2913, 'History of Adansi'.
63. Reindorf, *History*, p. 263.
64. Algemeen Rijksarchief, The Hague, Archief van het Ministerie van Kolonien 1814–49, MK/3965: Simons' Journal, 27 December 1831.
65. MK/3965: Simons' Journal, 13, 14, 15 September 1832.
66. Public Record Office, London, CO.96/7: Hill to Kwaku Dua, 19 December 1844; Hill to Stanley, 7 January 1845. CO/96/62: Kwaku Dua to Pine, 19 February 1863; Pine to Newcastle, 26 August 1863.
67. Asante Collective Biography Project: ACBP/97, Kofi Nti.
68. ACBP/602, Oti Panin.
69. MK/3965: Simons' Journal, 13 February 1832.
70. ACBP/10, Afua Kobi. Wilks, *Asante*, p. 360.
71. Wilks, *Asante*, chapter 9.
72. Ramseyer and Kuhne, *Vier Jahre*, p. 85.
73. *Ibid*, p. 143.
74. Asante Collective Biography Project: ACBP/4, Boakye Tenten.
75. The genealogical material in this section is based on Wilks, FN/39, interview with Nana Yaa Kyaa of Akorase; Manhyia Record Office, Kumase, 'The History of the Ashanti Kings and the Whole Country Itself', dictated by Nana Agyeman Prempe I, commencing 6 August 1907; and the numerous reports by nineteenth century European commentators.

Mama Khadija

A Life History as example of Family History[1]

PATRICIA W. ROMERO

Khadija lives today in Lamu, an island off the coast of Kenya, in East Africa. Kenya is bordered by Uganda and Sudan in the west; Tanzania in the south; Ethiopia directly north, with adjoining borders to Somalia on the north-east. The entire eastern part of Kenya rests on the Indian Ocean. Lamu is situated off the northern coast of the country—one of a small cluster of islands which for centuries have engaged in trade with India, Arabia, and the Persian Gulf. (Map 4).

People who were born and raised on the Kenya coast, and whose first language is Kiswahili, are called Swahili. So by birth and locale, Khadija is Swahili. Within Kenya the coastal Swahili are a minority and their Muslim faith is a minority religion. Most Kenyans are Christian and were originally rural. The Swahili were and are mostly urban, dwelling in cities and towns from north of Lamu all the way down the Indian Ocean coast into Tanzania.

But like many people who are called Swahili, Khadija's origins were from elsewhere.[2] The Swahili are a mixed people—local Africans who intermarried with visiting Arabian sailors and merchants in the Indian Ocean trade; slaves brought from southern and central Africa, who sometimes intermarried with the Afro-Arabs already on the coast. Sometimes they simply became known as Swahili because that became their only language. Khadija's family were slaves, and probably were from present-day Malawi. No one now remembers when her ancestors came to the Lamu area, but it is likely that at least two generations preceded her.[3] Her ancestors could have arrived by dhow before the ocean slave trade was abolished or they might have been brought out through the illegal caravan trade. Khadija's mother, at least, knew about the caravan trade and passed on some details to her daughter.[4]

In Lamu social stratification has been historically important. The freeborn are classified by who their families are, and how long they

140

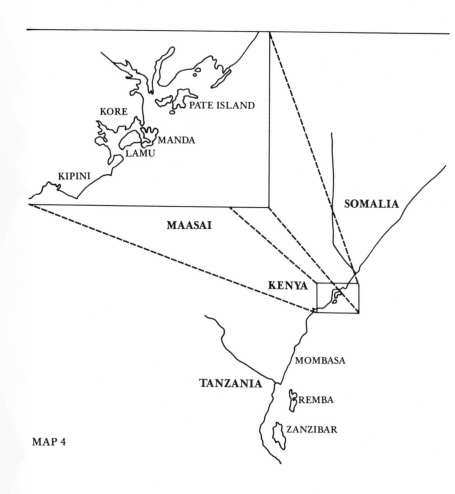

MAP 4

have been associated with the town. Slaves, of course, are kinless on arrival, but they tended to identify themselves with their owners in some cases, especially those who belonged to the aristocracy. Khadija's mother and father were owned by one such family, the BuSaid. They were relative newcomers, but they were related to the Sultan of Zanzibar, who was also the ruler of Lamu Island and whose family had been intermarrying with the old aristocracy since about 1820. Her mother was a house slave, meaning that she lived and worked in the town house owned by the BuSaid family, rather than on the small agricultural plots behind the town, which were mostly controlled by the old families. Although Khadija's mother remembered the old Lamu slave market 'where slaves were treated like cattle' it is not likely that she was bought there.

Marriages between members of the upper class were arranged—cousin marriage was preferred in order to protect property and the rights of daughters. Slaves were usually married either within the slave community of their owners, or between owners who were linked to each other by marriage. We know nothing about Khadija's father except that he was a coconut tapper on a BuSaid *shamba* (agricultural plot) on Lamu Island.

Khadija said her mother had been married twice—each time to slaves owned by a branch of the BuSaid family. The first marriage ended with the death of her husband and after the birth of seven children—five boys and two girls. After that, her mother was married to Athman, Khadija's father, by whom she gave birth to three children, one boy and two girls. Khadija was last and was born in 1919, the year referred to as *Lengelenge* (flu epidemic). Her father died soon after. (Large surviving families were not unusual among slaves or their owners in Lamu, possibly because of the nourishment provided by their diet of fish and fruit).[5]

By 1919, slaves had been officially emancipated for about ten years (or more, depending on whether owners were British subjects or subjects of the sultan).[6] But many slaves as well as their owners preferred to accept the word of the Qur'an, which held that only masters and mistresses could free their slaves. They therefore ignored the Proclamation of Emancipation issued in 1907 by the Sultan of Zanzibar. Khadija's parents were part of this group of slaves who voluntarily stayed on. Economic factors, however, influenced choices as to who could remain in slavery and who had to go free. Lamu's economy was in decline before Khadija was born, and several of her older siblings had been allowed to leave in search of paying jobs elsewhere. Most ex-slaves chose Mombasa, further down the coast, where a new port and railroad to the interior meant job opportunities, and this was where Khadija's oldest brother had gone.

When Khadija was only two years old, her mother left to join this brother in Mombasa. Her desertion was linked with the victimization of women which could (and did) occur under rules practised by Lamu Muslims. It was customary among the upper class for men to act as guardians over the financial affairs of their wives, sisters, daughters, or mothers. Having no example other than those with whom they lived, many slave and ex-slave families followed in this tradition. When Khadija's Mombasa brother began sending back a small stipend for their mother, another of her sons in Lamu took the money. When the eldest son discovered his mother was not receiving his gifts, he sent for her to join him.

Claiming her freedom from the BuSaid family, she departed— and in so doing began the process of establishing her own separate family group, rather than being mere extensions of the owning family. But she went alone, leaving two year old Khadija behind with an elder sister. Khadija had not been weaned until her mother's abrupt departure and she remembered that the separation was so painful that she 'cried from two years until twelve'.

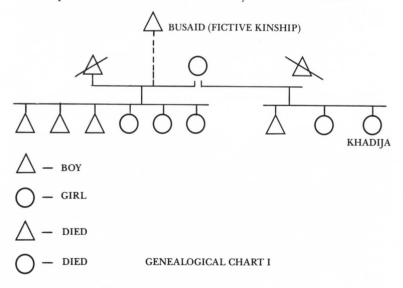

GENEALOGICAL CHART I

We meet Khadija in her small concrete house which is topped with a coconut frond roof. She lives in Langoni, the southern section of Lamu town which traditionally has been the home of newcomers and ex-slaves during the past one hundred years, or so. Her three room house consists of one tiny bedroom, the living room which also doubles as her own sleeping room, and the small kitchen behind. The entrance to her house is simply a dark drape which hangs from the top of the doorway—similar to the fashion of other houses in her neighborhood. The house is sparsely furnished. This is partly in keeping with Khadija's rejection of the emphasis on material goods found in the homes of the aristocracy; and partly because she is relatively poor. Her living room contains her hard bed, made from woven palm fronds, two simple small stools of the same material, and pictures of various members of her family along with framed verses from the Qur'an. Khadija's house, like her dress, reflects the simplicity of her taste. The bedroom, often filled with mats on which various grandchildren and great-grandchildren sleep, is small and dark. Because she is a traditional healer and midwife, she sometimes uses it for patients she is treating. Then she moves her bed in the extra room, joining the children on the floor mats when she sleeps. The kitchen is small, storing the few vessels she uses for cooking. Behind the house a small open area is enclosed with mats. This is where she cooks and where she does laundry for herself and any number of relatives.

Her present home is not far from the small hut in which she spent her childhood with her sister. Today, Khadija is working hard— continuing a pattern she was forced to develop from the time she was able to be useful in small tasks in and around her sister's home. She cannot remember when she was not working—from collecting pieces of firewood for cooking the noonday meal, to helping her sister collect and carry coconuts to the plant in town where they were processed for oil. She recalls her early love for learning: 'Teach me. I want to learn.' These were words she often said to callers, many of whom knew nothing they could teach the child, except the Qur'an. Her sister began her instruction early in the Qur'an and in the Muslim faith. She was pious and took religion from the beginning: 'I began to fast at the age of seven' she told me, unlike most Lamu children who do not carry out the Ramadan fasts until they are near or past puberty. Perhaps her early immersion in religion helped compensate for her missing mother.

Her childhood did include some time for play. She joined other children in the Langoni area in *koi*, which is the Lamu version of hide-and-seek. Out behind her sister's house, where sand is the only soil, she teamed up in a game called *washmalo* to throw as much sand on the opponents as she could. In the rainy season (usually May-June), they played *Salip*, which is something like 'one, potato, two potato', including songs about trips to Zanzibar and Pemba. Looking back on those carefree moments during her childhood, Khadija laughs and gestures as she describes the games—saying she was usually the winner or on the winning side.

Her sister married, but she continued to carry the coconuts for a pittance. Khadija learned to embroider men's caps when she was very small. She does not remember how she got the first one, but she said, 'one hat paid for another with always a little left over.' Usually someone else took the hats to local merchants for sale, but Khadija remembered what happened when the profit was small, or her hats were refused. 'I was hot tempered. When someone refused to buy, I would get very angry. I went to shops myself . . .' and usually got the desired price. She developed an odd buying pattern (for Lamu) with her profits. She seemed to find a measure of security in buying plates—even as a child. As she saw it, 'I had no mother and father. I had to take care of myself.' Those early years of hard work 'made me strong and long lived. People today engage in foolishness', including lack of desire to work and take care of themselves. 'I valued learning and learned whatever I could. I insist that my grandchildren and great-grandchildren to go school. I know how important an education is. They learn the Qur'an at Madressa (mosque school) which I never did. And they go to the government school.'

In Lamu today most daughters of the poor or the illiterate marry just past puberty. And most marriages are arranged, just as they were earlier in the century. In Khadija's case, however, there was an element of choice. When she reached marriageable age she met her future husband on the streets of Lamu. According to him, 'We fell in love'. Exactly whose permission was obtained is uncertain, but he was still a slave and he enjoyed the goodwill of his owners, the el Maawyia family, who gave a plot of land to his mother, so she could build a house for him. The el Maawyia family claim to be the oldest outside residents in the town, and Ahmed, Khadija's husband, belonged to the senior member of that family—a man regarded as something like a chief by the British civil servants who administered Lamu. His wedding present to Ahmed was his freedom.

Like Khadija's father, Ahmed was a coconut tapper and worked on the *shambas*, but he and Khadija moved to Langoni, to the tiny hut that his slave mother provided for them. They were fortunate for their class—and Khadija had her many plates to bring to her marriage as a kind of dowry. It was customary for free husbands to pay bride price to the woman's family, who in turn, bought furniture and other necessities with the money. Ahmed provided the almost unheard of present of a house, but it remained his and therefore was not considered bride price. They both worked hard. Khadija had to carry all of the water for every need from the local well. With that water she washed (by hand) their few items of clothing, cooked and cleaned. Muslims wash five times a day—before prayer—and so they always needed a store of water for ritual cleansing. In addition, she continued to find and carry firewood, sift and clean rice, and cook their main, midday meal which she often delivered to her husband in the *shamba*. At the end of their first year of marriage she gave birth to a daughter. The workload increased, but Khadija found time—usually in the dark of night when her only light was a small oil lamp—to embroider the men's caps, and thus to put aside a bit of money as often as she could. She used some of the extra money 'to buy goods we needed' otherwise, she saved. Before the second year was ended Khadija had given birth to her second child and her only son.

In the intervening months she discovered that her husband was unfaithful. This is not uncommon in Lamu, but Khadija was not a common wife. Her 'hot temper' warmed to boiling and after three months of argument, she finally convinced Ahmed he should divorce her. She remembered, and he confirmed, that he wanted to stay married. Divorce was very difficult for women. But a man merely said 'I divorce you' three times in succession if he wanted his freedom. Somehow she prevailed and Ahmed uttered the phrases—making it possible for Khadija to exercise negative choice over decisions affecting her life.[7]

Now she was on her own with two babies. She took her small savings and bought a run-down mud and wattle house near the Reiyadah Mosque, in Langoni. And after a quick trip to Mombasa to see her mother (with whom she had had little communication since that time long ago when her mother had deserted her), she returned and married again. This time it was to an ex-slave, who helped her put the little house in shape. That marriage 'was a mistake' and, although it produced a second daughter, it did not take Khadija long to convince her husband that he should divorce her. Again she was alone, and even though she had a home of her own, she had little opportunity to support her children.

She decided to follow in her mother's footsteps and move to Mombasa. But she still remembered the pain of being motherless when she was a baby, so she took the youngest daughter with her; leaving the older children with her former in-laws—still slaves of the el Maawyia family. In effect, there was a family relationship for these children on two fronts: the family of the owners, and the grandparents. The father was also in Lamu and no doubt took an interest in his children as time and inclination allowed. Her small house was habitable and she left it to a poor woman, whose only obligation was to keep it up.

This second trip beyond Lamu island was made by sailing dhow. She traveled in the special section reserved for women—meaning in the bow, behind a curtain, where it was dark and hot. On this trip Khadija remembered that women were seasick and fainting, but because she was an ex-slave, and thus of low status, she was allowed finally to crawl out on the deck for a breath of air; the trip 'was not bad' in comparison with that of her female companions.[8]

Khadija's nearly ten years in Mombasa forged links in the extended slave family which had been only dreams while she lived in Lamu. She established a close relationship with her mother, whom she was to care for in the old woman's declining years back in Lamu. Soon after her arrival, she began baking bread and sewing Muslim men's caps as a way of providing for herself and her daughter. Before long, she remarried, this time a man from the Comoro Islands—then a French colony in the Indian Ocean about seven hundred miles from Mombasa, but also Swahili in culture. She lived with him for nine years.

Back home her daughter and son were growing up, and she sent whatever small sums she could spare for their welfare and made a few trips home to see them during this period. This marriage also ended in divorce and although Khadija did not give her reasons, it is possible that her refusal or failure to provide more children may have been partly responsible. The next Mombasa marriage was to a tailor from the Bajun Islands, near Lamu. It 'was a mistake. I got annoyed with him and pushed him to divorce.'

After shedding her fourth husband, Khadija brought her mother and her younger daughter back to Lamu, where they moved into her small house near the Reiyadah Mosque, and where they were joined by her elder daughter and son. She continued to make Muslim caps and bake bread, and she soon found another husband, Salim. He was a poor but respectable member of one of the old families—an aristocrat who had a house in town to which he brought Khadija and her family.

During the nine years she was married to Salim, two tragedies of very different sorts occurred. Her son, who had spent nearly ten years without his mother, was especially close to her on her return. She doted on him. At the age of twelve, he drowned in the bay off the Lamu seafront. Perhaps a twinge of guilt as well as normal grief colored her memories of his death. 'He was swimming. He called to his sister, saying he wanted "to say goodbye to the sea" and dived in again. He never came up.' Search parties attempted to find his body among the mangroves near the seafront, but when all appeared in vain, a group of men went to Khadija and told her that her son had drowned. 'For four days I went to the seafront to look for him, hoping he was in the mangrove. By the fifth day I prayed that he was dead.' There was a sense of incompleteness that never left her—no body to bury and no final rituals to help with her mourning. In 1983, after a lapse of thirty-two years, Khadija could only say, 'I knew my son was dead, but it would have helped to see his body.' But, it was also 'Allah's will' and she is sustained by Muslim fatalism.[9]

Soon after her son's death, and while she was still married to the upper-class man, she had to face a crisis of another sort. Her elder daughter, now having reached puberty, was beautiful, well built, and developing the charisma which made her mother so attractive to men. But because she was still young, she frequently went about the Langoni area without the requisite veiling required of upper-class women. She captured the eye of one of the descendants of the revered Habib Saleh, who had founded the Reiyadah Mosque, and whose children and grandchildren enjoyed much prestige in the ex-slave community because of his saintly reputation and because they were descended from the Prophet Mohammed.[10] When Seyyid Bwana came to Khadija for permission to marry her daughter there was little she could do but refer him to the child's father, Ahmed. Ahmed bowed to the request and a small wedding was arranged. There was no bride price—the honor of marrying into this Sharifian family (ie. into the Prophets' by extension) was regarded by the groom as sufficient. On her daughter's wedding night Khadija and a few female members of the family remained outside the door long enough to receive the blood-stained sheet which proved her daughter's virginity, then they retreated to allow the couple their honeymoon. And honeymoon was all there was. Within a few days, the Shariff retired to the home he maintained with his permanent wife and deserted Khadija's daughter along with the son she bore him. He never inquired after her, nor acknowledged the child.

Years later, Khadija acknowledged that because of her position in Lamu society, she could not have refused the Sharif her daughter. She knew when he came to her that he never contracted long marriages with ex-slave girls, and her daughter 'was so far down the line of wives that he did not remember how many came before her.'

Khadija and her husband took the abandoned daughter into their home which also contained her mother and her youngest daughter. When the baby boy was born, Khadija's husband immediately became attached to him. In fact, friction involving the child eventually brought an end to the sixth marriage. The boy was ill with a cold. His mother repeatedly called him to come in from a rainstorm. He refused and his mother spanked him as she forced him inside. Khadija's husband was so angered at seeing the child smacked that he, in turn, slapped the mother. Khadija 'had an attack of temper' and stormed out of the house vowing not to return and called for divorce. Eventually the old man gave in, divorcing Khadija, but arranging for one of his houses to be given to the small boy. 'He really took care of Aisha's boy' and 'he was good to the girls, but he was old.' In fact, when the old man was suffering his final illness, Khadija vacated the house in Langoni into which she had moved and her two daughters remained and cared for him until he died. (In Lamu divorced men and women are not allowed to see or talk to each other again—thus she had to move out if he was moving in).

Khadija's next foray into marriage was with a Kipini man from the nearby mainland who was probably an ex-slave since she said he was a Swahili. He was a carpenter and dhow builder who put his skills to work in repairing her house in Langoni, moving in with her during their brief time together: he soon proved to be 'another mistake.'[11]

Her last husband was a Kore—an outsider who came to Lamu from the Kenya mainland during the manpower shortage of World War II.[12] The Kore husband was 'the best' and 'the only man who

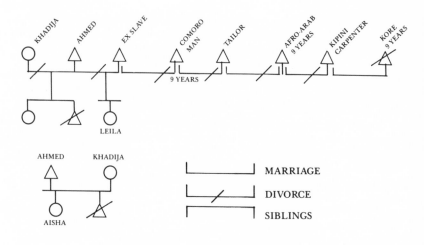

GENEALOGICAL CHART II

ever made me happy.' Sadly this marriage lasted nine years, ending not in divorce but with her husband's death.

The Kore were originally Maasai. After capture and enslavement among the Somali, they obtained their freedom around the turn of the century and returned to nomadic cattle grazing. Eventually some reached the mainland not far from Lamu island and settled in small hamlets, farming a bit of deserted land and mostly tending their livestock. When an epizootic plague wiped out their cattle, some came to Lamu to work as herders on the shambas behind town. The importance they attach to cattle especially, and livestock in general, cannot be overemphasized. Soon after Salaal's marriage to Khadija they began to acquire a small herd of their own: 'One cow led to another and so on until we built up to eighteen cows.' But, Khadija saw the cattle as a way of acquiring land and argued that they sell their herd to buy a shamba. 'We really fought' and 'his brothers and sisters fought with me' to keep the cattle. 'I told them land is money. The cows are just like humans, they can die . . . but you can get money out of land.' Eventually Salaal capitulated and they sold all but four of their cows, purchasing a *shamba* about two miles from their Langoni home. The remaining cows were 'sent to graze and one died. The land is still there. We put coconut trees in. When a tree dies you replant. When a cow dies you cannot quickly get another.'

They also built a small house for themselves and gave Khadija's small home in the Reiyadah area to her second daughter, Leila. Leila followed her mother in marrying a Kore man and soon became pregnant. It was the birth of this grandchild which launched Khadija into her next career—that of midwife and traditional healer.

In Lamu it is customary to have a 'family midwife' on the order of the family doctor. Their midwife was off tending to another birth when Leila started labor. Khadija stepped in and delivered the child—following the procedures she had witnessed at the births of her own children as well as countless others she had seen. When the midwife arrived she was so impressed with Khadija's work that 'she certified me' on the spot. Soon her services were much in demand. 'She was more famous than all the others' and if they were jealous, it mattered not at all to Khadija's who received 'spiritual pleasure from helping other women.' The fees were small but welcome, and the price structure reflects on the value put on the sexes in Lamu: for a boy Khadija was paid goods or money equalling twelve shillings; for a girl the fixed amount was only ten. (The value of the shilling has changed, but it was roughly $1.75 for boys and $1.50 for girls until the 1970s when the shilling dropped against the dollar, making the amounts less than a dollar for either sex.)

Her daughter, Leila, provided her with an abundance of sons-in-law—eight altogether—and a continuing stream of deliveries, for a total of eleven children. The first baby Khadija delivered—a girl—married a Kore, giving him three children. Now Khadija was tied to the Kore by three generations of marriages—although both her daughter and grand-daughter were divorced from the Kore husbands after bearing them children. Then, following in her mother's footsteps, the grand-daughter married a man from the Hadramaut in southern Arabia by whom she has six children. Khadija has been responsible for looking after any number of these children by both her daughter and her granddaughter—keeping them by day, if not full time, and often contributing to their support.[13]

Meanwhile, Khadija's first grandson (by the Sharif) has married and four children were born to him and his wife. All of these children have been delivered by Khadija, not counting the scores she has delivered to ex-slave women, their descendants, and to the Kore—with whom she gained extended kin status through her marriage and those of her children and grandchildren.

Although Khadija never delivered babies for the Afro-Arab women, her skills for postnatal treatment were valued by those in her former family. In Lamu, women, and especially upper-class women, are kept on a strict regimen for forty days after delivery. Treatment includes salt for healing the vagina, and daily massage to help restore the new mother's strength as well as making sure all afterbirth is expunged from the body. After each birth, Khadija is sent for; and for forty days, she goes daily to the town house of her former owners' daughters, rubbing them with oil, and skillfully massaging their bodies back into shape. In so far as is practical she tries to follow the same course with the poorer women—most of whom do not have the support system necessary to allow them forty days of rest. For her own daughters and grand-daughters she spent precious money buying liver and chicken for broths that she prescribes to upper-class women—broths which are consumed daily as part of the restoration process.

Her experience as a midwife also made her something of an expert on troubled births. Early in her career a patient came to her for prenatal examination. Khadija discovered 'no movement in the mother's womb,' but said nothing except to request her return in a few days time. When the woman returned and there was still no movement, Khadija dealt with her first stillbirth by 'massaging' until parts of the fetus began to appear. Although problems such as this are rare in Lamu, traditional healers had medicines for women to drink which 'cleansed the womb and prevented infection.' In this case, Khadija's combination of herbs and water worked and the woman subsequently gave birth to five healthy children.

Khadija enlarged her study of traditional medicines and her practice to include other forms of treatment. She became expert at treating her mostly female patients for colds, sore throats, malaria, and even problems with the spirit world. In order to keep other women from successfully putting *hudsa* (a curse) on new babies, she learned to draw designs with incense on their eyes, cheeks and foreheads.[14] For the common cold she has two prescriptions: first, she breaks egg in honey which the patient drinks for relief from congestion. If this mixture produces no results, she has 'an Arab

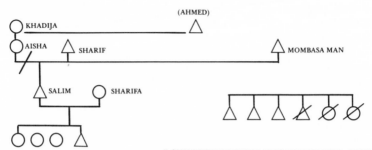

7 CHILDREN BORN TO FIRST DAUGHTER; 3 DIED
4 CHILDREN BORN TO FIRST GRANDSON

GENEALOGICAL CHART III

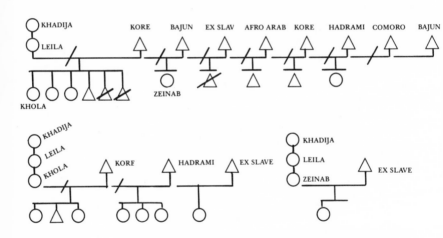

11 CHILDREN BORN TO SECOND DAUGHTER; 3 DIED
7 CHILDREN BORN TO ONE GRANDDAUGHTER
1 CHILD BORN TO ANOTHER GRANDDAUGHTER: 1 MISCARRIAGE

DIVORCE

MARRIAGE

SIBLINGS

GENEALOGICAL CHART IV

medicine, *samgha larabi*, [a sort of gum resembling a cough drop], which the patient sucks at night for relief.' For malaria, she uses roots and leaves from a special tree, *mtu*, in the mangrove swamps near the seafront. 'I boil the leaves and roots in water, and then I completely cover the patient with a cloth. If the patient is well enough, I make her sit, covered over, on a stool, and put the steaming medicine under that. If she is too sick, I put the steam pot under her bed. The combination of steam from the medicine and sweat from the cover forces the fever out' and with repeated treatment, the malaria is gone.

Although venereal disease is said to be uncommon among Lamu women, Khadija had a cure. Near her house there grows a small vine-like plant called *kiuno pembe*, the root of which resembles a white radish. This root is boiled in water and given to the patient to drink: 'once you drink that—a strong medicine—you are cured.' For abortion, also rare, there are herbs she claims are successful. One is a combination of herbs, sesame and a small amount of water which 'will abort up to two months'; and *shimari*, when taken in combination with Arabic incense and water, will usually 'abort into the fifth month of pregnancy. No abortion is possible after that medically' and mechanical means are not employed. Although every effort is made to stop miscarriages, including mixtures of herbs and water, when it happens it is 'Allah's will' and it remains for women to get pregnant as soon after the miscarriage as they can. One of Khadija's grand-daughters was in process of losing her baby when I visited her in September 1985. She did everything in her power to save the baby—in the fifth month of pregnancy— including putting the girl to bed in her house to 'rest', but unfortunately she lost the baby, and a pall of stillness remained over the house for several days. This was the first miscarriage among her own family and Khadija was unusually distressed since the girl was slow to become pregnant.

Most poor patients come to Khadija for treatment, although she goes to them for deliveries. She keeps her medicines and herbs in a closet off her tiny kitchen, and her 'office' is her living-bedroom. Patients come when she is at home preparing for the large midday meal, or in late afternoon after she has returned from work in the shamba.

Despite her heavy workload, Khadija enjoys merriment and often participates in wedding celebrations when they occur among the family of her former owners.[15] She often insists on dancing the role of *malishma* (head slave) during pre-wedding dances among the women (although she never held that position in the household). This is her way of illustrating that she still has ties to the old family; and re-inforcing the position of importance and respect she has come to enjoy with them.

On the other hand, when she intermingles with the Kore, she is also viewed as a leader as well as extended kin. Whereas her behavior during the upper-class weddings is restrained and controlled, when she participates in Kore weddings she lets go and has a rousing time. In 1983 the grandson of her former Kore husband was getting married. His family was very poor, and his earnings were small as a livestock herder on the shambas. Khadija, knowing the Kore wedding customs, came to his aid and in so doing she was the first to bridge the wide social gap between the aristocratic old Afro-Arab families and the outsider group of Kore. (The Kore work for the old families, but generally their only association with them is to deliver milk to their town houses daily.) Knowing that the Kore especially value a calf to slaughter on the night of consummation, she approached her former owners and they gave a calf. Because the Kore put emphasis on gift giving to family members of the bride as well as the bride herself, Khadija reached into her own meagre savings and provided some of the expense money. Then, she went to friends in the ex-slave community—mainly women who had married among the Kore—and raised a few shillings to pay for Kool Aid and cookies (wedding refreshments for guests).

Finally, and significantly, she invited aristocratic women and ex-slaves to the wedding celebrations out in the shambas—far from town and to an area almost never frequented by the Afro-Arab women. Several young women from the old families joined ex-slaves in their trek through the heavy sand to the groom's hut. The music consisted of Afro-Arab and ex-slave women beating buffalo horns together while the Kore women ululated in high shrill tones, creating sounds no Lamu woman had heard before.

Khadija, in keeping with Kore tradition, produced a drum (which Lamu women do not use), and began beating it to the slow, monotonous beat of the buffalo horns. No one danced. Clearly, Kore women did not know Lamu wedding songs: and Lamu women did not understand that ululating was song. Quickly sizing up the impasse, Khadija bounded into the middle of the circle and began to dance. She was joined by another old ex-slave woman who had placed a shilling note (local money) in her mouth. Before the combined audience, gathered mostly at her initiative, Khadija swayed and revolved around her partner on the dance floor of heavy sand. At sixty-five, the spider-like figure was agile and quick. She leaned forward, grasped the money in her own teeth, and while the Kore ululated, and the Lamu women beat their horns, Khadija began her slow descent. Without so much as a teeter, Khadija leaned low over her partner, carrying out a parody of sexual intercourse which featured mostly Khadija's gyrations. The eyes of every woman present were riveted on her. Forgotten momentarily were the divisions between them. Through Khadija these women have attained a sense of community—although not equality. At the conclusion of her performance, knowing the barriers were down, she returned to her former controlled manner, symbolically celebrating all of her families with the repetitious beat of her drum.

Within the framework of Lamu society, Khadija is an unusual woman. Born a slave, freed during childhood but deserted by her mother, raised amid poverty, denied education, she might have been destined to the anonimity of her countless unfortunate sisters who also dwell in Lamu. But her life has been full of adventure— she has dealt with tragedy and with triumph. She has touched and healed female members of her community in ways that make her unique among them. Her many marriages are behind her. She sees her future in the education of her many descendants—male and female—for whom she provides as generously as she can. Perhaps the most descriptive phrase that can applied to Khadija came from the philosopher, Paul Tillich: she had 'the courage to be.'

Notes

1. Enid Schildkrout generously worked out the genealogies in this paper and I am very grateful to her. All names except for the owning families have been changed to protect the privacy of Khadija and her family.
2. For various definitions of Swahili see Chittick, Neville H. and Rotberg, Robert I. (ed.), *East Africa and the Orient*, (New York:

1973), p. 43. Lofchie, M, *Zanzibar: Background for Revolution*, (Princeton: 1975); Prins, A. J. H., *The Swahili Speaking Peoples of Zanzibar and the East African Coast: Arabs, Shirazi, and Swahili*, (London: 1960); Nurse, Derek, and Spear, Thomas (ed.), *The Swahili: Reconstructing the History of an African Society 800–1500*, (Philadelphia: 1984).

3. Slaves did not usually live and work on Lamu island unless they were proficient in Swahili. The presumption is that her grandparents on both sides probably came as slaves to the Lamu mainland, where they learned the language; and their children—Khadija's parents—lived and worked for their owners on Lamu island. Interviews with Khadija took place in Lamu between March and June, 1980; January–February, 1981; February, 1982; October–November, 1983; and September–October, 1985.

4. For Lamu and the slave trade see Patricia Romero, 'Lamu (Kenya) Slave Trade and British Efforts to Suppress,' paper presented at the Colloque International sur la Traite des Noirs, Nantes, 10 July, 1985.

5. For fertility and nutrition see Bogarts, John 'Does Malnutrition Affect Fecundity: A Summary of Evidence' *Science* 208, 9 May 1980; Frisch, Rose E. 'Population, Food Intake, and Fertility' *Science* 199, 6 January 1978. Although there is still some controversy over whether nursing mothers conceive, evidence in these papers supports our findings that they do. This was also the case with Mama Khadija and Hajiya Husaina (See Schildkrout, this book).

6. Romero, Patricia, 'Where have all the Slaves Gone: Emancipation and Post Emancipation in Lamu (Kenya)' *Journal of African History*, 1986.

7. This concept is also found in Makhlouf, Carla, *Changing Veils: Women and Modernisation in North Yemen*, (Austin; 1979), p. 41.

8. For conditions pertaining to women traveling by dhow see Villiers, Alan John, *Sons of Sinbad*, (New York; 1940).

9. Marcia Wright believes that women who accept conventional roles in African societies are subject to a degree of fatalism. See Wright, Marcia, 'Women in Peril: A Commentary on the Life Stories of Captives in Nineteenth Century Africa' *African Social Research* 20 (December, 1975), p. 805.

10. Lienhardt, Peter, 'The Mosque College of Lamu and its Social Background' *Tanganyika Notes and Records* 53 (1959), pp. 228–242.

11. Martin Ottenheimer has written about men from the Comoro Islands who move into their wives' homes, thus maintaining matrilocal residence. This is also reflective of the Lamu ex-slave community, where most husbands move into and out of their wives' homes. See Ottenheimer, Martin, 'Matrilocal Residence

and Nonsororal Polygyny: A Case from the Comoro Islands' *Journal of Anthropological Research* 35 (1984), pp. 328–335.

12. Romero, Patricia, 'Generations of Strangers: The Kore of Lamu' *International Journal of African Historical Studies* 18 (1985), pp. 455–472.

13. Megan Vaughan found elsewhere what I discovered in Lamu—that there can be a chain of women, mothers, daughters, grand-daughters, all dependent on one of them for support. See Vaughan, Megan, 'Which Family: Problems in the Reconstruction of the History of the Family as an Economic and Cultural Unit' *Journal of African History* 24 (1983), pp. 275–283. Divorce is common among Muslims in East Africa, although traditionally divorce has been attributed to the men, who cannot afford more than one wife at a time. Khadija's divorces were almost all at her instigation, although she forced her husbands to take the initiative. For a traditional view of divorce see Caplan, Ann Patricia, *Choice and Constraint in a Swahili Community: Property, Hierarchy and Cognatic Descent on the East African Coast* (Oxford: 1975).

14. Drawing traditional designs on babies faces and across their eyes with kohl is practiced among the Afro-Arabs, the Hadramis, and the Indians in Lamu. When Khadija extended her care to the Kore, she brought the practice to them. This does not seem to be universally successful medically, however, because various of Khadija's great-grandchildren almost constantly have eye infections. Eye problems are a considerable problem among Lamu people.

15. Romero, Patricia, 'Weddings in Lamu, Kenya: An Example of Social and Economic Change' *Cahiers d' Etudes africaines* 94 (1984), pp. 131–155.

Mercha:

An Ethiopian Woman Speaks of Her Life

ANNE CASSIÈRS
Translated by
CHRIS PROUTY ROSENFELD

Man, God, the natural, and the supernatural are for many Ethiopians all one and the same. Their lives are lived as much with those invisible forces that surround them as with what is visible and tangible. So it was with Mercha. Her story will show the strength of her spirituality and her acceptance of the supernatural.

Mercha is a potter, which places her in the artisan caste long disdained by many Ethiopians, who are wary of those who make their living by manual skill. I first met her in 1970 when she came to work at the Ceramic Workshop I set up in Addis Ababa to produce pottery that combined Ethiopian designs with modern techniques. She was about forty, tiny, but well proportioned. When she spoke, in her sweet, modulated voice, it was with her whole being—wrinkling her nose, arching her eyebrows, a palm upheld. Her arms, legs, the line of her throat had a sculptured perfection. She was dark skinned, except around her eyes and nose, where her tint shaded to copper traced with red. Her frizzy hair was cut short. Dressed always in rustic clothes, she was barefooted. Her bearing expressed the deep humility characteristic of many who live close to the soil. An astonishing grace of movement added to her beauty, and her usual pensive expression bespoke piety.

During those months when we worked side by side, I often went to her village near Addis Ababa where I watched traditional ways of working clay. Mercha sat on the ground on a potato sack, one foot stretched out and the other, knee bent, tucked under her hip, her clay and work tools in front of her. In an old saucepan full of water floated her tools—a piece of bamboo, piece of gourd, a corn cob. Behind her were some black pebbles, gleaming, polished, and smoothed by long use. Rocking her whole torso backward and forward she kneaded the clay. Then, taking the kneaded ball, she

159

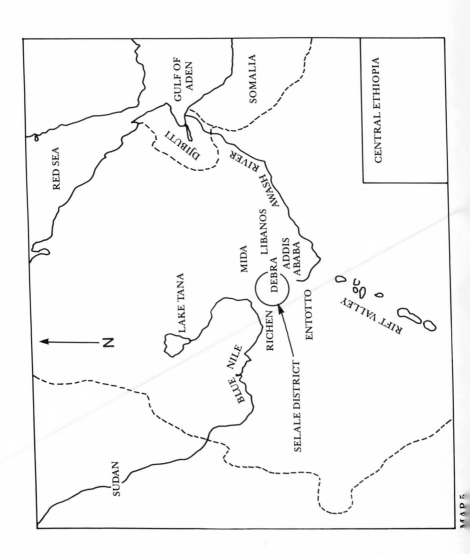

RED SEA

GULF OF
ADEN

DJIBUTI

SOMALIA

AWASH RIVER

LAKE TANA

MIDA

LIBANOS

DEBRA

ADDIS
ABABA

RICHEN

ENTOTTO

N

BLUE NILE

SELALE DISTRICT

RIFT VALLEY

SUDAN

CENTRAL ETHIOPIA

MAP 5

struck it with the flat of her hand—clac! clac!—and threw it on the scant wheel.[1] Then she began the pot. Her right hand gave it form while the left supported, steadied, and propelled it around. The hand was sure and firm. With the gourd fragment she carved out and smoothed the interior. The thumb and index finger modeled the upper rim, and the nail of the index finger creased it while the wide part of the thumb gently pressed out the shape. Often the little finger was extended, held as a balance, a rudder, while the other fingers worked directly on the clay. The gestures were precise, delicate, and efficient, like those of a midwife. The upper part of her hand, rough and brown with short nails, was a poem to the earth, while the palm, delicate as a beach of white sand, sheltered the spirit. Mercha breathed form into clay.

As the hours passed, the small courtyard filled with pots, marmites, and pitchers which she left to dry in the sun while waiting to add a spout or a handle. Before firing them she smeared them with a paste of clay and oil. Often her daughters came to help her. With a pebble they pumiced the dry pieces and they became shiny, a job that took a long time. On Fridays, Mercha did the firing, for the traders came on Saturday to buy. In the courtyard a pit was dug, and there she placed very carefully on a stand of faggots the pots ready to be 'cooked'. She slipped underneath a handful of dry leaves, lit them with a match, and the fire crackled. With a stick in her hand, Mercha watched the fire, poking it to calm or encourage it as needed, in spite of the flames and dense smoke. Sometimes one heard the dull thwack of a pot breaking.

The firing took about an hour.[2] When she took the pots off, they were as incandescent as red metal. With the tip of her stick she rolled them gently on the ground to a mound of grass from which she recovered them. She set fire to the grass, and immediately stifled it, creating heavy smoke. In an instant the pots turned black as ebony, the way the buyers preferred them. Mercha passed the whole day doing this task, untiringly repeating the whole process for another firing.

At dawn, as I left the quarter, the mass of each of these little ovens blurred and seemed to grow narrower. In the darkness the flames glimmered and danced across alleys and lanes. One could understand the confused feelings of ordinary people, the fear, the distrust, toward those who work the transmutation of earth into those ebony shapes.

Our friendship grew, and Mercha began to tell me about her life, her parents, where she came from, and her own family. At first, it was just 'woman-talk', but as I became deeply interested in her story I began to take notes and, ultimately, used a tape recorder.[3] It was always very relaxed, sitting on the ground, preparing food, and going on pilgrimages together. Although very poor, she would always invite me for a meal even though she might be fasting for religious reasons. Eventually, these casual conversations became more revealing and intimate. As I was soon to find out, Mercha was reluctant to divulge anything pertaining to her spiritual life, but she would talk very freely of her everyday life, including her marriages, her relations with men, and her family.

My father was born at Amelsa, in Borana Gojam. My father's mother was from Mida, on the frontier of Menz. My mother was born at Derra near Fitche. (Map 5). My parents met by chance. He was called Tekle Maryam and he left the place where he was born because his neighbors tried to cast an evil spell on him. He had no children so he migrated to the village of Entotto. It must have been during the time of *Atse* Menilek.[4] My father was a weaver and made fabrics for the church and also worked for the palace. While living and working at Entotto he believed he was sterile so he thought to himself, 'Why stay here when I can have no children?' So he went to the monastery of Debra Libanos and became a monk. It was there he began to have dreams. In his dream he saw a big female bird. With a lance he killed it, and it lay on its left side. Then many little birds came out of it and they played around their mother. They say this bird is very pious because it is seen around churches. My father told this dream to some friends. 'You will have children,' they said.

Then he had another dream. A voice called him: 'Tekle Maryam.' 'Who is it?'

'Your destiny is not to be a monk. You will have many children.'

He told this dream to his friends who said: 'Very well. It is clear. It is only a matter of time.'

In the monastery, a monk also had a dream about this. Yes, everything combined to show he would not become a monk, but would have many descendants.

As for my mother, she was a young divorcée. For her second marriage they gave her to this old man, Tekle Maryam my father. [Laughing] They had twelve children! The very first time she was pregnant, she left him and returned to her family saying, 'I do not want a husband so old.' She stayed with her family and gave birth to a son. After two or three years, my father, who still loved her, sent the *shemagalle*[5] to seek her out. She returned to my father's bed. Again she became pregnant and again she returned to her parents. The *shemagalle* came again, and again [laughing] she returned to him.[6] After she had four or five children she remained with her husband. After their twelfth child they separated their beds because she wanted no more. She was still young and my father, who was sweet and kind, let her do what she wanted.

My parents settled in Selale district. We lived on a hill in an isolated place. There were about ten families nearby, but I remember only the two or three who were closest. A little brook ran below our house where we went to get water. Our nearest neighbors were Amhara, but all around us lived Gallas.[7] We all lived in accord, sharing our pastures. When the animals wandered, whether ours or our neighbors, a call would come across the hills: 'Oooooowoo-yay . . . have you seen our cow?' Or one of us would shout: 'This brown one . . . is it yours?'

My father led an austere life. He ate very little . . . a few beans, a little *talla*.[8] He hardly ever touched meat. All the food prepared in the house was for us children. My father took life one day at a time, without ever getting angry or joyful over anything. When we were ill, he did not weep. If he was happy he never showed it. He never laughed. If we burst into laughter, he just grimaced. Thus he lived, and never, never did he embrace us.

We children amused ourselves in the fields and meadows. We pretended to make bread from the 'flour' dust of crushed white stones. But this was only on rest days when our parents slept. All other times we worked for our parents and were not allowed to play. Our parents were very pious. They went to church often and ate and fasted according to its laws.

When my father's time came to die, he assembled us and commanded us to respect religious customs: fast on Wednesdays and Fridays, observe the Sabbath, and never marry a slave. This last command does not apply anymore, as today everyone is equal. To treat someone as a slave, that is not done any more, is it? In former times, no one wanted to marry a person whose ancestor was a slave. Now it is common. In our religion they do not buy and sell slaves.[9] My family bought no slaves.

On his deathbed, my father also told us not to drink coffee and to respect the law of Genesis. So my father ordered, yet none of us lives according to these laws. Only my sister, perhaps, who is a nun, respects the will of my father. This is why she does not want to tell you about her life. For that which one does for God, one does in the secrecy of one's heart.

Mercha did not like speaking of these things. I knew that coffee was considered the drink of Muslims and pagans in traditional Ethiopia, but I did not understand the 'law of Genesis'. Twice in the course of that conversation she told me: 'Today you really make me talk my heart out!' We laughed. She kept silent for a while, then when I urged her, she told me this.

When a woman has her period, she must stay alone for seven days and not meet any man. He who touches her becomes impure. Nowadays, when a woman has her period, they simply say, 'One sees the flower', as religion is no longer respected. When Eve bit into the apple, a white liquid ran out. It was the blood of the apple. That is why God said, 'May your blood run for seven years.' But Eve pleaded, 'Make it happen for only seven days.' And God replied, 'Go, and return pure after seven days.' The ancient Hebrews built a house to one side to which women could withdraw. Our grandmothers did that. My mother also. My father insisted that we follow these customs.[10]

In the past, everyone went to church, both men and women, and if they could not go, they recited the Psalms at home. My parents recited in Gi'iz[11] 'Our Father', 'I honor you, Mary', 'The Golgotha', 'The Praise of Mary', and 'The Creed'. All of these prayers were learned by heart and they said them every day. My parents did not know how to read. There were no schools at that time. We lived like animals! My mother's uncle was the only one in the family who had any education and that was because when he was a baby, four months old, he caught smallpox and became blind. His mother then was divorced and took him to Gondar where he learned *qenē* and became a wise man.[12] This uncle never married. He remained chaste his whole life. He listened to everything said by the priests, and when they made a mistake, he corrected them. Eventually, he returned to his native hamlet and started teaching others. He had the spirit of God in him and people considered him a saint.

Sometimes I resent that my parents did not provide any instruction for us, not even in the priest's school. They fed us and clothed us but should also have arranged for some teaching. It would have been a good thing. But who knows? Even if I had gone to school I may not have been able to learn anything.

My father was an honest, hard-working man. His skill was weaving but after marrying my mother he turned to farming and became rich. We lived well. At harvest time, he employed other workers to help out, paying them off with a percentage of the harvest—wheat, beans and sorghum. We owned five pairs of oxen. My two brothers and two salaried men worked our land and often a day-worker was hired. Each used a pair of oxen.

People would help each other with such chores as pulling weeds. It is called the *debo*.[13] When they came to our place, my mother was always fixing food and drink for them, for my father would tell her, 'Prepare food plentifully, so that God will also give us our daily food.' After they finished their work they were given some money.

While they were getting in the harvest, my father turned to his weaving. For a *gabi* he would accept six days work on the land with the client providing the cotton. Others would pay in cash—six *birr*.[14] My father was much in demand as a weaver and when he had to decline orders because he had too much work, they would say to him, 'Oh, just weave it whenever you have the time.'

For our clothes, the women spun the thread and my father wove the cloth. We all ate together—all equal. The only difference was in the division of work. Our life was harmonious. The older people would get together to arbitrate village affairs. Everyone went to church together and had fun together. I grew up in innocence and did not even know the name *Amlak* [God]. I heard only the name of St Mikael to whom our church was dedicated. I even thought [smiling] that Mikael was the Creator.

They say that my father was about 120 when he died. He had married off all but two of his children. He was still robust, his hair not yet white, and he was not even bent over. You might ask how we knew his age. It was dated from the famine they call 'qamoud' and they said that at that time my father was thirty years old.[15]

That famine was severe. Many animals died. Wild beasts attacked people even in their houses. Parents put their smallest children high up, in hollows carved on the walls of the house. Mothers could not nurse their babies so they got rid of them. There was no water so they drank the urine of horses.

At that time, my father worked for the palace and was given butter, spices, and some dried meat as well as seven *birr* a month. He had a donkey on which he carried his cloth, and during the famine he slept beside it for fear people would steal his donkey and eat it. People were so weak, yet they walked long distances to find water. When they brought back water after a long day's search they armed themselves with sticks and lances to fend off attackers who wanted their water. One day, when my family went to look for water, a woman followed them with her little girl trailing behind. Once in the forest, she began to beat the child, saying, 'Stop following me.' My parents were upset. 'I cannot feed us both,' she said. 'We will both die. It would be better to abandon her.' My parents cursed this woman and took her child. She grew up with us and worked hard, but she died at a young age.

I was told these stories when I was small, and though they made me cry I liked to hear them. While my brothers and sisters were playing or sleeping, I sat near my parents to listen, and they were surprised at what I already knew.

After the death of my mother, my father had a dream. He heard my mother say: 'I was mistaken by one *semuni*[16] in my accounts. This money does not belong to us. Let Mercha take it to the church of the Holy Trinity.' Then my mother said—see how obstinate she was—'I died without having given life to the thirteenth and fourteenth children I should have put into the world.' Even though she would meet them in the company of the Trinity,[17] the loss of this money and the thought of those two babies troubled her.

I began to make pottery when I was quite small. I learned from my mother. Her side of the family were also weavers, but she had learned to make pots by watching our neighbors. When she picked up clay, my sisters and I would hurry to help her. We would play around making little crosses or little dolls out of clay. In the country where my sister lives, she could show you a water pitcher she made when she was a child. She keeps it for the milk to make butter. My brother and another sister also have a jar made before I was born. Isn't it amazing that they lasted so long?[18]

When my mother went to market, she left me in charge of the house. I would hurry through the work and begin my pots. When I had the chance, I would sell them to make a little money. In our family, we were all encouraged to work. In truth, what little money I made went back to the family. [Laughter] If I saved enough to buy a sheep, we would all eat it together. Or rather, my parents would take the sheep and give me a cloth in exchange.

A potter's work is very tiring, it is true. But I prefer 'mixing up mud' to any other work, for it gives me independence and I can observe all the religious days.[19] I will do it till I die. I love my work. While working with my hands, I can have my thoughts, far from the quarrels of others. That brings me peace and brings me closer to God. Besides, the vision of what I want to create is born in my quiet moments. A small job, or a big order—it does not matter. From the very depths of my being comes my inspiration. 'He who is not illuminated by God will not be a good worker.'

When I was old enough to be married, my father chose my husband. I did not stay more than two or three months with my first spouse. He was a eunuch![20] [Laughter].

His family were rich weavers. He was quite handsome, quite young, and he wanted to get married. I was quite pretty. When I tell you that I do not like to be photographed now, it is because of that. Now my beauty has passed, and no one ever took my picture when I was young and pretty!

This boy, this eunuch, wanted to enjoy his life. He asked his parents to look for a pretty girl and they found her in a far-off village—me! My parents did not know he had been castrated, so they agreed to the marriage and that I should go with him to Addis Ababa where his family lived in the quarter called Kechine Medhane Alem.

It is customary to have two wedding parties, one at the home of the girl's parents and another at the groom's parents. When my husband-to-be's family arrived on a Saturday, my parents gave a large party. The next day we all set out for Addis Ababa and I wept at leaving my own family. I was small and they placed me in front of my betrothed, in the saddle of his mule. Two of my relatives came with us, a woman to look after my clothes and jewelry, a man to cut the throat of the sheep in the orthodox way, for the wedding celebration.

After two days riding, we reached Entotto where friends of my husband were waiting for us. They welcomed us with food and drink. All the way from my home, I was dying of fear that on the way someone would cheat me or even cut my throat! During the daytime, I had a nice time watching the girls dance and play the drum, but when night came I was terrified of what would happen to me when I was alone with this strange man, my husband.

My parents had told me nothing. My sisters had given me frightening ideas. In those days they never spoke of such matters as 'pleasure'. My sisters said, 'When a virgin girl sleeps with a man for the first time, it hurts a lot,' and 'if your husband wants to sleep with you, you must resist him, for if a girl accepts him at the first try, he will make fun of her.'[21] Indeed I was really scared.

The first night, the second and the third night, nothing happened. I was well fed, well dressed, and tranquil, and I began to think that this was what marriage was. It is usual that soon after a marriage the girl goes home to visit her parents. I did this and returned. I was just a country girl and lived in Addis Ababa like country people do and did not go out of the house. But the young women of the neighborhood came to visit me. After a bit, they began to speak frankly to me.

One of them said: 'Your husband's parents are going to give you a potion.'

'Why?'

'Because your husband is a eunuch.'

'What is a eunuch?'

'A man who has no sex organ. Have you had sexual relations?'

'What are sexual relations?'

They explained that it meant doing this and that, and repeated that I would be made to drink this liquid to keep me there. They told me I should run away to my parents. Now, just at this time, I received a message from my father in Selale telling me that a relation of ours lived in the district of Zebegna Sefer, not far from where I was, and I should pay him a visit. Then and there I made up my mind and said to the friend who told me about everything, 'I have a relative, but I do not know him personally.' She said she would go with me to visit him.

I had never before heard the word 'potion'. My friends were not speaking of a drink that would kill me but only of a philter that would tie me forever to my husband. I did not really understand, but I was afraid. I thought I had already been through the ordeal of marriage, but now I realized this test was still ahead of me.

We found my relative, an uncle, and he asked, 'To whom are you married?' When I told him, he snorted, 'That man is a eunuch! My brother puts daughters into the world and gives them to eunuchs?' The next morning, he brought me back to my husband's house. It was empty. My husband, thinking that I had run away, had disappeared and so had his father. They were afraid of punishment, for the law forbids a eunuch to marry. After all, how can a girl marry a girl?

At the time of the wedding, my husband's father had given me 30 thalers. My uncle spoke to them—my husband and father finally came back from where they were hiding—and they gave me all my things—my clothes, my jewels, the 30 thalers, everything. They wanted to hush up the affair, and asked my family to annul the contract. The next day they came with the *shemagalle* and said, 'Here, take the money, but do not denounce us.' My uncle calmed down and said, 'The only wrong you have caused is that people call my niece the wife of a eunuch.'

Before returning to my father's house, I lived at my uncle's house for a while. Many men came to ask for my hand. But I did not want to marry. I stayed a month and cried much of the time. Finally, my brothers came to take me home. A little later, my father married me off again and I began to hate men.

My second marriage was also by contract. My father gave me a heifer as dowry but suggested that we leave the heifer with him to be fattened up. This husband was called Damiye, and he was a weaver in our area. We did not get along. Was he rich or poor? I don't even remember him. I knew only that there was day and there was night and I was no longer a virgin. But conjugal life did not appeal to me. I can't remember if I left for that reason. Perhaps it was from fear, perhaps from lack of interest. How can one remember what one was thinking in one's youth? I was closely watched for it was suspected that I might run away. If my husband went to market, he made me go too, and when I was in the house, he stayed on guard. I used to hide in the bushes and one day, when it got dark, I left for my father's house.

I had stayed with Damiye only one month! With us, many girls leave their husbands. I knew one who left the same day as her marriage. Now, they still call that girl the wife of so-and-so, even though she spent only one night with her husband. [Mercha laughed a lot during this story]. That is what happens when parents give their daughter to a boy the girl has never met.

I was married a third time, to a man called Seyfu. He was a merchant of Fitche. This marriage was not by contract but a salaried union. If we got along well, we could change this arrangement later into a civil contract. At that time his father gave me some money, for a young woman does not give herself away for nothing. In the city they give a ring, in the country they give money! A virgin girl could command sixty thalers, but for a non-virgin like me, only twenty.

This third marriage of Mercha's was *bedemoz*, 'by salary', and was respectable and particulary common for divorcées in the poorer layer of the population. Her part of the obligation was to keep house. It could be ended at the wish of either one at the end of the time period agreed upon. Her first marriage before the age of puberty was very common. Sometimes they were arranged before birth. One friend would say to another, 'if it is a girl your wife gives birth to, she will be for my son.' During the ceremony of betrothal that seals this informal agreement, dowries of both are agreed upon. Breaking the agreement is a serious matter because it affects not just the individuals but the families involved. In Mercha's case, she knew a lot about keeping house so did not require an apprenticeship with her husband's family, and because of the peculiar circumstances of that marriage she did not have to be protected from premature sexual relations, as the in-laws of a pre-puberty bride would normally insist. All of the usual requirements for a first marriage were violated in her case—proof of virginity, for example. Mercha continued her story about Seyfu.

This merchant loved coffee, but I told him, 'No, I will not fix coffee for you.' His mother was a *zaram*.[22] She made and drank coffee and he went to her house to drink it. I did not like my third husband, so I left him. It must be my character that I could not stay with a man. Even though my father arranged my marriages, they were not my wish. I found it easier to think of being devoured by a hyena than to live with a man. In the country they are not gentle like the husbands in the city who are less harsh.

My parents struck me when I said I wanted to leave this man. My father was very angry and wanted to drag me back to him. My father asked me, 'What is the matter?' I answered, 'He drinks coffee and he smokes.' I said these things not understanding they were against our religion. I said them because I knew those habits displeased my father and I sought only to leave my husband. My father then repeated the proverb, 'The barley which grows, the suitor who asks for the hand—are just alike. Soon bad weeds invade the barley and the son-in-law shows his bad habits.' After that, because my father loved me very much, he said, 'Leave him then and live alone.'

I stayed a long time with my father. I had the reputation of being a good housekeeper but now had the mark of not liking conjugal life. Then I left for Addis Ababa again. Let me tell you how it happened.

During my first marriage, when I lived in Addis Ababa, my husband took me to the theater. The spectacle left such a great impression on me, especially the warrior songs, that I wanted to see it again. I headed for the city. On my way, I stopped to visit my sister. It was at her house that I met the man who would father my two eldest daughters. He was related to my sister's husband and was called Kebede. He never took his eyes off me. Quickly he proposed marriage, but I did not like him and I did not want to get married again. Then I noticed that preparations were going on for some kind of celebration. 'Eutiye,[23] what are you up to?' She told me they were getting ready for a saint's day so I helped her with the food. Then some young man came over to me and said, 'So it is for your marriage that people are coming.' 'What marriage' I said. 'Your marriage to Kebede.'

I said nothing when I returned to the kitchen but I heard the women speak of a wedding. Then I just ran away. I was only half-dressed. I left the food burning and ran away, just like that, without knowing where I was going. My sister's husband and her son-in-law ran after me, shouting 'Stop her! Catch her!'

They caught me and they beat me. They called me bad-mannered and tied my hands behind my back. They said, 'Wash yourself.' I refused and would not even dress myself. They forced my clothes on me, then brought on the wedding food. Then I was taken to his house.

I was wearing a tight pair of pants under my skirt and would never take them off. They were dirty. After a few days, my new mother-in-law, who was very kind, said, Give me your pants and I will wash them for you.' I took them off after two weeks! My mother-in-law treated me well. She taught me good posture and how to eat correctly. My husband was good also, not like the others. He loved God and he did not force me. I stayed with him because he was kind and because I loved his mother. It was the will of God. We slept beside each other for three weeks and he did not touch me. Nonetheless, I always became anxious as bedtime neared. But he would say, 'Sleep, sleep. I will not do anything to you.'

His mother would ask me to prepare things to eat and we all ate together. While Kebede slept soundly, I was wakeful but eventually I got used to him. I lived with him much longer than the others. We lived together for twelve years, then we were separated. It was the will of God.

At the beginning of our marriage, Kebede's father did not like me. He thought I was sterile, but my mother-in-law was much more understanding. She would say, 'This little one is so young, she has not yet had her period. Leave her alone.' 'She is a mule,' my father-in-law would say. 'Do you think a mule has blood?'

Because of these quarrels I did not want to stay with them. Kebede and I left for Addis Ababa, and on this trip I had my first period. Before I had my second, I was pregnant. I went to stay with my mother to bring my child into the world. After I had this little girl my father-in-law began to like me!

Before this time I did not know how to count. At the time of my confinement, a man with some education told me that I was twenty-one years old, for at the time the Italians entered the country [1935] I was a child of five. When my daughter was born I had been married for five years, I think. I had my period very late, about age twenty. With my daughters it has been the same. Azeb will be fifteen soon but she has not yet developed, and the elder one, Debre Zeit, had her first period at age nineteen. Her *kosso* was not seen before that age.

Mercha links the word *kosso* to the onset of menstruation. This was the first time I had heard that word in that context. It is a word used both for tapeworm and the medicine that Ethiopians take to expel it. I asked Mercha if there was a connection between *kosso* and menstruation.

The fruit that Adam ate was not completely swallowed. He wanted to spit it out, but it stayed . . . there! [She touched her Adam's apple.] But Eve, she swallowed hers. That which Adam spit out was transformed into a tapeworm. But since it was the woman who picked the fruit, she, ever since then, bleeds. I am not educated. I only hear about these things. When a person has the *kosso* she cannot receive the blessed bread on the day of *mahber*.[24] On that day they prepare two kinds of flat bread. One is large, the other is small. Everyone can eat the big one. But those who have tapeworm, as well as women who are menstruating, may not touch the smaller bread. Also those who have recently had sexual relations must not touch it.

After our daughter was born, Kebede and I had a son. At that time there was an epidemic. I myself was ill. The child was not full term and was born at seven months. Still, he was well formed. They told me, 'He will live and can grow if you give him milk.' This I did. But he fell ill and died. His time had come.

I did not have enough milk. We knew nothing then about bottles. Our daughter was not yet three. Kebede and I were very sad, though I was sadder than he. Even though a woman, I did not love girls so much. The idea of being a girl often made me angry. My father was disappointed that I was a girl. I don't know why. Later, my husband and I had another daughter. But before she was born we had separated.

Between Kebede and me, the time of our happiness was short. It lasted as long as my mother-in-law was alive—four, five, maybe six years. During those years we did not quarrel and money problems did not divide us. He would buy grain for the whole year and let me use it in my own way. He did not bother me even if the grain ran out before the end of the year. I knew some men who would not let their wives enter the grain store-room, for fear they would squander it.

But we prayed together and lived our lives together thinking each of the other, and of both the material and spiritual side of life. What should we eat? What should we wear? How should we organize our work? That was the material side. The spiritual side was to fast together, go to church, and do good works. Of all my husbands, only with Kebede did I share these things. Some couples live in hypocrisy. They do not have mutual trust.

We were like brother and sister. By that I mean we lived in complete freedom through the best and the worst. Some couples

live without love. The wife says, 'A husband is a stranger.' The
man says, 'A wife is an enemy.' Some stay together only because
of the grain and water, for the daily bread.[25] It is God's order but
not love that makes them live together.

Those who are lucky stay together their whole life from
infancy to death. Kebede and I continued to see each other for
five or six years. For me, those twelve years passed like twelve
days. Since then, I have suffered for fifteen years. If I had stayed
with Kebede, my misfortunes would not have happened. I have
had so many troubles. My life has been like clapping with one
hand. When I compare those dozen years of happiness and the
next fifteen years of misery, only the misery do I feel. We had, at
one time, thought to wed by Holy Communion,[26] and if he had
died I would have become a nun. If I had died he would have
become a monk.

But, for reasons both painful and unforeseen we separated.
Now he weeps . . . and so do I. A long time ago he pardoned
me, but I cannot pardon him. When we were in Selale, Kebede
became lazy. He no longer got along with his father. He began to
go with other women. The devil slipped between us. I have
stayed bitter too long, I know. But when I love someone, I give
my whole trust. When I love a man, I do not want to do him
wrong, for even if a human does not see the evil, God does. I
loved him very much. When others came to tell me what he was
doing I could not believe them. When he went too far, I asked,
'Why have you done such thing?' He denied it, and I believed
him. [Mercha began to cry. The tears coursed down her cheeks,
and she did not try to hide them.]

Here is how our separation came about. I had a dream one
night. Wanting to make *injera*[27] I prepared the batter, then took
down the cooking pan. A rat ran into it. In my dream I did not
want to throw out the batter and decided to have the container
blessed.

Near us lived a woman who interprets dreams. I said to her,
'Eumaye Addougna, I am desolate about the dream I had last
night. The pan in which I cook *injera* was profaned by a rat.' She
told me, 'You live as a good Christian which is pleasing. Now
when your receptacle was profaned, it was a sign that your trust
has not only been shaken, it has also been badly violated. The
receptacle represents your husband. The rat is the bad spirit. You
are going to separate, and he will marry another.' I told her that
was impossible and I did not believe it.

In our village there was a place where neighbors gather together. One evening, some people ran to my house to tell me that my husband had been beaten. He had been sitting beside a woman, paying court to her, when some people came up and struck him.

I told them it was impossible. But my dream had been interpreted the same way. It was a sign! My stomach turned over when I heard these words. Bitterness settled inside me. I tried to reason with myself but my heart said no. I was pregnant. As soon as the child was born I took her to my mother. Kebede tried to reconcile with me through the *shemagalle*, but I would not accept him.

When, two and a half years later, the little girl died, I had already returned to my husband in Addis Ababa because he had sent not only his parents and the *shemagalle* but also his confessor. But it was not long before Kebede and I began to quarrel frequently. By then, you see, our thoughts were as different as heaven and earth. We had made a promise to live together in the same flesh and spirit. He had broken this promise. I tried to resume our common life so as not to be at fault before God.

Six months after my return to the city, my daughters got the measles. They were sick a long time. I said to God, 'If one of them must die, take the little one, but leave me the older one.' The little one died. At this time I had another child in my belly.

You see, in the dream of the rat, I had thought of having the cooking pan blessed. Thus the woman who interpreted the dream told me, 'Since you thought of the blessing, it means you must reconcile with your husband.' Had I thrown the rat and the mixture out without the blessing, I could not have had another child from that man. But such was God's will.

When I returned to Addis Ababa to live with Kebede, I saw that he was earning money in a manner which did not please me.[28] I tried to be patient and sent him to the *shemagalle*, who asked him for my sake to change his work. He refused, so we separated permanently.

I had been patient and had not said anything when he wronged me. I wondered, 'Is it my fault, or is it the devil?' I was sure I had done no wrong, but others said to me, 'Don't be upset. Rancor is not good as it does not please God.' How could I change? My character is what God gave me. I no longer wished to go back with my husband.

It is true that I had only tended to my work and did not take care of my appearance. But I never thought that would lead him to commit adultery. He respected me. He did not neglect me. It was not a dispute that separated us. It was because he did things contrary to our religion.

I admire work done by the sweat of one's brow. When God condemned Adam he told him, 'You will earn your living by the sweat of your brow.' That is what pleases God.

Kebede used to say prayers to honor God, and read holy books. When he came to Addis Ababa, where everyone loves sorcery, those who saw him reading these books said to him, 'My daughter is ill', or 'My son is ill', and would ask him to come and read a passage over their sick child from the holy book. He would tell them that an evil spirit had entered into the sick one. He would sprinkle holy water and he would pray. Thus, those whom God wanted cured would get better, and others would die.

When I saw all this coming and going in our house, with Kebede reading prayers for them, I asked, 'What do they all want?' He said, 'They are sick and I read to them from the holy books.' I asked him, 'Have we the right to cure the sick, or are you doing sorcery?' 'It is nothing,' he said.

From that moment I stopped being happy. I said to him, 'When people quarrel, they can solve their conflicts through the *shemagalle*; when one offends God, confession can reconcile. As for us, the whole point of our lives has now been destroyed. You, who are so clever, could choose between several kinds of work—as a weaver, or work for the church—and I would be happy to work with my hands to make us a little money. Let us raise our children in honesty, so as not to be condemned on earth or in heaven.'

For a week, a month, I watched his behavior. Then I stopped asking him for money for housekeeping. When people asked me why, I told them, 'This man does not work. What is this money he brings in?' They said, 'What do you care where it comes from?' I answered that, since we are of the same flesh and soul, when he is condemned then I would also be condemned. If he is insulted so also would I be insulted. I would never take money from a sorcerer. I earn money from my sweat and so should he. Let him not use the holy books for making money.

I went to find the *shemagalle*. I was advised to stay with my husband, so I sent a message to Kebede. 'If you stop doing this evil thing, I will stay as your wife. Otherwise I will not have relations with you. If we talk to each other peacefully we can live together, but if you try to use force on me, I will leave you.'

As he was a patient man he permitted me to live alone for a while, to reflect. I kept an eye on his conduct, but he never stopped using holy books to make a lot of money. When I went to market, or to get water from the river, or to have my grain ground, someone whose child had died would say to me, 'Here is the wife of the sorcerer.' Or someone whose child had survived would greet me cordially with, 'Here is the woman of the priest.'

I thought, for sure I am known as the wife of a sorcerer! If he wants me to stay with him, he must stop this work. I went back to the country and, after a few months, my daughter was born.

Kebede married another woman. So God decided, as always. It was only in a single weak moment with Kebede that I conceived my daughter, Azeb. For this child I have known much shame, much difficulty. But all this is the will of God. One person is born to work, another is born to be happy, another to enter paradise, while paradise is forbidden to still another. Those who seek pleasure from the world may never find it. God decides everything. That is what I think.

Mercha, the most devout of Christians, was nevertheless considered in her quarter as 'the wife of the sorcerer'. This is not so surprising, for was she not one of those artisans who, for centuries, have occupied an unenviable place in Ethiopian society? People living on the high plateau—warriors and cultivators—have long held the trader and the artisan in low esteem. The child of the tanner, the blacksmith, or the potter was looked down on by those whose children are called *ye-tchewa lidj*, or well born. Not too long ago, artisans could not own land, nor could they become priests or soldiers. Their children could not marry those from a higher social stratum. It was believed they could cast evil spells just by looking at a person, and artisans were reputed to be able to take on the appearance of a hyena at night. Such fear or revulsion very likely stems from the fact that artisans work with fundamental elements—fire, clay, metal. Even though they provide such necessary and useful objects as ploughs, iron lances, cooking utensils, cloth, and water pouches, the barrier of fear and prejudice remained against them. It is curious that the word for the despised artisan, *teib*, derives from *tebeb*, the Gi'iz word for wisdom.

Most artisans belonged to populations peripheral to the highlands or occupying 'pockets' on it, and it is rare to find artisans
among the Amharas, such as Mercha's father. He was ostracized in
his home village because he opted to be a weaver, so he took his
family to live in an Oromo village. Fortunately, they settled among
kind and friendly people, for even some Oromo farmers could have
the same antipathy as Amhara toward manual workers.

In Selale, the Gallas were friendly to us. We became like relatives, working together, eating together. We all spoke Gallinya
and family members often became god-parents of their neighbor's children, who would then suck their breasts.[29] Our young
people married theirs. These Gallas did not have any prejudice
against our work. If I had stayed in Selale, I would have married
off my daughters to Gallas in that region, for we lived with them
in peace. It is we Amhara who are harsh. We don't like our
children to marry theirs. My elder brother had daughters old
enough to marry, but he would not give them to any Galla.
Artisans always looked for other artisan families to marry into. I
cannot understand it. In Selale no one spoke about *buda*.[30] True,
in my childhood, nothing disagreeable ever happened. It was
much later that I heard of these hatreds. I have heard that in
Derra, Amelsa, and Merhabete, the artisans still suffer from these
prejudices. Once my father confessor told me, 'You artisans, you
are only refugees.' He repeated, 'You artisans are not Ethiopians,
you are refugees.' I asked 'What does that mean?' He said, 'You
are refugees from Israel.'[31] I, I did not understand this. I know
many artisans and see only that they live for their work and do
not want to take anything from anyone else. But each time
someone became ill, the others would accuse us of having 'eaten
him' with our eyes! They would then tell us to come and spit on
him, and we would spit, to calm them down.[32]

Truly all this business astonishes me. How could we possibly
'eat' them? [Laughter] What part of the body would one want to
eat? Yet these people would get very excited, even kill each other
because of this nonsense. Personally, it not only makes me laugh,
it amazes me that they could believe such things. But Amhara do
not like artisans. That is why they live by themselves. Nowadays
these beliefs are fading away.

Where does it come from, this way of treating artisans? Truly I
don't know. I have never understood it. My whole life I have

tried to find out where these ideas come from, but no one can tell me. Seeing how my parents, my grandparents and their ancestors lived, it is difficult to see any reasons for it. We are all made of the same clay, only our work is different. I don't know why they think we are *buda* and have the power to eat with our eyes. Who knows whether our so-called victims died of illness or not? [Laughter]

To create and take life, to make ill and to cure is the work of God, not us. How strange to believe that man is capable of such things. Rather than hate us, those who fear us should ask, 'How do you do it?' The most amazing thing is that these foolish ideas go from region to region.

Mercha is a skilled potter, working long hours with very few breaks to produce the ebony pots and jugs that the traders of Addis Ababa prefer. She earns enough to provide decently for her family, living with her three daughters in a two-room house like most of those in the quarter, along the main road but hidden from view by a high, corrugated iron fence.

The main room, about 15' x 20', has a bed, a single chair, a few stools, and some wooden boxes. Although the floor is of rough wood, it is, in itself, a mark of comfort as many houses still have dirt floors. This is the room where visitors are entertained, and an occasional chicken will flap in from the yard to peck for crumbs on the floor. Here also is a small wooden sideboard with cups and saucers of European make visible behind its cracked glass doors. In the second room there is a large bed under which a number of recently made pottery pieces are stacked to dry.

Beyond the house to the rear is a small shed, the *tchis bet*, or 'house of smoke'. Here meals are prepared over an open fire. There is a long table, and under it a pallet, piled with rags, which serves as a mattress. Occasionally, Mercha will sleep on this with her youngest daughter when her oldest daughter's husband, an intinerant trader, comes to stay with them. 'Out here,' Mercha says laughingly, 'I sleep as the peasants do. We are earth and we shall all return to earth. Soon we shall sleep deep inside the earth!'

It is in the company of her children that Mercha, today divorced, finds most comfort, especially in that of her youngest daughter. Werqnesh is tiny, with timid gestures. Her large, melancholy eyes stand out in her thin face. She is a little girl who knows what hunger means. She was born as the result of a strange encounter of

Mercha's. The memory of it brought a smile to Mercha's face and she told the story with humor and some self-mockery.

One night I had a dream in which I had gone down to the river to look for clay but found a big chunk of gold in the ground. So I went to the old woman who interprets dreams and she told me, 'You will have a child from a man who has never fathered a child.'

At this time I was separated from Kebede and was living alone. My work was not going well. All my pots were breaking. I thought God was trying to test me, so I resisted the wish to go to a sorcerer. Instead I made some *katikala*[33] and took it to sell in the market. I did this for about three years, instead of making pots.

Near me lived a man called Gebre Sellase who had studied to become a priest. He was in the house next to mine and we met often. I would get a strange feeling every time I saw him. I would sweat and tremble. I was sure this was not love, for I was not a young girl. I had already loved. Though I had been apart from my husband for six years I had no thoughts of pleasure. I was chaste, working very hard to make a living. Me, I'm just a plough-ox!

For about a month I tested my fears. I thought this man must be possessed of the devil. Or was it me? I said to myself, 'I must leave this neighborhood.' Then my fear disappeared. We began to greet each other and talk. He was always reading his prayer books. He lived alone and bought prepared food so I had sympathy for him. When I prepared *injera* I would take him some. I had no thought of sin. He was poor, dressed in tatters, and he had no attraction for me. Besides, I was proud, living an enclosed life, with no interest in mixing with people, gossiping. I also wore old, country clothes. It is only recently that I began to take a little trouble with my dress, my hair. Still, I was proud!

Shortly I had another dream. A little white calf left my stomach without my feeling the birth. On the threshold of the house a red cow wanted to enter to lick the calf, but I said, 'This calf left my womb, that cow wants to take it. Close the door so it can't take it.' My sister, in the dream, shut the door. Still the cow came in and began to lick the calf. Then I woke up. I was scared. I had a ringing in my head and in my ears. [Mercha grimaced, covered her ears with her hands, and imitated the buzzing sound.]

Today I say it was a dream, but at that time I considered it a nightmare.

Because of my friendly respect for Gebre Sellase I used to address him as *Abbaye*.[34] One day I said to him 'Abbaye, last night I had a nightmare. Can you interpret it?' As we spoke of God together, it was to him I wanted to tell my dream.

'In my dream, a woman I know well put into the world a calf, without being pregnant.' I hid from him that the woman was me, so that he would answer me with complete sincerity. He said, 'I understand your dream. But go ask Eumaye Addougna.' Then he asked me what sex the calf was. But I did not know.

I went to the old woman's house and told her the dream without hiding anything. 'What sex was the calf,' she too asked me. Then she said, 'You will have an infant blessed by Mary and by God. For the red cow was Mary, and in dreams, the white is for angels.' True, as the proverb says, 'For the body the remedy is the cow, for the soul the remedy is Mary.'

Little by little, the man and I became closer. Before, we had spoken as brother and sister, but after that he began to look at me the way a man looks at a woman. He taught me special prayers, like 'I salute you Mary.'

'You are not pronouncing it right,' he said. 'If you drink this potion, you will pronounce it better.'

'Is that true?' said I.

'Wise people use it.'

'Where will I find this potion?' I asked.

'I will give it to you; prepare some *injera* with red tef. Prepare some *besso*.'[35]

He took out of his pocket some kind of black spice. He took some water, cut the *injera* into four pieces, mixed it up with the black stuff, and said, 'Eat.'

I ate it. An hour later I prepared and ate the *besso*. An hour after that I began to feel strange. I began to laugh and giggle. I saw a field covered with dew, the meadow surrounded by leafy trees and I was laughing in the middle of it all. It was marvelous. When I kept my eyes fixed, I saw this vision, but whenever I turned my head, the vision disappeared.

The man asked, 'What is happening to you?' Then I was frightened and would not open my eyes again. I wrapped my *shamma* around my head and did not move at all. I began to cry. Suddenly I saw my future. I saw that I would have a baby from

this man. I saw what would be my life, that one day I would be
blind. I said to God, 'Why do you take my eyes when I want to
work.'

For five days I felt as though I was drunk. I felt I lacked blood
and would have to drink *talla*, that I would eat very little, even
that I would enter a pottery factory. Actually all this has happened to me. The only thing left is for me to become blind.

I had shouted out what I saw in the vision, and those words
about having a child by this man were engraved on my heart.
After several days I asked Gebre Sellase, 'Is it true we will have a
baby!' He replied, 'I knew it even before you told me your
dream, but I had you drink the medicine so that you would
know it also.'

Thus began our liaison. The day of the Festival for God in
October we slept together. Nine months later, to the day, I
delivered this infant. I am still astonished. It is the work of God.
Since the separation from Kebede I had not known any man.
One does not usually become pregnant from one single en-
counter.

I lived with this man for a year and a half. Before we began to
live together we felt shame. We cried. But it is the will of God
that man and woman live together. We were nearly the same
age. He was about thirty-five and I, thirty two, but he looked
much younger. I was no longer young and this displeased him,
as in an Ethiopian household the man should be much older than
the woman. So we never thought of marrying in the church. In
the beginning this man esteemed me. He said to me, 'Promise
not to deceive me and I will not deceive you. Let God curse me if
I betray you.'

He was a virgin and had never known a woman. In our
country many men and women remain chaste for fear of God.

He told me that once he went into retreat for forty days, but
on the thirty-seventh day God said to him, 'Your destiny is in
Addis Ababa, where you will be a weaver. You will meet a
woman but you will not stay together.' Because of those words
he believed he would not stay with me, and soon he began to
show me less respect.

For my part, I did not want to marry him. When I lived with
Kebede, we had thought of marrying in the church. That was
what I wanted. But my husband went off with another woman
and that gave me terrible pain. Then I thought about becoming a

nun, but I was still young and I wanted more children. The memory of Kebede prevented me from marrying Gebre Sellase, so I said to him, 'I don't want us to be tied by communion. That had been my hope with Kebede but he betrayed me. Let the future decide itself. If it is the will of God, we will live together, but I cannot promise you in the name of God to marry you.'

Both of us were very poor. We agreed that we would share whatever we earned. Our contract was in Christ! For my part I thought, if I live with a man I will become pregnant. So I told him, 'You must work. What I earn we will spend on house-keeping; what you earn, we will put aside. My heart is pure. God knows I have never broken my word.'

Years earlier, Gebre Sellase had studied to become a *debtera*.[36] When he came to Addis Ababa he learned how to be a weaver. After we began living together he would pay one month's rent and I would pay the next. But when we separated, he took all of our savings and all the cooking utensils!

I was left without anything. 'May God judge you,' I said to him. Later he gave me half of the 150 *birr* in our savings, but without any of the interest it had earned.[37] Last year he came back and asked me to marry him. I refused. I no longer trusted him and was sure he would eventually betray me. His character did not please me and I remember saying to him, 'One cannot love God and money at the same time.'

When I had our little girl, he said to me, 'I am going to support her, but not the other two.' At the time of our separation he told me to get out. Werqnesh was only four months old and I was very tired. Because of the baby I did not want to move but he said, 'Throw the baby down the sewer.' I told him, 'Even a monkey does not reject its dead baby. God will nourish my child.' A week before Christmas I left with my three daughters. I had nothing. I began to make pottery.

For a long time I believed that little Werqnesh was her mother's favorite. Only later did I come to understand the complex relation-ship between Mercha and her eldest daughter, Debre Zeit. At the time I first met her, Debre Zeit was about twenty, and about eight months pregnant, lying down most of the day in the room next to the main room where Mercha and I were talking. With no door between us, Debre Zeit could hear all we said, and Mercha did not lower her voice when castigating her daughter. Debre Zeit remained silent and discreet, coming out occasionally to serve us some tea.

Debre Zeit had only a slight resemblance to her mother. Her posture was slightly stooped, but she was a beautiful girl with a glossy, golden complexion. Her mischievous eyes were underlined with khol, and her languid walk expressed her tendency toward the easy, pleasurable life. Her apparent nonchalance, Mercha said, was inherited from her father, Kebede.

I met Kebede only once when I was just about to leave Mercha's house after one of our talks. We were making our farewells while Mercha held Debre Zeit's baby in her arms. A man came up to us, took the baby's foot in his hand and began to rub it gently. Mercha, without a word, signaled him to leave and, with a faint smile, he did so. 'That is the father of my oldest girls,' Mercha whispered to me.

The bitterness Mercha retained from her break-up with Kebede seemed to spill over on Debre Zeit. She thought Debre Zeit too much like her father, indolent and without the 'worker's' spirit.

Kebede is not a bad man; his character is innocent. But he is lazy. He opens his Psalms and reads them. He does not organize his day. He just lets it happen as children do. At the beginning of our marriage, when we lived with his parents, I did not know his character well. I did not notice if he was a hard worker, but I remember that on holidays it was never he, but always his father, who cut the sheep's throat. But as he was pious and patient, he pleased me, and he was good natured. But his laziness led him to take up evil work, though he could have been a good weaver. He was clever, but so lazy. If he wanted something, rather than go get it he would sit there and give orders, 'Bring me this, bring me that.' Even if his clothes were hanging just over his head he would say, 'Give me my *shamma* if you please.'

Our daughter, Debre Zeit, resembles him completely in this way. If she continues like this she will end in misery. I am her mother and I love her, and I say to myself, 'Oh well, let her live in her thoughtlessness.' But soon I get angry. She also is clever and can work very well. But she prefers to wash her Sunday dress while I do all the housework. My daughter takes everything lightly. Life, however, is a burden one cannot escape. How can I explain this? Words fail me. This idleness of my daughter is the cause of our quarrels. Seeing it I am wounded for I raised her.

So I am responsible. Still, I love her in a way I cannot describe. I love all three of my girls, but it is the oldest I favor. I don't know why. It seems it is the will of God. The love one has for a man can fade, even disappear. I used to love my husband, but his love has passed, while I cannot stop loving my daughter. The times we spend together are for me the best. I wait for and look forward to them. On Easter and Christmas, my favorite holidays, we chatter the whole day and into the night, even until the cock's crow. And if she is not with me on those feast days, I do not even want to get dressed, or be happy.

In front of me, mother and daughter never quarreled. To the eye, they got along well. However, their disputes became more frequent than they wanted to tell me. One day, Debre Zeit arrived at my house covered with bruises. Mercha had beaten her! It was true that Debre Zeit was thoughtless and lazy. Where the mother was so industrious, the daughter would rather play with her baby, fix her hair in ten different ways, crochet little napkins. It was Mercha who eventually told me the drama that had torn them apart.

I prefer to think no more of what will be the future of my children. I always believed that Debre Zeit would turn out alright but she disappointed me. She was born at a place near where a number of hermits lived and one of them predicted that she would have a future blessed by God. When she was a little girl, she had visions, saw angels and saints. I saw none of these things but I believed what she told me. They taught us that church is the dwelling place of many angels and saints and that one must not disturb them. They stand around the altar, and if one touches them they will strike you with a sword, so you must not move. I had been told these things, but Debre Zeit had not, although she had these visions.

Just before our quarrel, Debre Zeit had said to me, 'Don't you see an old man sitting there?' 'No, I don't see him.' 'Well, he is telling you to buy 25 kilos of wheat and make little bread cakes to give to the children of the neighbors, in observance of tomorrow's holiday,' she said. 'But tomorrow is not a holiday so I will not do it.' Then Debre Zeit argued that the old man had said, 'If you don't do what I ask, you will be terribly sorry and have much pain,' and then disappeared.

Not long after she and I began to fight and she left for

Nazareth.[38] This was around Christmas and she did not return until Easter. In Nazareth she got married without telling me about it. She sent her aunt and cousin to me to announce her return. When she showed up, alone, she said she had been working in Nazareth, but she said nothing about her marriage. I learned of it from someone else. Then I prepared the *mals*[39] but the husband never showed up.

The first time I met her husband was the following Christmas when I went to Nazareth because Debre Zeit had sent me a message asking me to come because she was pregnant. As was customary, my son-in-law killed a sheep in my honor, but I was still angry and could not hide my annoyance with him. So I returned to Addis Ababa the next day. Easter came, but I did not invite them. I had the feeling he did not like me. Perhaps he was even ashamed of me because I was very poor. It was not too long before Debre Zeit fought with him and left him.

The man she lives with now, Girma, is her second husband. He urged my daughter to leave her first husband. They have known each other a long time. They had met at school. When Debre Zeit flew away to Nazareth, she said nothing to Girma. He looked all over for her until he found her. As I did not care for her first husband, and since Girma was pressing Debre Zeit to marry him, I let things take their course. But this boy is too young. He is like a child beginning to walk. Girma is a nice boy, but he has no skill or livelihood.

My daughter's first husband who lived in Nazareth had some good points. For one thing, he was older and he is a Christian who fasted every Wednesday and Friday. He was well brought up and he earned a good wage. But the second husband holds her by strong feelings. There was physical warmth between them and they have married to satisfy this desire, not according to tradition. Young people of today—one doesn't know where or how they get together! My oldest daughter married against my wishes, against tradition. This second husband does not go to church or observe religious occasions. He smokes, and drinks coffee. Maybe my daughter is happy but I am not. What is going to be the fruit of this marriage?

As Mercha talked, twilight descended. I could hardly see her face against the dark earthen wall and only the folds of her *shamma* retained the last bit of daylight. In the dusk, one object could hardly be distinguished from another. This is a time of quiet, of lowered voices and silence. Seated on a low stool, Mercha grasped her knee in her familiar gesture. In this moment of trust she will surrender the heart of her torment.

> The true name of Girma is Hussein Ahmed. He is a Muslim. He changed his name, but he is not yet baptized even though he no longer eats meat butchered by Muslims. If he was baptized it would be a great thing for God. I ought to hate him because he is a Muslim, yet at the same time I did not like my daughter's first husband even though he was Christian. Girma is young and innocent. When my daughter married him I did not know he was not a Christian. If I had known, I would have preferred to see my daughter dead. But now Girma is like my son. He respects me a great deal. When I say 'Come,' he comes. When I say, 'Go,' he goes. When I discovered that he was a Muslim I wanted them to separate but he pleaded with me to let him stay and he promised to be baptized. So I thought, 'Why forbid him the bounties of God?'
>
> Until last year, I believed that Girma was a Christian. One Friday I had prepared food for our meal after the day's fasting. When I returned to the house from work, I discovered that the meat had disappeared, so I asked Debre Zeit why she had touched that food on a fasting day. She replied, 'My husband is not baptized so why not eat it?' That really shocked me. So we have continued to exist, trying to keep the neighbors from knowing our shame.

Mercha asked me for her sake to use his Christian name whenever I came to the village. Now I understood the anguish of the mother and the meaning of her 'curse'. For a woman so attached to her Christianity, the marriage of her daughter to a Muslim was a true drama, a tragedy. Mercha was deeply troubled about the fate of the child already stirring in Debre Zeit's womb. She dreaded this pregnancy as if Debre Zeit were going to give birth to a monster. The child came into the world still-born.

A year later, another child was born, a vigorous handsome boy. If Debre Zeit had fallen in love with Girma, that young Muslim trader, was it not partly because of her refusal of a life like her mother's—a life 'in the mud'? In the Addis Ababa of the 1960s she was attracted by new values that offered the false possibility of a life less harsh. At school, artisans were in contact with children from other social backgrounds, richer, more 'modern'. But, as Mercha needed her services at home, Debre Zeit attended school so irregularly as to obtain small benefits. She finds herself now as an adult without enough training to find 'modern' work. Truly, it is not the potter's work she rejects, but the state of misery it entails. Now, Debre Zeit speaks.

When I was little, my mother made pottery. She had no money. She rented a tumble-down shack of straw for 2 *birr* a month. When we found something to eat, as we had no receptacle, my mother used her cloak to hold it. At night she put her dress on the ground and we slept there covered with her cloak. I believe I will never forget this to the end of my life. I was only an infant but I will remember it forever.

As my mother was very poor I was not married young. Men look for someone who has a little wealth of her own—me, I had nothing. Had I married very young, an artisan, as my mother wanted, I don't think I would have been happy because I see that among artisans the woman is oppressed. I never wanted to marry a weaver because their wives are not very happy. In the first place, what a man earns alone is not enough to live on. In the second place, the wife must help her husband making the *araq*, the *talla*, or the pottery. In the third place, there is even more work for the weaver's wife, who must separate the cotton thread—that is extra labor. That is why, since my infancy, the wish I made to God was never to marry a weaver.

Life for the wife of an artisan is hard, for in addition to the work she must put children into the world. The artisan women have children without stopping. The men do not wish to prevent it. A woman can have twelve or thirteen births. And when I see these little ones growing up, I pity them. The woman does not have the right to say, 'Let us not do that,' for her husband would beat her! It is different with my husband. If I say that one or two children is enough, he agrees. But if I were married to an artisan, I could not even speak of these things.[40]

As I was of a poor family, I would surely have gone to a poor man and he would never understand these problems. Artisans say that to prevent children from coming into the world is a sin. I think it is a sin to raise more children than you have the means for.

I know the work of a potter very well. I was good at it. But one is not paid according to how tiring it is; one has no rest, no hope of bettering one's situation. That is why when one sees a profit, one wants to work; when one sees nothing, one despairs. You ask me if working on religious days, one would earn more. That is certain. But only the young people think this. Don't think that the young do not like the work of the potter. But they earn too little considering their pain. As we are not rich I would like to find a little job to help Girma. If I could earn a little, our life would be easier. We have a son. If we had more money, as it is not good to have only one child for who knows what can happen, I would like to have one or two more.

In former times, people showed openly their contempt for artisans. Now there is a law. Those who scorn artisans are obliged to keep their aversion to themselves; so they can harm us no more. At one time they even killed artisans. In our country that existed. I never saw such a thing, but they said things like, 'Your eyes have eaten our son, our daughter, come and spit here.' For everyone believed that our saliva could cure them. But the artisans refused; if they had agreed, that would have perpetuated the belief. In truth, I do not know what the word *buda* means, but that was what they called tanners, iron-workers, weavers, and potters. When those workers passed in the street, people hid their children. They believed in the power of their eyes. Today, all those who are educated do not believe in such things. And others, even if they believe them, can no more insult us or show their hatred.

Apart from the financial problem, for my husband and myself, there is the one of religion. Our religions are different. When I asked him to convert to Christianity he refused. And I could never accept becoming a Muslim. That is our problem. Before my marriage, I followed the religion of my mother. I went to church. I fasted. Now I have abandoned all that. I only pretend to before my mother because I am afraid of her. Today I am neither in the religion of my mother nor in the religion of my husband. He and I are between two religions.

Between two religions, between two worlds; such has become Debre Zeit's reality. I frequently met Mercha and her family in 1974, the year the Ethiopian revolution started. The events of this troubled period only increased Mercha's difficulties. Her financial problems were exacerbated by the rising cost of living as well as worry for the future of her daughters. Schools kept closing and opening, and in the artisan's quarter there developed an atmosphere of unrest and dissatisfaction that fed on the growing misery and confusion.

The town, Mercha knows from her experience, is for her family the agent of misery. That 'modern' life which attracts her daughters is, for Mercha, only disillusionment. Deep in herself she is drawn to the wisdom of the traditional life in which she grew up, and she longs to return to the country. But, after so many years in town, with her parents dead, her brothers and sisters scattered, and with no money, returning to village life seems impossible for her.

Long ago, when I left my natal hamlet to come to the town, I did not do it with joy. If I came back to Addis Ababa, I must have been pushed by some diabolical force! At that time, my life was so difficult that I dreamed of ending it. Only the fear of God kept me from it. I have not forgotten anything about what I saw and understood in my youth—each tree, each blade of grass, each twig is engraved on my memory. I would very much like to return and settle there. One finds *tef*, honey, and animals, and for eggs one keeps chickens. While there, everything is bad. See this tiny courtyard. I cannot even keep a sheep. I bought a ewe. It got thin instead of getting fat. I can hardly feed my family. You see how the little one has gotten thin? It is not because I neglect her. Sometimes she is hungry and just sits there. It can be read on her face. Before I had a little money; today I have none. I ruin my eyes working until late at night, but I have no choice. My soul is confused. Where shall I go? Where shall I go? I have lived too long in the city. Even if I had family in the country, I would have no house. No one would build me one. I have no cow. Who would give me one? Seeing me arrive from Addis Ababa, people would think me rich and they would try to make me go away. If I had a husband, if I had some belongings, I could remake my life in the country. I have less energy. My eyes are bad for I have wept too much in my life. Yes, I have always cried too much and, today, my situation leaves me no hope. I have to stay here. Misery forces me to.

Today, the customs of our country and our religion have changed a great deal. That makes me very unhappy. That which in my memory was beautiful bears no resemblance to what I see today. It seems it is another country. I feel as if I no longer existed. My daughters say, 'It is not normal for you to think as you do.' I say, 'Yes, my children, perhaps you are right that my way of thinking is not correct.' [Mercha smiled sadly.]

I wish I had been born in another epoch, for nothing of the time in which we live pleases me. In my life, as soon as I find the least joy, it is effaced. What can I do about it? I was young and my youth led me into error. I put in the world these children and now I curse my life. For, without having sought a profound knowledge of life, I was trampled in the mud of this world. In itself, the coming into the world of these children is a wonderful thing. But their future torments me so much. God knows where they are going—hell or paradise?

Note: The story of Mercha is based on her conversations with the author that extended from 1970 to 1976 and is excerpted from the author's manuscript, 'Mémoires Ethiopiennes.' The real names of participants have not been used. Reprinted with permission from *North-east African Studies*, Volume 5, Number 2, 1983.

Notes

1. This 'wheel' can be, for example, just a piece of broken pottery.
2. Small pots took about forty minutes, and some took more than an hour. The pit's size was about 50cm by 2m 50cm. In the city nowadays they use corrugated iron in place of the base of broken pottery.
3. I recorded between 1974 and 1976. Despite the affection between us, Mercha would never use the verb form for intimate friends. We used the form 'antu,' which marks a certain deference.
4. Menilek, when king of Shewa province, made Entotto his capital about 1882 and had a residence built there. Two churches were also built there.
5. A *shemagalle* is a mediator, an elder of the village.
6. Mercha rarely used her father's name in telling the story. Ethiopians believe in the power of the spoken word. If a woman has lost a child, she will call her next baby 'dirty rag', or 'little rubbish', so that the angel of death will not appropriate this one.

7. Mercha, in what was typical Amhara fashion before the revolution, used the word 'Galla', although they refer to themselves as Oromo and resent Amhara usage.

8. *Talla* is a home brew made from barley.

9. Slavery existed for centuries and was not effectively stamped out until the 1940s. The *Fetha Negest*, a religious law book, has numerous references regarding conduct toward slaves, conditions of manumission, and inheritance rights of children conceived between a slave and a free person.

10. So the 'law of Genesis' was actually the law of Leviticus, XV: 19–24. The belief that menstruation was a penalty inflicted on women because Eve ate the apple is widespread. An even longer purification period is required after childbirth. A menstruating woman cannot enter the church.

11. Gi'iz is the Latin of Ethiopia, understood by very few, but prayers in Gi'iz are learned by rote.

12. Gondar, Ethiopia's capital in the seventeenth and eighteenth century, and now the capital of Begemdir province, has long been famed for its religious schools. *Qenē* is a verse-form which calls for much skill in the use of puns and double meanings.

13. *Debo* is an association based on exchange of services.

14. A *gabi* is a blanket-like cloak. A *birr*, or silver, was a Maria Teresa thaler; the term is used today as the unit of currency, as in ฿10.00.

15. Famines and epidemics are given proper names. It is probable that the famine she refers to was the one of 1888–93, so his age must be exaggerated. Mercha said her father died in the late 1960s. Mercha's claim that he was in his eighties when she was born was probably wrong. He was more likely about a hundred when he died, if we make him thirty in 1890.

16. A *semuni* is one-quarter of a *birr*.

17. In paradise.

18. This is amazing because Ethiopian pottery is extremely fragile. The method of cooking the pottery over an open fire covered with cow dung can generate at most between 600° and 800°. Yet at our ceramic workshop, even though our higher temperature firing made stronger pots, we were unable to achieve the blackened, smoked finish that the country potters made and which were much preferred.

19. There are from 165 to 220 religious days a year.

20. Eunuchs are not rare in a country where eviration had long been practiced on conquered peoples, where a castrated slave was worth ten times more than others. Mercha did not know the circumstances in which the young man had become a eunuch.

21. For many Ethiopian women, the first wedding night is an ordeal. In the highland culture, one of the duties of the best man is to subdue the recalcitrant bride, who, as Mercha recounted, was

supposed to struggle against being taken by her husband. The boy, for his part, is raised with the idea that he must 'force' his bride. One of the preparations for this 'battle' is to cut the bride's fingernails and toenails so she will not scratch the groom. She may also be given a purgative to weaken her. She faces this test with the understanding that it is an inevitable, but temporary, trial.

22. A *zaram* is a kind of magician. Recall that Mercha had been cautioned about coffee by her father, for its association with Muslims. Coffee was connected with some magic rites; sorcerers and diviners read the future in coffee-grounds on Wednesdays and Fridays, precisely the days on which the Ethiopian Christian commemorates Christ's sufferings.

23. A pet name for an older sister.

24. *Mahber* is a religious gathering at which prayers are recited. A priest is present to bless the food eaten after the prayers.

25. The words for grain and water, spoken together, also mean 'destiny'. When a couple divorce, they say 'ehel-weha alqo new' or 'What they shared is now finished between them.'

26. Holy Communion marriage is the indissoluble bond in Ethiopian marriage. It is a serious, permanent act, usually taken after a couple has lived together for many years. Divorce after a Holy Communion marriage is allowed only in rare cases that have been appealed to church courts.

27. *Injera* is a fermented bread, looking like a large pancake, that accompanies stews.

28. As a sorcerer.

29. By this action, an Oromo custom, the adopted child becomes as one of the family, with the same rights as the natural child.

30. An evil spirit, much feared and considered a form that could only be taken by the despised artisan.

31. Among the best-known groups of artisans are counted the Falashas, who call themselves 'Bet Israel' or 'House of Israel'.

32. It was the belief that the *buda* had no saliva, so if artisans promptly spat for their accusers, it proved that he or she was not a *buda*.

33. An alcoholic liquor made from distilling grain.

34. *Abbaye*: Little father.

35. A snack of roasted grain taken on journeys.

36. A *debtera* is a layman who, because of his learning, works for the church without enjoying the respect Ethiopians give to priests.

37. The money was in the local co-operative association called an *equb*.

38. Nazareth or *Nazret* is a town about sixty miles from Addis Ababa.

39. The *mals* is a feast given by the bride's family soon after the wedding to become better acquainted with the son-in-law and urge the couple to keep in frequent contact.

40. Though schooled young people know about the 'pill,' which is openly sold in Addis Ababa.

Index

195

[1] Official titles are listed by designation (ie., emir-ruler); otherwise only proper names are included. Mothers, fathers, husbands and children of the subjects are also specified in the index. In Muslim Africa and in Christian Ethiopia first names are actual names of the person; the second name is the father's given name and not the surname. Thanks to Jeffrey Romero who contributed to compilation of the index.